THE QUEEN BEHIND
THE THRONE

THE QUEEN BEHIND THE THRONE

Michael De-la-Noy

HUTCHINSON
LONDON

© Michael De-la-Noy 1994

The right of Michael De-la-Noy to be
identified as Author of this work has been asserted
by Michael De-la-Noy in accordance with the
Copyright, Designs and Patents Act, 1988

2 4 6 8 9 7 5 3 1

This edition first published in 1994 by
Hutchinson

Random House (UK) Ltd
20 Vauxhall Bridge Road, London SW1V 2SA

Random House Australia (Pty) Ltd
20 Alfred Street, Milsons Point, Sydney, NSW 2061, Australia

Random House New Zealand Ltd
18 Poland Road, Glenfield, Auckland 10, New Zealand

Random House South Africa (Pty) Ltd
PO Box 337, Bergvlei, 2012, South Africa

A CiP record for this book is available
from the British Library

ISBN: 0 09178557 X

Set by Deltatype Ltd, Ellesmere Port
Printed and bound in Great Britain by
Clays Ltd, St. Ives PLC

Contents

List of Illustrations

For Bruce

A Preface

THE WIVES OF MANY monarchs have brought their influence to bear on the throne; the wives of Charles I and George II come immediately to mind. But no queen consort has exercised so much influence for good as Queen Elizabeth the Queen Mother. At more than one moment of national crisis she has seen with startling clarity what had to be done to steady people's nerves, in particular those of her husband, King George VI. This is the story of her contribution to the development of modern monarchy and of the way in which, by the force of a powerful and astute personality, she has become a phenomenon in the life of the British people.

Hundreds of books have been written about members of the Royal Family, and to produce a full bibliography would be tedious. However, a number of characters who have played important parts in the drama of Queen Elizabeth's life have been served by writers of distinction. Elizabeth Longford's Life of Queen Victoria (still alive when the Queen Mother was born) has not been superseded. Edward VII has been admirably portrayed in modern times by a number of distinguished writers, including Christopher Hibbert – perhaps the most consistently entertaining and reliable of all modern popular historians. Edward's wife, Queen Alexandra, has also been sympathetically dealt with, by Georgina Battiscombe. The official biography of George V by Harold Nicolson remains an elegant model of its genre, as does John Wheeler-Bennett's official biography of George VI. James Pope-Hennessy's life of Queen Mary is one of the best accounts of a modern queen consort yet written. In 1983 Kenneth Rose produced an updated and extremely well-researched biography of George V, and in 1989 Sarah Bradford contrived a major modern portrait of George VI. In some ways – perhaps because his story remains so riveting – the twentieth-century sovereign who least deserved to wear a crown, Edward VIII, has been served most comprehensively of all. Frances Donaldson's biography of Edward is a fair and balanced study of a basically unbalanced man, and Philip Ziegler has excelled himself – his earlier life of William IV was a brilliant examination of nineteenth-century regal madness – as Edward's official biographer. And anyone writing about the life or times of Edward VIII will always be indebted to the editing by Michael Bloch of Edward's letters. Anthony Holden's 1979 life of the Prince of Wales, now inevitably somewhat out of date, remains a model of lucidity.

As the daughter of a baron, Queen Elizabeth the Queen Mother was born the Hon. Elizabeth Bowes-Lyon. On the accession in 1904 of her father to the earldoms of Strathmore & Kinghorne she assumed the courtesy title Lady Elizabeth. On her marriage in 1923 to the Duke of York she became Her Royal Highness the Duchess of York, and on the Duke's accession to the throne in 1936 she became, of course, Her Majesty the Queen. At the time of the King's death, in 1952, his mother, Queen Mary, was still alive, and the Queen let it be known she wished to be styled in future Queen Elizabeth the Queen Mother. To members of her family and to the various Royal Households she is always known as Queen Elizabeth. This book is not strictly chronological; indeed, the narrative quite deliberately moves backwards and forwards in time, and almost always I refer to the Queen Mother by whatever title she enjoyed at the time I am writing about.

Letters in the Royal Archives are reproduced by gracious permission of Her Majesty the Queen, and to the following I am particularly indebted, for their time and trouble or for their consent to reproduce copyright material: Sir Alastair Aird (Private Secretary to Queen Elizabeth the Queen Mother), Lady Elizabeth Basset, Sir Michael Burton, Mr Michael Bloch, Miss Charlotte Cotton of the Victoria and Albert Museum, Comtesse Anne-Pierre d'Harcourt, Mr James Fergusson, Sir Edward Ford, Mr Dick Francis, the late Dowager Viscountess Hambleden who died while this book was going into production, the Hon. David Herbert, Mr Michael Meredith of Eton College, Mr Nigel Nicolson, Viscount Norwich, Bishop Simon Phipps, Sir Ian Rankin, Bt, Sir Kenneth Scott (Deputy Private Secretary to the Queen), Miss Ann Sebba, the Reverend Victor Stock, Mr William Tallon (Page to Queen Elizabeth the Queen Mother), Group Captain Peter Townsend and the Superintendent of Windsor Castle.

Michael De-la-Noy
Hove, 1994

I

A Most Terrible Omen

THE FIRST PERSON TO whom Queen Elizabeth the Queen Mother wrote on becoming queen was the Archbishop of Canterbury, a sanctimonious old snob called Cosmo Lang. 'I can hardly believe that we have been called to this tremendous task,' the Queen told the Primate of All England, 'and (I am writing to you quite intimately) the curious thing is that we are not afraid.' By 'we' she meant of course she and her husband, the new King, George VI, who the previous day, 11 December 1936, had succeeded his brother, King Edward VIII. The reason neither she nor the King were afraid – and this was entirely genuine and typical of both of them – was because, as she told the Archbishop, 'I feel that God has enabled us to face the situation calmly.' At 1.52 pm, the moment at which Edward's Instrument of Abdication, which he had signed on 10 December, became law, George VI assumed among his other titles (Emperor of India, Defender of the Faith) that of Supreme Governor of the Church of England. For the King, as for his wife, the Church of England was a living embodiment of a personal religious belief. Neither of them ever entertained any serious doubts about the truths of revealed religion; both were uncritical Christians who accepted the Faith at a simple emotional level. But the situation God had enabled them to face so calmly was one which in the recent weeks had shaken the nation and its still colossal Empire to its foundations. The 'tremendous task' to which the Queen referred was not the job of reigning in the usual way but of restoring confidence in a monarchy reduced in a matter of months from the sanctified mystique of George V to the shambolic funfair presided over by Edward VIII.

But in many respects the world into which the Queen had awoken the day she wrote to the Archbishop was exactly the same world as the one on which she had closed her eyes as Duchess of York. It was a world in which, despite the best endeavours of a younger generation to dance until they dropped (and if that didn't kill them, to smoke themselves to death), authoritarianism and rigid rules of social conduct still held sway. It is extremely difficult today, when half of all those who even ask for a church wedding are already living together, and a third of all marriages end in divorce, to realise that before the Second World War a woman who was not a virgin on her wedding night was regarded as little better than a prostitute. The very idea of divorce was so scandalous that no divorced person was even admitted to the Royal Enclosure at Ascot. Yet the King of England had announced his intention of marrying a woman who had divorced one husband and was on the point of divorcing a second. So determined was he to marry her that having failed to negotiate a morganatic marriage he had abdicated and sailed away to France.

Yet it would be true to say that only one half of society was shocked by King Edward's behaviour; the elder half. Many of the younger generation, with whom the King himself, although entering early middle age, liked to identify, believed that Edward, until a mere 325 days before the most popular Prince of Wales in history, had been harried from his throne by a pack of fogies, a martyr to the cause of love. The new King and Queen were caught somewhere in the middle of this rather arbitrary divide. King George was three days away from his 41st birthday. Queen Elizabeth was 36. Incredibly youthful in appearance, both veered by temperament, however, towards the conventions. Both possessed an inherent regard for institutions and an intuitive knowledge of protocol. Neither ever had to be taught how to behave, how to perform their public duties or how to conduct themselves in private. Queen Mary, to whom Queen Elizabeth became very close, may have passed on tips about carrying out royal chores, but the essential technique seems to have been at the Queen's fingertips since birth. Both King George and Queen Elizabeth possessed a rigid sense of moral duty, an attachment to family and Crown, and it was this which decisively set them apart from the sovereign who had just departed. Just as it is quite impossible to imagine King Edward VIII writing to the Archbishop of Canterbury in the way his sister-in-law had done, so it is equally incredible to think of either George VI or Queen Elizabeth corresponding in disparaging terms about the Establishment. But Edward, as Duke of Windsor, had no such qualms. 'Let us . . . enjoy our lovely full life together far removed from the boredom, the restrictions and the intrigues of the Royal Family and the Court,' he was write to the Duchess in 1953 after attending his mother's funeral.

The Duke, as Prince of Wales and briefly as king, had not the faintest idea about the proprieties or his constitutional duties. When his father succeeded as king (in 1910), Edward had to ask his mother how to address her (he was by then 16). When he received Archbishop Lang the day after his father's funeral, in 1936, Edward VIII told the Archbishop he understood he now had to appoint bishops, and to Lang's astonishment, he 'asked me to tell him how it was done!' Lang records in his diary that he tried to enlighten the King, and that Edward spoke of one or two clerics whom he had met, 'but even of these his knowledge was very faint. It was clear that he knows little, and, I fear, cares less, about the Church and its affairs.' (The King's duty was in fact only to ratify the appointment of diocesan bishops on the advice of the Prime Minister.) Much has been made of George VI's remark to the effect that before coming so unexpectedly to the throne he had never seen the contents of a State Paper, but although it seems the education of both the heir apparent and his heir presumptive had been woefully neglected by George V, the difference between the two brothers was that one, the Duke of York, was capable of making up for lost time, the other was not; although, to be fair to Edward, the Archbishop did concede that he was impressed by the young King's alertness and obvious eagerness to know and to learn. But, Lang added, rather oddly, 'he was very pleasant and *seemed* to be very cordial.'

It was hardly surprising that the King and Lang had got off on the wrong foot. Within minutes of succeeding, the first thing Edward did at Sandringham was to have all the clocks turned back half an hour to GMT (George V had kept the clocks half an hour fast to increase the time available for one of his favourite pastimes, shooting; the other was philately), thus ensuring that in the morning the Archbishop was very nearly late arriving at the parish church, where he was due to celebrate holy communion. Lang was not the only person to wonder 'what other customs will be put back also!' And Edward was well aware that in 1935, at Balmoral, Lang had enjoyed with his father 'a long and intimate talk' – about what Lang always referred to as The King's Matter, in effect, about Edward's relations with an American divorcée, Wallis Simpson.[1] So, as what we now know as the Abdication crisis unfolded, Lang's advice never seems to have been sought, no doubt because the King resented the fact that he had discussed his affairs with his father.

The Duke of Windsor, as Edward became when his new title was gazetted on 8 March 1937, developed a positive aversion to all archbishops, expressing himself in language somewhat intemperate for a former Supreme Governor of the Church of England. When Queen Mary was dying, the Duke wrote to his wife to say that while he was at Marlborough House 'the Archbishop of Canterbury [Geoffrey Fisher] showed up to "give Mamma a blessing" as he called it and Mary [the Princess Royal] and I had to kneel in the next room while he said some prayers. An unctuous hypocrite like all the rest I should judge and he reminded me of "Auld Lang Swine"!!'[2]

Lang had been so christened in a popular ditty written by Gerald Bullett but not published until 1959 (it had gone the rounds verbally), which made clever play on his episcopal signature Cantuar. He had quite unintentionally whipped up popular sympathy for Edward, thus making life more difficult for the new King and Queen, whom Lang revered, by delivering from the Concert Hall of Broadcasting House a high-flown and disastrously ill-judged sermon just three days after the Abdication. The ditty went:

> My Lord Archbishop, what a scold you are;
> And when your man is down, how bold you are;
> Of Christian charity how very scant you are;
> You Auld Lang Swine, how full of cant you are.

'Seldom, if ever,' the Archbishop said, 'has any British sovereign come to the throne with greater natural gifts for his kingship,' an opening gambit some historians might wish to dispute; it seemed to take little note, for example, of the gifts, and even genius, of Henry II, Henry VIII, Elizabeth I or Charles II. 'Seldom, if ever,' he went on, 'has any sovereign been welcomed by a more enthusiastic loyalty,' a remark which was scarcely calculated to reassure the Queen's apprehensions about popular support for her husband. 'From God,' the primate explained, '[Prince Edward] had received a high and sacred trust. Yet, by his own will, he has abdicated. He has surrendered the trust. With characteristic frankness he has told us his motive. It was a craving for private happiness. Strange and sad it must be that for such a motive, however strongly it pressed upon his heart, he should have disappointed hopes so high and abandoned a trust so great.'

Continuing to throttle the English language, Lang warmed to his theme. 'Even more strange and sad it is that he should have sought his happiness in a manner inconsistent with the Christian principles of marriage, and within a social circle whose standards and ways of life are alien to all the best instincts and traditions of his people. Let those

4

who belong to this circle know that today they stand rebuked by the judgement of the nation which had loved King Edward.' Finally he resorted to the last refuge of the pompous, self-justification. 'I have shrunk from saying these words,' he dared to suggest, 'but I have felt compelled for the sake of sincerity and truth to say them.'

Like the former King, Lang too moved in a certain social circle; he once gave a luncheon party at Lambeth Palace exclusively for dowager duchesses. 'As I fully expected,' Lang wrote in his diary, 'my words about the late King let loose a torrent of abuse from the less reputable Press and from a multitude of correspondents. On the other hand, there were just as many letters of gratitude.' This was not the case; his protective chaplains made sure that Lang saw only a few of the abusive letters. He was, however, more than content with a pat on the back from the Prime Minister, Stanley Baldwin, who told him his sermon had been 'the voice of Christian England'. According to the Archbishop's biographer, while Lang was writing this wretched sermon a chaplain entered his study to find the old boy on his knees in prayer.[3] But Lang was not all sanctimonious rectitude. 'My heart aches for the Duke of Windsor,' he wrote in his diary afterwards, 'remembering his childhood, his boyhood, the rich promise of his services as Prince of Wales . . . I cannot bear to think of the kind of life into which he has passed.'

It was because King Edward VIII chose the life of an exile – not that he gave the boredom such a life would entail a moment's consideration at the time – that Elizabeth Bowes-Lyon, Duchess of York, was transported, as in a fairy story, from 145 Piccadilly to Buckingham Palace. But, although in the last few hours events moved towards their climax at what for those closest to the centre of the storm must have seemed a terrifying speed, the Duchess was far from unprepared. She was too shrewd a judge of character not to have appreciated well before it struck the press and the public the flawed nature of her brother-in-law's essentially immature and selfish make-up. His was a character that had never been tested by a single personal sorrow or by the need to make any kind of sacrifice. This is not to say his life had been happy. His relations with both parents were sometimes uncomfortable, his father sending a footman whenever he wished to speak with him, his mother finding it impossible to extend ordinary maternal physical affection. Babies at York Cottage, the ugly suburban house on the Sandringham estate where Edward and his brothers and sister were brought up (it has in recent years been transformed into flats and an estate office), were objects bathed and put to bed by servants, likewise fed and exercised. (Sandringham House itself, purchased by Edward VII when Prince of Wales, has won few prizes for its architectural merits, much though the Royal Family seem to love it. 'On the whole', Alan Lascelles, Assistant Private Secretary to George V, told his wife, writing from Sandringham on 17 January 1936, 'this is one of the least attractive places I have ever seen.' It reminded him, he said, of Government House at Simla, 'all pitch-pine and trophies'.)

David, as Edward VIII was always known to the family, was indulged by his paternal grandparents, King Edward VII and Queen Alexandra, but he walked in permanent fear of displeasing his father. Writing of the time, in 1915, when the Prince of Wales was on active service, Frederick Ponsonby, who served the Court for more than 40 years, knew the Royal Family intimately and is one of the most amusing and reliable witnesses of royal conduct, remarks, 'It always seemed to me that the Prince was at that time very nervous before his father; he remained singularly silent, only opening his mouth when he was addressed and then weighing carefully each word he uttered.'[4]

David was not the only York child to suffer. George and Mary's second son, Albert, always known to the family as Bertie, struggled all his life with a debilitating stammer. Henry, later Duke of Gloucester (and father of the present Duke), born in 1900, the first British prince to go to boarding school, took to the bottle. It was no coincidence that George, later Duke of Kent and again father of the present Duke, born in 1902 and hence eight years younger than the Prince of Wales, was David's favourite brother, for until redeemed by his marriage to Princess Marina of Greece he was nothing more than a drug-addicted playboy. The saddest boy of all, Prince John, was an epileptic who lived in seclusion at Wood Farm, Wolferton, on the Sandringham estate. He died in 1919, at the age of 13. (His namesake and uncle, Prince John, third son and sixth child of Edward VII and Queen Alexandra, had died at Sandringham, in 1871, aged only one day. Edward VII's elder son, the dim-witted Duke of Clarence & Avondale, also died at Sandringham, as did Bertie, eventually.) The most conspicuous outcome of David's emotionally starved childhood was, in consequence of his father's brash and bullying manner, a contempt for authority (which ironically, as king, he would himself one day be expected to embody), and as a result of his mother's frigidity, an inability to establish a sexual relationship other than with a mature, and usually married, woman. His cousin Lord Louis Mountbatten drew up for him a list of 18 unmarried European princesses, but he was wasting his time; David craved love, and starved of his mother's love he turned to surrogate mothers. Eventually it cost him his throne.

Having been baptised Edward Albert Christian George Andrew Patrick David, the last four names being those of the patron saints of England, Scotland, Ireland and Wales, Edward was known as David because he was destined to be created Prince of Wales. On becoming king he could have chosen to be known by any of his seven Christian names, and it is interesting that he decided not to follow his straightlaced father as 'George VI' but his jovial, fun-loving grandfather as Edward VIII. Bertie, on the other hand, whose names were Albert (he had had the temerity to be born on the anniversary of the Prince Consort's death) Frederick Arthur George, did not hesitate to assume the name of his father, with whom he closely identified.

The Archbishop of Canterbury was not the only friend with whom King George V discussed his worries about David. His pronounced opinions on the imperfections of the young ('Good God, *look* at those short skirts, *look* at that bobbed hair!' the King could be heard bellowing, for the benefit of visitors, from a window overlooking the North Terrace of Windsor Castle) were just as likely to be voiced at the dinner table as in private audience with the Archbishop of Canterbury, and one of his favourite dinner companions was his daughter-in-law since 1923, the Duchess of York. High on the list of the young of whose conduct he disapproved was his eldest son and heir. David walked around unaccompanied, he went to night clubs, he took needless risks at point-to-points, he made a fuss when forced to accept both the Military Cross and the French Croix de Guerre for non-combative duties in the war, he wore baggy trousers and enjoyed jazz. Worst of all, he was clearly determined to ignore his matrimonial duties. Most young men were married by 25, to well-bred gals of 23. But the Prince, like his grandfather, seemed to prefer the company of married ladies with a ready-made family. His latest companion was not only married, she was a divorcée and an American. Her name was Wallis Simpson. Even the name Wallis sounded unsuitable.

One or two years younger than the future Edward VIII (there is controversy about the date of her birth), Wallis Simpson was born Wallis Warfield in Baltimore (probably out of wedlock), and grew up in poverty. Her father died of tuberculosis when she was two, her mother ran a boarding house, and Wallis escaped into a gruesome marriage with an alcoholic pilot, Earl Winfield Spencer. After living alone in Washington for a number of years, she obtained a divorce, and decided to seek security and respectability. Hence in 1928 she married a stolid former Coldstream Guards Officer, Ernest Simpson, whose mother was American, and, when they settled in London, on modest means with which to satisfy upper-middle-class pretensions, it was mainly among Americans that they circulated. One of Wallis's American friends was Anne Bigelow, an actress and the widow of Stephen Bigelow of Boston. Few people had a good word to say about Anne Bigelow. 'Vulgar' and 'as hard as nails' seem to have been the general verdict, but the same year that Wallis married Ernest Simpson, Anne Bigelow wed a widower, Lord Sackville, and became the mistress of Knole, one of the largest and most romantic houses in England. On visits to Knole, outside Sevenoaks, Wallis met useful contacts in the aristocratic world, and through the First Secretary at the American Embassy, Benjamin Thaw, she met the Prince of Wales's current mistress – another American, Thelma Furness. Lady Furness, twice married before, was Thaw's sister-in-law.

Wallis Simpson had few if any women friends, yet Lady Furness seems to have regarded Wallis as one of her closest companions. She certainly did her a good turn when she introduced her to the Prince of Wales. The date has been pinpointed by Edward's official biographer, Philip Ziegler, as 10 January 1931, the occasion being a dinner party at Burrough Court, Lady Furness's house near Melton Mowbray.[5] According to Lady Furness's memoirs, *Double Exposure*, Wallis and the Prince then saw one another 'at least once a week for the next three and a half years'. Love certainly didn't bloom at first sight. The Prince, who was 36, had only been in love twice before, which hardly indicates a promiscuous or headstrong nature. Between 1915 and 1918 he was head over heels in love with a married woman 12 years his senior, Viscountess Coke, the daughter-in-law of a Norfolk neighbour, the Earl of Leicester, but this was really puppy love. In 1918 the Prince briefly switched his affections to Lady Rosemary Leveson-Gower, daughter of the Duke of Sutherland – the only occasion, as another of his biographers, Frances Donaldson, points out, 'that he showed more than a passing interest in an unmarried girl'.[6]

The first woman to become his mistress was Freda Dudley Ward, married with two children. Her husband was a Liberal whip, so that like the wives of so many members of parliament, Mrs Dudley Ward spent more evenings apart from her husband than with him. Her meeting with the Prince, during an evening air raid in 1918, took the form of those apocryphal stories people like to tell about someone sitting next to Princess Margaret, and, desperately trying to recall where they have met before, saying, 'And what does your sister do?', to which the Princess is supposed to reply, 'Oh, she's still queen.' The Prince of Wales came up to Freda Dudley Ward in the semi-darkness of a cellar in Belgrave Square, where everyone had taken shelter, and asked where she lived. She in turn enquired where the young man lived (she had, in fact, no idea who he was) and he said in London, and sometimes at Windsor. She ended up dancing the night away with the most eligible bachelor in town (perhaps in the world), who drove her home in the early hours. Their affair lasted 16 years.

There were other quirks of fate attached to the life of the Prince of Wales that a novelist would have been hard pressed to invent. Maud Kerr-Smiley, the Prince's Belgrave Square hostess on the night he met Mrs Dudley Ward, was none other than the sister of Ernest Simpson. So totally involved with Mrs Dudley Ward did the Prince become – seeing her every day when he was in London – that no thought of marriage between the years 1919 and 1934 ever entered his head. He followed her like a lap dog (he followed Wallis like a lap dog, too, from the day they were married until the day he died, hardly being able to bear having her out of his sight), staying wherever she stayed, occasionally having an affair with another woman (including Lady Furness) but essentially remaining devoted to an ultimately unattainable ideal. Exceptionally pretty, discreet and blessed with genuine charm, under different circumstances Mrs Dudley Ward might have made a very suitable queen. She was liked and admired by the Duke and Duchess of York and the Princess Royal, and like the woman who did become queen, Elizabeth Bowes-Lyon, she was adored by all who met her, in particular by servants, to whom she never condescended. Lady Donaldson makes the witty observation that the only way in which Freda Dudley Ward's influence upon the Prince was not a good one was that it was she who set him free to renounce the Crown in order to marry Mrs Simpson.[7] Edward always intended to marry for love, but had he fallen in love with an unmarried woman the composition of the present Royal Family would be very different indeed. The Queen Mother would still be Duchess of York for a start. It can however be argued that Edward had no intention of falling in love with anyone suitable to share the throne, for the last thing he wanted was to be king.

By the time the Prince of Wales was in love – probably for the third, and certainly the last, time in his life – with Wallis Simpson, relations between George V and his eldest son were strained beyond repair. The King, like everyone else, knew about the affair with Mrs Dudley Ward, the greatest objection to which, as far as the King was concerned, was the barrier it placed between the Prince's eventual

9

marriage and the production of a direct heir to the throne. So King George and Queen Mary were hardly in a mood to celebrate when Mrs Dudley Ward was dropped precipitately by the Prince of Wales, for she was dropped so that he could concentrate all his affections on an American divorcée, an 'adventuress' in the opinion of Queen Mary. So far as the King and Queen were concerned, things had simply gone from bad to intolerable, and the King increasingly came to look upon his second son, the Duke of York, since 1930 the father of two children, as the son he would prefer to see on the throne.

Like Mrs Dudley Ward, Wallis Simpson had charm. She also had an acerbic sense of humour. But people other than royalty disliked her, and some were quite rude about her. Henry Channon, a socially ambitious host and Member of Parliament for Southend-on-Sea, who was knighted in 1957 and fathered the Conservative cabinet minister Paul Channon, knew the Prince of Wales well. He lived in some splendour at 5 Belgrave Square, next door to the Duke and Duchess of Kent, and thought Mrs Simpson 'a jolly, plain, intelligent, quiet, unpretentious and unprepossessing little woman'. Always assuming he did not doctor his copious diaries with the benefit of hindsight, he appears to have had remarkable prescience, for he added, some two years before the Abdication, 'She has already the air of a personage who walks into a room as though she almost expected to be curtsied to.' At any rate Channon, known universally as Chips, thought Mrs Simpson would not have been too surprised to receive a curtsey. He considered she had 'complete power over the Prince of Wales, who is trying to launch her socially'.[8] But Channon's diary entries sometimes contradict one another. One minute he tells us that Mrs Simpson was a 'nice, quiet, well-bred mouse of a woman, with large startled eyes and a huge mole', but when he realises her importance to the Prince she becomes 'a woman of charm, sense, balance and great wit, with dignity and taste'. Wit she certainly possessed. Shortly after her marriage to the Duke of Windsor she signed a visitors' book on the Fourth of July: 'Here on the Fourth with my third.' When King Edward told the up-and-coming society photographer Cecil Beaton, who in 1939 was to transform – indeed, create – the image of the new queen, that he wanted prints of all the photographs he had taken of her during a sitting in 1936, Mrs Simpson quipped, 'Oh, Sir, wouldn't that be too much of a Wallis Collection?'

But it would probably be more accurate to describe her as clever and amusing, and it was clever and amusing people who appealed to Edward VIII. Intellectuals and artists he never cultivated. He was, like most of his family, a philistine, which was one reason he was to find exile so excruciatingly boring. He never read a book if he could help it. Told by James Pope-Hennessy he was writing a biography of Trollope, the Duke laughed and said to his wife, ' 'E's writing a book about a trollop.' But he appreciated fine cuisine and elegant furnishings, and these the future Duchess of Windsor was to supply in Paris, aided by an army of servants, with a panache matched only by that of her estranged sister-in-law, the Queen Consort of England.

Precisely why the Prince of Wales decided to marry Mrs Simpson no one will every know for certain; that he became besotted by her is common knowledge. Mrs Simpson was quite capable of receiving a kiss from another woman without returning it, for there was within her personality a certain chilliness that may have reminded David of his mother, the woman whose love he really craved. Mrs Simpson's apparent attempts to dissuade the King from marrying her may have made him all the more determined, and his determination to get his own way, combined with 'an unusual certainty about what he wanted',[9] was one of the most marked traits of his personality. Perhaps at a deep subconscious level, never really wanting to be king, with all the constraints on his personal freedom which kingship, even in an era he hoped to modernise, was bound to entail, he realised that Wallis Simpson was the perfect let-out. Had Edward been imbued with the stoical Hanoverian sense of duty that even some of his most disreputable relatives possessed, he might have resisted the call to happiness and resigned himself to the lottery of birth. But for a man who longed to have a home, not a palace, the idea of a lonely bachelor occupancy of two castles and a country house in addition to Buckingham Palace appalled him. Besides, as his brother King George VI was to complain in 1939 to his Secretary of State for War, Leslie Hore-Belisha, David had never had any discipline in his life.[10]

It is conceivable that Edward's emotional needs would have been met as king had Mrs Simpson consented to be his mistress. But when the Prime Minister, Stanley Baldwin, made so bold as to hint at the feasibility of such an arrangement, the King professed shock. And in 1937 he sued Geoffrey Dennis, Chief of Document Services at the League of Nations, for suggesting in a book called *Coronation Commentary* that Mrs Simpson had been his mistress before their marriage, something which he always vehemently denied. 'We cannot afford any more scandals and insinuations,' the Queen wrote to Walter Monckton, Attorney General to the Duchy of Cornwall, on 21 September 1937, hoping the case against Dennis might be kept out of court, but the Lord Chief Justice delivered himself of the verdict that the libels (Dennis had maintained the King had drunk too much as well) warranted 'a thoroughly efficient horse-whipping', and David won his costs and substantial damages. His denial that Mrs Simpson had been his mistress may have been an act of gallantry to protect her reputation. He was fiercely protective of her in every way, almost demanding that people accept her as some sort of deified being, as someone who had done him a great honour by marrying him, someone of whose love he was quite unworthy. He had also been terrified of an accusation of collusion which might have jeopardised her second divorce. Michael Bloch, to some extent a partisan of the Windsors but whose knowledge of their private affairs is considerable, doubts if before marriage the King and Mrs Simpson 'ever made love in the full sense of the term'.[11] On the other hand, her conduct towards the King was so markedly proprietorial as to suggest some quite definite sexual bond or hold, and at least two people who stayed with the King and Mrs Simpson at the King's Windsor home, Fort Belvedere, went on holiday with them and in fact knew them both extremely well, Duff and Diana Cooper, had no doubt whatsoever that theirs was a sexual relationship long before marriage. Their son, the writer John Julius Norwich, has written, 'I don't believe that either of my parents had any doubt at all that she was his mistress ... Given both their backgrounds, a sexual relationship would only have been to be expected. I am sure that there was one, and equally sure that my parents thought so too.'[12]

If 'in the full sense of the term' they were not lovers, then the King had resigned himself to several years of celibacy, a self-discipline which might have surprised his brother Bertie. A rather cynical argument for believing Edward's denial that Mrs Simpson was his mistress (although it must be said that he was capable of lying over other matters, most notably financial) would be that Wallis calculated that if she capitulated to the King sexually he might well rub along as a bachelor king and she would not become queen; that her best hope of achieving the ambitions Queen Mary was convinced she entertained was by withholding her favours until she was safely married. As things turned out, the 'king' slipped through her fingers and she had to make do with a royal duke. Whatever the truth about the King's and Mrs Simpson's pre-marital relationship, he felt he had no alternative but to 'surrender his high and sacred trust', as the Archbishop of Canterbury saw the matter. To that extent it is possible, although hardly fair, to blame the Abdication on Mrs Simpson; the King became hell-bent on marrying her, and abdicated before ever she was free to marry him. But many did blame her, including the Duchess of York, who for many years harboured a resentment against a woman who had been put in a practically impossible position by a man she gave scant evidence of loving at the time of her marriage to him. Cecil Beaton, who attended the Duke of Windsor's wedding, thought the Duke's expression 'though intent, was essentially sad', and many of the wedding photographs taken by Beaton look as if they were shot at a funeral. That Wallis did come to love him is a matter of thankfulness, as is the fact that despite all the bitterness that developed between the Duke of Windsor and his family, he never ceased to worship the Duchess.

Much nonsense has been written about the way in which Mrs Simpson 'improved' the Prince of Wales. To many observers, there seemed to be no obvious improvement. While waiting for George V to die, Alan Lascelles, who had resigned as Assistant Private Secretary to the Prince in 1929 in disgust at his moral conduct and indolence, sent a weary letter to his wife on 18 January 1936, in which he referred two days prematurely to the future King. 'We are all rather sad at the general demeanour of Edward VIII,' he wrote, 'specially myself, who had hoped for some alteration after eight years; but *plus ça change* etc . . . If he asks me to stay on with him now I feel I must do so, more than ever; for if the Crown is to survive the next reign it will need honest men to hold it up, if it ever did.' Lascelles, a cousin of the Princess Royal's husband, not only stayed on with Edward VIII but in 1947 was knighted by George VI and served as Private Secretary to Elizabeth II for the first year of her reign. It is believed it was he who commented that Edward's 'mental and moral development just stopped dead when he was about 15.'[13] But Alan Lascelles, who came to dislike and distrust the Duke of Windsor intensely, was one of those who initially fell for his famous charm. When he was appointed Assistant Private Secretary in 1920 he wrote in his diary, 'He won me completely. He is the most attractive man I ever met.'

Many others were also to be cruelly disillusioned. What Mrs Simpson did, by publicly acting the role of a friend so intimate she was at liberty to adjust the Prince's tie and tell him who to meet, was to create a scandal which eventually men like Lascelles were powerless to avert. Discretion was not Mrs Simpson's forte. Marie Belloc Lowndes, sister of Hilaire Belloc and herself a prolific writer, was told by friends that one Christmas the Prince of Wales had given Mrs Simpson £50,000 worth of jewels, and a week later, to celebrate the New Year, a further £60,000 worth.[14] He was spending enormous sums on gifts she did not hesitate to flaunt, sums which must have led people to wonder whether such presents were being paid for privately by the Prince or out of state-allocated funds. His income, a large amount of which he had managed to save, came from the revenues of the Duchy of Cornwall, and was in essence intended to defray the costs of his office.

In 1930 the King had allowed the Prince to set up home at Fort Belvedere, at that time a grace and favour residence six miles from Windsor Castle, originally a gazebo built for the Duke of Cumberland, fourth son of George II, overlooking Virginia Water. It had been enlarged considerably by George IV's architect, Jeffry Wyatville, and eventually became the home of Edward's nephew, the Hon. Gerald Lascelles, but it no longer belongs to the Crown. Here it was that the Duke of York, who shared his mother's aversion to ivy, helped the Prince of Wales hack down the undergrowth so that he could replant the garden. Here, as early as the summer of 1934, the compliant Ernest Simpson and his wife were constant visitors, and before long Wallis had moved into the position of hostess, thus upsetting the servants by organising menus and rearranging the furniture. The Prince was delighted. He must have been even more delighted when in the autumn he managed to present Mrs Simpson to his parents – at a reception at Buckingham Palace on the eve of the wedding of the Duke of Kent.

But with Mrs Simpson adopting the role of chatelaine at the Fort, the Prince was becoming increasingly isolated from his family – and royalty perhaps need family relationships more than anyone else: who but their brothers and sisters and their spouses can even address them by their Christian name? It was estrangement from his family after the Abdication that caused the Duke of Windsor such anguish; not that he was particularly fond of them (although he had been very close to his youngest brother George), but they represented relationships which at least were rooted in some sort of reality. Now the only member of the Royal Family (although he was no longer strictly even that, his father having been compelled in the war to exchange his Battenberg title for an English marquisate) who called at Fort Belvedere was Louis Mountbatten. But perhaps it was the timetable as much as the presence of Mrs Simpson, now increasingly in attendance without her husband, that kept them away. Lunch was a hit and miss affair. Tea was served at 6.30 pm and dinner at 10 pm. Informality of a sort that shocked and horrified the King and Queen was the order of the day, the Prince mixing cocktails himself, and marching round the table after dinner wearing a bonnet and playing the bagpipes.

When Wallis was not staying with the Prince at Fort Belvedere she was overseas on holiday with him, cruising in the Mediterranean. The

King was under no illusion that the friendship between the heir apparent and Mrs Simpson was not serious. Indeed he is said to have told the Prime Minister the boy would ruin himself within 12 months of succeeding, apparently adding, very shortly before that event, 'I pray to God that my eldest son will never marry and have children, and that nothing will come between Bertie and Lilibet [Princess Elizabeth, the Duke of York's elder daughter] and the throne.' That Bertie and his wife were aware of the King's sentiments cannot be in doubt; George V was a feisty man who bellowed and roared like the sailor he was, for all to hear, servants, Household and family alike. It is revealing of the King's hopeless inability to guide and train his eldest son, however, that while he could summon up the energy to criticise his clothes or his deportment, on a vital matter of state he remained tongue-tied. Not once was the subject of Mrs Simpson discussed between the Prince and his parents. Nor indeed did any other member of the family raise it with the Prince. Nor did the Prime Minister or the Archbishop of Canterbury. Matters were just allowed to drift until, as king, it became overwhelmingly the responsibility of Edward himself.

George V died late at night on 20 January 1936, eased from this world by an injection of morphia and cocaine administered by his doctor, Lord Dawson. It was a year that was to see no fewer than three monarchs on the throne. To the surprise of some of the family, the new King Edward VIII displayed an almost hysterical grief. In recent years this has been attributed to a realisation on the King's part that he was now trapped in a role he never wanted, caused by a failure to renounce his right to succeed sooner. But a more plausible explanation, surely, is that he was overwhelmed by feelings of guilt about a father he had never loved. At all events, his conduct was in marked contrast to that of his mother, who confined her true feelings to her diary. 'Heartbroken' she wrote. Her outward composure remained serene and dignified, but Edward's emotions were entirely focused upon himself. He had now to square up to the loss of a father with whom he had not enjoyed a happy relationship and to the fact that he intended to marry Wallis Simpson, as king if possible, after abdicating if he had to.

For the next 325 days it seems as though for much of the time he was living in a trance. He spoke to nobody about his plans or apprehensions, and nobody, not even his Prime Minister, spoke to him. Yet anyone who at the time had seriously raised the possibility that King Edward VIII would not reign for the next 30 or even 40 years might have had their sanity questioned. He had been the most popular member of the Royal Family who had ever lived (Elizabeth I and Victoria, although respected and widely acclaimed in old age, were never popular in the modern sense of enjoying the common touch), harnessing to his own youthful looks and aspirations the attitudes of a post-war generation, not only at home but throughout the Empire; in Canada, in particular, he was idolised. He had identified with a generation disillusioned with war and politicians, a generation that longed for a Brave New World.

Edward had been 25 when he undertook his first overseas tour, to Canada, where he understood instinctively a far less formal attitude towards royalty than anything ever experienced by his parents. As he told his father, writing from Government House on Vancouver Island on 23 September 1919, 'it is all so different out here & . . . one thing above all others that won't go down & which one has to be careful not [to] put on is "side" & pompousness!!' Sixteen days previously, Queen Mary had reacted with suppressed anger at 'the amount of handshaking and autograph writing you seem compelled to face! In one place I see you had to give yr. left hand as the right was swollen! This does not sound dignified, 'tho no doubt the people mean it well.' Neither George V nor Queen Mary had ever shaken hands with anyone who had not been formally presented to them, but their son had cheerfully entered an era in which the relationship between royalty and commoners would have seemed as incredible to Queen Victoria as the sight of Concorde flying over Windsor Castle.

The Times greeted the new reign with words which might today be regarded as sycophantic but in reality were nothing short of the truth:

> His winning smile, 'the smile that conquered Canada', his laughter-loving habit of identifying himself with the different nationalities of the United Kingdom and the Empire, his thoughtful tact, his kindness and sympathy, his affection for children, his delightful sense of humour, his bodily activity and love of sport, his ready memory for faces, his freedom, for all his dignity, from personal or official side, his powers of conversation, and his remarkable talent of voice, memory and quiet resourcefulness as a public speaker in other languages besides English [he spoke German and Spanish, and bad French] . . . have endeared him to all who he met on our tours.
>
> But it is not only in the nations of the Empire overseas that he has won the hearts of unnumbered men, women and children. Here, at home, in countless ways, he has no less securely established his hold on the affections of his people. Day in and day out he has never spared himself. He has traversed and studied the country from end to end, has made friends with all sorts and conditions of its workers, has gained an inside

knowledge of its industries and has taken his place under the King, his father, at the head of every national movement for the relief of sickness and suffering and want. As a man he has a real British love for sport and every form of healthy exercise, and to all outward appearance does not seem to know the meaning of physical fear. As a King the people will be able to look up to him as one who has a statesmanlike knowledge and sympathetic understanding of the people of all creeds and races over whom he has been called to reign.

Such a paragon of virtue will strike the modern reader as a product of journalistic hyperbole, but these words reflected exactly the feelings about King Edward in the country, and no such words could conceivably have been written about any other member of the Royal Family. To compare them to anything felt or written about the Duke of York might seem unfair. The Duke was dutiful. He had undertaken overseas tours. At home he had taken a serious and practical interest in the welfare of boys from industrial cities. But the strain of public engagements nearly always showed through. He was shy. He stammered. The stammer had been brought on by idiotic and unsuccessful attempts to alter his natural left-handedness. He had inherited, too, a fair share of Hanoverian temper and neuroticism. Although good-looking and always impressive in uniform, he had the presence of a stand-in, a perfectly acceptable younger son but without the innovative flair and genius for informality of his older brother, of whom the Duchess of York was to tell King Edward he was more fond than anyone.[15] Indeed, Bertie hero-worshipped his brother, which was not surprising. Just ahead of him in age, David had led the pair of them through childhood and adolescence, and far from developing any jealousy about David's future as king, Bertie had been only too relieved to realise, with his physical imperfections, that his was destined to be a relatively relaxed and private life. How ironic then that at the new King's first meeting of the Privy Council, attended by all the members of the Council on the accession of a new sovereign, Clement Attlee thought Edward looked 'very nervous and ill at ease', and that his hand shook so much that eventually he laid his speech on the table. But no doubt he recovered his composure in the evening: he dined with Mrs Simpson.

Unprecedented though the new King's popularity may have been with the public, there were members of his Household, Members of Parliament and Church leaders who entertained serious doubts about his staying power, and one of the most extraordinary incidents of the King's brief reign provoked little surprise to those who witnessed it.

As the gun carriage carrying the late King's coffin was hauled through the gates of New Palace Yard for the lying-in-state at Westminster Hall, the Maltese Cross became dislodged from the top of the Imperial Crown and landed in the gutter. 'Christ! What will happen next?' exclaimed the King, walking with his brothers behind the gun carriage. Walter Elliot, the Minister for Agriculture, who was standing on the pavement, remarked, 'A fitting motto for the coming reign.' 'A most terrible omen,' Harold Nicolson, the former diplomat, now National Labour Member of Parliament for West Leicester, noted that night in his diary.

Elliot, nevertheless, helped swell the King's fan mail by writing to him to say he came into power 'as one of the younger generation' and to assure him that his own generation would serve him in the years ahead 'as loyally as any generation ever served a King'. A former Foreign Secretary, Sir Samuel Hoare, told the King's Assistant Private Secretary, Sir Godfrey Thomas,[16] that Edward would make a great king. How great a shock must the Abdication have been to men like him, for Sir Samuel added, '. . . those of us who know something of his work and worth have no anxiety for the reign that is now beginning.' Winston Churchill, a hopeless romantic, went right over the top when he prophesied that the King's name would shine in history 'as the bravest & best-loved of all the Sovereigns who have worn the island Crown'. The Empire was safe in his hands, Churchill assured the King; he began his reign from a position 'which no King of England has ever had on his accession before'. And so the eulogies, sincere as they were, poured in. Yet even as they did so, on 2 February 1936 the Earl of Crawford & Balcarres, a member of the cabinet from 1916 to 1922, was noting in his diary that if criticism of the King's relations with Mrs Simpson became insistent the King might do something fatuous by talking of abdication. 'He has done so *en famille* before now.'[17]

As if in anticipation of a short reign the King was in no hurry to take up residence at Buckingham Palace, allowing Queen Mary a dilatory eight months to remove herself to Marlborough House, and in the event he only lived at the Palace, which remained effectively an office, for two and a half months. Until October 1936 he retained apartments at York House in St James's Palace, and one day he caused a sensation by walking to Buckingham Palace from St James's. He was to be the only sovereign never to sleep at Windsor Castle, spending every weekend at Fort Belvedere, where fun and relaxation were virtually enjoyed by royal command.

Lady Diana Cooper, the presumed daughter of the 7th Duke of Rutland, and her husband Duff Cooper, the Secretary of State for War, stayed at the Fort in the middle of February, where they found the servants 'a bit hobbledehoy because HM wants to be free of comptrollers and secretaries and equerries, so no one trains them.' Despite the fact that her father was in fact Henry Cust, a minor poet, dilettante editor of the *Pall Mall Gazette* and a Unionist Member of Parliament until he lost his seat in 1906, Diana Cooper was always styled Lady Diana, as though she really was the daughter of a duke, and even after her husband was created Viscount Norwich she retained her courtesy title because, according to her son, 'she never liked the name Norwich and, as she said, she had been Lady Diana for sixty years and was too old to change!'[18] During Duff Cooper's introduction into the House of Lords, Henry Channon thought 'she looked lovely but furious.'[19] Lady Diana, whose maternal grandfather had been an equerry to Queen Victoria, had been blessed with good-looking and talented parents (her mother was a very fine sculptress) and she was herself one of the noted beauties of her day. She also had a great sense of fun and command of style, which was one reason why, despite her early allegiance to Edward VIII, she later became a great friend of the Queen Mother. Duff, too, had distant royal connections; his uncle, the Earl of Fife, had married Edward VII's eldest daughter.

Not only did a reluctance to move into either Buckingham Palace or Windsor Castle, let alone discuss his coronation, suggest an equal reluctance on Edward's part to remain very long on the throne; a certain gaucherie began to suggest he did not care much about the niceties, indeed, had hardly bothered to acquaint himself with how to behave. When he went to the BBC to broadcast a message to the Empire he asked the Director General, Sir John Reith, if he should begin, 'Ladies and Gentlemen'. Nobody would ever need to teach the Duke and Duchess of York how royalty were expected to carry on. But when it came to personal bravery, there was nothing between the two brothers. The Duke of York had fought at the Battle of Jutland, thus becoming the first sovereign, albeit uncrowned at the time, to go into action since William IV fought at the Battle of Cape St Vincent. On 16 July 1936, as the King and the Duke were returning to Buckingham Palace on horseback, an Irish journalist by the name of George McMahon drew a loaded revolver. It was knocked out of his hand by an alert Special Constable, and went skidding under the King's horse. Neither the King nor the Duke turned a hair, and their calm behaviour only served to enhance the King's already spectacular popularity.

And on the score of popularity, there was just no comparison between David and Bertie. Bertie simply did not cut the sort of heroic or easy-going figure that had so distinguished the Prince of Wales, and which, so far as the public were concerned, never deserted him as king. Only a month before the Abdication, Edward VIII spent two days at Portland with the Home Fleet. We have the memoirs of the First Lord of the Admiralty, Sir Samuel Hoare, to remind us of his hold over people's affections. 'The King seemed to know personally every officer and seaman of the Fleet. On one of the evenings there was a smoking concert in the aircraft carrier *Courageous* . . . The vast underdeck was packed with thousands of seamen. In my long experience of public meetings I never saw one so completely dominated by a single personality.' At one point the King started up community singing to the accompaniment of a seaman's mouth organ. 'When he came back to the platform, he made an impromptu speech that brought the house down.' When one of the sailors proposed three cheers for the King, 'there followed an unforgettable scene of the wildest and most spontaneous enthusiasm. Here, indeed, was the Prince Charming, who could win the hearts of all sorts of conditions of men and women and send a thrill through great crowds.'[20]

For all his popularity with homespun sailors and out of work miners, what the King still lacked in early middle age (and his heir presumptive so conspicuously possessed) were two things nearly always seen as essentials in a sovereign, a happy home life and an heir. One reason for George IV's unprecedented unpopularity had been his virtual bachelor status. 'Good riddance, say I' the sister-in-law of one of the canons of Windsor remarked as she saw the King's mistress, Lady Conyngham, beating a hasty retreat with wagonloads of furniture when George IV died. 'I am glad we are going to have a *Queen*.' And in this respect one of George V's most unlikely friends, J. H. Thomas, at one time General Secretary of the National Union of Railwaymen, who used to be invited to stay at Balmoral for a fortnight every summer, had his finger firmly on the national pulse. Thomas, a rough diamond, played a rather similar role with George V as that enacted by John Brown in the case of Queen Victoria, and in modern times by the Queen's life-time confidante, Margaret McDonald, daughter of a railwayman, who spent 67 years as her nurse and personal maid. Without undue deference but imbued with heartfelt devotion, he kept the King informed of opinion outside the restricted world of the Court. In return, the King could talk to him (as Victoria had talked to Brown) with that easy familiarity adopted by upper-middle-class families towards their servants.

When George V died, Thomas told Harold Nicolson he had lost one of his dearest friends. 'And what makes it so odd,' Nicolson told his wife, the writer Vita Sackville-West, 'is that it is true. The King adored him.' It is easy to see why. One day King George was regretting that the princes didn't like Balmoral. 'I don't wonder at that, Sir,' said Jim Thomas. 'It's a bloody dull 'ouse.' On another occasion the King told Thomas an interesting story, of how he had defied his redoubtable grandmother, which led, when Thomas came to recount the tale to Harold Nicolson, to an even more revealing comment on the current position of King Edward VIII. ' "J.H.", 'e says to me one day, "did I ever tell you that my grandmother asked me not to call myself George but Albert? I found a letter on my dressing table at Windsor saying that it was her dearest wish that I should change my name. But I said I wouldn't. I had been Christened George, and George I would remain." 'E was like that, you know, 'arold, not afraid of people, if you know what I mean. And now 'ere we 'ave this little obstinate man with 'is Mrs Simpson. Hit won't do, 'arold, I tell you that straight. I know the people of this country. I *know* them. They 'ate 'aving no family life at Court.'[21]

King Edward was in fact desperately trying to manufacture some sort of 'family' life, even going so far as to insert Mrs Simpson's name in the Court Circular, on one occasion giving her precedence over the Duke and Duchess of York. Such conduct was in contempt of all known rules of proper behaviour, a gauntlet thrown down in the face of protocol. It followed an incident which did as much as any other to blacken Mrs Simpson in the eyes of the Duchess, although the true cause of the brouhaha was the King himself. Edward had declined an invitation to open an extension to a hospital in Aberdeen while in residence at Balmoral, and asked the Duke and Duchess of York to deputise for him. 'I do wish that David could have done it,' the Duchess wrote to Queen Mary on 19 September, 'as they have all worked so hard for so long, and it will be one of the best in Scotland, and it would have given such enormous pleasure to the countryside.' In 1993, as Queen Mother, the Duchess returned to the hospital when she required a general anaesthetic for the removal of a blockage from her throat. Meanwhile, she was not the only person who wished 'that David could have done it'. While she and the Duke were at the hospital, the King drove 60 miles to Aberdeen to meet Wallis, to save her the minor inconvenience, to which members of the Royal Family were perfectly accustomed, of changing trains at Ballater. The train was late, so the King had to hang around, not very successfully disguised in motoring goggles, an incongruous adornment to his Highland dress. Of course he was recognised, and two photographs appeared in the local newspaper, one of the Yorks performing their royal duty, the other with the caption: 'His Majesty in Aberdeen. Surprise visit in car to meet guests.' 'Aberdeen will never forgive him,' Chips Channon predicted.

The Yorks were staying at Birkhall, a 6,500-acre estate purchased by Queen Victoria in 1852 for the Prince of Wales. The house is a small, white early eighteenth-century building well secluded in woodland, with terraced gardens that descend to the River Muick. Since 1952 it has remained a summer residence for the Queen Mother.[22] Aware that Edward had no intention of inviting anyone to Balmoral other than personal friends, and that the Archbishop of Canterbury, still grieving for the loss of George V, would be bound to miss his summer holiday with the late King, the Duke and Duchess of York had invited Dr Lang to stay with them at Birkhall. 'They were kindness itself,' he noted. 'The old house is full of charm and the Duchess has done much with the garden.' On the second day of the Archbishop's visit, after tea, the two Princesses, Elizabeth and Margaret Rose, as the younger daughter was still known, sang 'action-songs' for his entertainment. Some presentiment must have occurred to the Archbishop, for he wrote in his diary, 'It was strange to think of the destiny which may be awaiting the little Elizabeth, at present second from the Throne! She and her lively little sister are certainly most entrancing children.'

When the Yorks arrived at Balmoral Castle for dinner three days after the fiasco in Aberdeen, Mrs Simpson, ignorant of protocol as ever, instinctively, as though hostess, stepped forward to greet them, instead of waiting to be presented by the King – or for the royal couple to greet her. Many versions of the Duchess's reaction have circulated, including one which has her openly showing her resentment. She was too well-mannered to have done that. But on 11 October the Duchess let down her hair to Queen Mary, her closest confidante in the family. Wonderful weather notwithstanding, she told her mother-in-law, 'there has also been a great sadness and sense of loss for all the people . . . David does not seem to possess the faculty of making others feel *wanted*. It is very sad, and I feel that the whole difficulty is a certain person. I do not feel that I *can* make advances to her and ask her to our house, as I imagine would be liked, and this fact is bound to make relations a little difficult . . . The whole situation is complicated and *horrible*, and I feel so unhappy about it sometimes, so you must forgive me, darling Mama, for letting myself go so indiscreetly. There is nobody that I can talk to, as ever since I have married I have made a strict rule never to discuss anything of Family matters with my own relations – nor would they wish it, but it leaves so few people to let off steam to occasionally.' She wondered if anything had 'transpired about Xmas' and hoped they could all spend it together. 'Do suggest it to David,' she wrote, 'as he loves and admires you and I am sure would arrange what you wish.' By Christmas, the Yorks would be King and Queen and David would be kicking his heels in Austria.

The incident at Balmoral had not been the first occasion on which Mrs Simpson had put her foot in it. During tea at the Royal Lodge, the Yorks' home in Windsor Great Park, Wallis, not invited but wheeled in from Fort Belvedere by the King, had volunteered advice on improving the landscape, a task already undertaken with exemplary knowledge and skill by the Duke and Duchess themselves. (The Duke's horticultural expertise was demonstrated in an ingenious and original letter of thanks for a stay in May 1935 with the Countess of Stair, in which he wrote 'in the language of rhododendrons'. It is reproduced as Appendix A.) The children's governess, Marion Crawford, was present, and recorded, in *The Little Princesses*,[23] '[Mrs Simpson] had a distinctly proprietary way of speaking to the new King. I remember she drew him to the window and suggested how certain trees might be moved, and a part of a hill taken away to improve the view.' There is no reason to disbelieve this account of events, and it has been interpreted as an attempt to impress upon the Duchess that Mrs Simpson was well aware that the Royal Lodge was Crown property, and so was she. 'I have never admired the Duke and Duchess more than on that afternoon,' Crawfie wrote. 'With quiet and charming dignity they made the best of this awkward occasion and gave no sign whatsoever of their feelings. But the atmosphere was not a comfortable one.'

Crawfie's indiscretions as an authoress – mild by any standards – were to lead to employees of the Royal Family eventually being compelled to sign a declaration that they will not divulge anything of a personal nature learned in the course of their duties. When the Duchess of York, after she had become queen, heard that the formidable Member of Parliament for Plymouth, Nancy Astor, had somehow acquired a copy of the manuscript of *The Little Princesses* she wrote to Lady Astor to say:

Thank you so much for sending on the manuscript of Miss Crawford's story. Perhaps you have heard the whole thing has been a great shock to us. We have worried greatly over this matter and can only think that our late and completely trusted governess has gone off her head, because she promised in writing that she would not publish any story about the daughters and this development has made us very sad. We have to trust people completely and such a thing has never happened before.

Poor Crawfie was dislodged from her grace and favour retirement apartments and went back to Scotland in disgrace, there to pursue a new career, as a journalist. But in 1955 the Queen Mother received a pleasant surprise. Idly turning the pages of *Woman's Own* she discovered that, according to Marion Crawford's account of the Trooping the Colour, the 'bearing and dignity' of Queen Elizabeth II had 'caused admiration among the spectators'. Ascot, too, the Queen Mother read with an understandable smile on her face, had had 'an enthusiasm about it never seen there before'. Both items of information came as news, however, to Her Majesty, for a train strike had caused cancellation of the Trooping, and Ascot, for the same reason, had been postponed. Alas for Crawfie, such magazines as *Woman's Own* are printed well ahead of publication date, and Crawfie's contract was promptly terminated.

Whatever the truth about the Duchess of York's reaction to Mrs Simpson's conduct at Windsor and Balmoral, clearly her relations with the King remained as snug as ever at this time. On 4 October she was writing to him to say, 'Darling David, I do want to thank you most gratefully for lending us Birkhall this year. It is the most wonderful holiday for us, and I cannot tell you how much better we both feel after 6 weeks of complete peace. I honestly don't believe that I could cope with all the problems of modern life if it wasn't for Birkhall, & it was ANGELIC and kind of you to let us have it.

'I do thank you from my heart; you are always so sweet and thoughtful to us, and I wish that I could thank you as I would wish.'

She went on to ask if she might bother him with something: 'It really isn't my business at all,' she said, but could he inspect some of the St John Ambulance volunteers in Hyde Park 'who give up their hard-earned leisure to cope with accidents & public occasions' and 'hardly ever get a pat on the back'? They would, she told the King, 'feel so set up if you *could* have a look at them'. If we take the Duchess's letter at face value, and there seems no reason not to, it is a testimony both to her genuine personal touch and to the King's. '*Please* don't give me away,' she implored him, 'as it really has nothing to do with me. I am being an interfering busybody, but the St John order is run by *old old* men, & they forget the rank and file! I felt I would like to ask you this – it means so much to these excellent people.' She signed herself, 'Your loving sister-in-law.'

On 16 September Wallis had written to Edward from Paris in a serious attempt to break off their relationship, but had returned under relentless pressure from the King, whose every move was motivated by the fear of losing her. In 1935 he had written to Wallis saying, 'I love you more and more every minute and no difficulties or complications can possibly prevent our ultimate happiness.' There were actually two fairly major difficulties in the way; Wallis was married, and Edward was heir to the throne. Wallis, to her credit, was less selfish and more pragmatic. 'It's a tragedy that he can't bring himself to marry without loving,' she told her aunt, Bessie Merryman.

Charting the course of the King's eleven-month reign, Michael Bloch observes, 'When he was sure of her, when she was standing by him, he was a good king; otherwise he was hopeless.'[24] There have been those – the late Dowager Lady Dashwood was one – who believed that a public subscription should have been organised to raise a statue to Mrs Simpson in gratitude to her for organising his removal.[25] It was probably only about a month into the reign when Wallis realised her husband Ernest was in love with another woman, and seriously contemplating divorce. At a meeting at York House in the early spring between the King and Ernest Simpson, witnessed by the editor-in-chief of Reuters, Bernard Rickatson-Hatt, Simpson asked the King whether he meant to marry Wallis. The King, rising from his chair, apparently said, 'Do you really think I would be crowned without Wallis at my side?'[26] However, the Royal Family and the politicians were still hopeful that the problem of 'a certain person' would just somehow go away.

The Simpsons were both half-hearted about separating. And the last thing the Royal Family wanted was a divorce, for they assumed the King was unlikely to commit bigamy. In the end, it was the King himself who organised the divorce, mustering lawyers when he should have been attending to the Red Boxes, never mind discussing arrangements for his coronation or giving his mind to the formation of a new, more youthful Household. It is significant that he promoted or reappointed so many of his father's inflexible courtiers. He seems to have been convinced he would marry Wallis, and at the same time to have been subconsciously doubtful about staying on as king, although in the end he did not give up his throne without a fight. 'Sooner or later my Prime Minister must meet my future wife,' he told Mrs Simpson, having invited Mr and Mrs Stanley Baldwin to dinner on 27 May. 'The idea is impossible. They'd never let you,' Wallis tells us she replied. To which Edward responded, 'I will manage it somehow.'[27] Including the King and his equerry there were 17 at the dinner, and Mrs Simpson found the Baldwins 'pleasant but distant'. They thought she had 'stolen the fairy Prince'. Everybody's names appeared in the Court Circular, including that of Mrs Simpson's cuckolded husband. Six weeks later, after another dinner party attended by the Duke and Duchess of York, Mrs Simpson again appeared in the Court Circular, but this time her husband's name was missing. He had taken himself off to the Guards' Club as an essential preparatory move before divorce.

'The Simpson scandal is growing,' Chips Channon noted. In August, the King set out on holiday, attended by two private secretaries and a cabinet minister (Duff Cooper; Lady Diana went too), and accompanied, among others, by Mrs Simpson. The King had chartered from Lady Yule a yacht called the *Nahlin* (the entire holiday is said to have cost £10,000), which he and his party boarded at Sibernik in Yugoslavia. The society hostess Lady Colefax (quoted in Harold Nicolson's diary) had thought that until July 1936 'there was no indiscretion at all, and that Wallis seemed really to understand the responsibility of her position.' But on 6 October Nicolson was writing, 'Since the *Nahlin* things have gone more recklessly. Rob Bernays [Robert Bernays, the National Liberal MP for Bristol; he was killed in 1945] thinks that the thing is really serious and will shake the foundations of the monarchy.' Much of the King's indiscretion he attributed to the fact that 'The King resents the suggestion that Wallis is not as good as anyone else.' This would account for his insistence on having her name blazoned in the Court Circular. 'There is,' Nicolson wrote, 'seething criticism which may develop into actual discontent.'

The seething criticism had been fanned by American newspaper reports of the notorious *Nahlin* cruise. The King appeared in public in nothing but shorts, and according to Diana Cooper, Mrs Simpson 'looked a figure of fun in a child's piqué dress and a ridiculous baby's bonnet. As her face is an adult's face *par excellence*, the silly bonnet looked grotesque.'[28] Lady Diana did not enjoy the trip at all. Shabby clothes, she found, were *de rigueur*, the other guests were not in the least interested in sightseeing, and the catering on board seems to have been as chaotic as at the Fort, the King being served last and seldom getting anything to eat at all. But he seems to have enjoyed himself if nobody else did, ignoring the heat, fishing, rowing about and walking when the others were wilting.[29] As he wore round his neck two crosses on a gold chain, and Mrs Simpson wore identical crosses on her wrist (not to mention the fact that they occupied a suite at the opposite end of the boat from all the other guests), it is hardly surprising that Mrs Simpson was now regarded as his mistress. After a final five days in Vienna, even the King realised things could not go on like this for ever. He flew home from Zurich 'to resume my duties and to deal with a personal problem which it had become increasingly clear could not be held much longer in abeyance.'[30]

Once the King had sorted out his personal problem by abdicating, Alan Lascelles wrote to Diana Cooper – from Buckingham Palace on 12 December 1936 – to say, 'It is my belief that he – Edward – what does one call him? – will, if things go well, know greater happiness in the future than he has ever known in the past. This is some consolation. For years I have felt that kingship could never bring him happiness, any more than the papacy could bring it to Duff or me.' He said that in all the time he had known Edward (17 years, on and off) he had never seen him content 'save in those days in the *Nahlin* when there was nothing to remind him that he was a king.'[31]

2

A Pretty Kettle of Fish!

THE SIMPSON DIVORCE PETITION was heard in Ipswich on 27 October 1936. At dinner the next night at Lady Colefax's home, Argyll House in Chelsea, Harold Nicolson discussed with Diana Cooper's mother, the Duchess of Rutland, 'the great Simpson question'. Afterwards he recorded serious rumours that the King intended to create Mrs Simpson Duchess of Edinburgh, a dukedom traditionally reserved for royalty, which had been in abeyance since the death, 36 years before, of Queen Victoria's second son. As a peeress in her own right, Mrs Simpson would have been entitled to take her seat in the House of Lords, so if the King seriously intended using his own prerogative to ennoble Mrs Simpson without consulting the Prime Minister he was heading for a constitutional crisis. The King was rumoured also to be contemplating a morganatic marriage – a marriage between a person of high rank whose wife is not elevated to a similar rank, and whose children have no rights of succession to the higher party's titles or property. The King was in fact advised that if he were to enter into such a marriage with Mrs Simpson it would require the sanction of parliament.

Apparently at this stage Mrs Simpson did not think the King would be so foolish as to contemplate a morganatic marriage, but Nicolson gathered from other people that there was 'considerable danger'. The danger lay in the fact that there is no provision in English law for the morganatic marriage of the Sovereign, and, under common law every wife automatically enjoys the status of her husband. The clear implication of a morganatic marriage (for which, as a last ditch attempt to save his crown, the King did eventually ask) was that the King's wife was unfit to be queen. That would have placed her on a par with George IV's embarrassingly bawdy wife, Caroline of Brunswick-Wolfenbuttel, who was locked out of Westminster Abbey on the day of the King's coronation.

While waiting for the divorce proceedings, Mrs Simpson lodged in a rented house in Felixstowe. The King became restless, fulfilled no public engagements and lost all consideration for his Household. Indeed, the management of Buckingham Palace became a shambles. No one knew the King's intentions. Cars, footmen and equerries were kept waiting. Everyone whispered in corners. The British press refrained from speculation (a state of affairs impossible to imagine today), and one reason, perhaps, why the press harried Princess Margaret when she was deciding whether to marry Peter Townsend, and with even greater virulence pursued the private lives of the Prince and Princess of Wales and the Duke and Duchess of York in the dying years of the twentieth century, was because they have never forgiven themselves for their reticence in not reporting the most dramatic royal love story ever. Meanwhile, the American press were having a field day, and letters from 'Worried of North Dakota' were beginning to land through the letterbox at 10 Downing Street, Lambeth Palace, and even Marlborough House. Yet, at an audience with the King on 14 October, Stanley Baldwin funked raising the question of the monarch's matrimonial plans. So badly briefed were those whose responsibility it was to warn the King of danger that neither Baldwin nor Alexander Hardinge (who had served George V as Assistant Private Secretary since 1920 and whom Edward had appointed as his Private Secretary) knew of the pending divorce date. As soon as Hardinge did find out (on 15 October) he urged Baldwin to see the King and try to have the proceedings stopped. Another audience was arranged for 20 October, at Fort Belvedere. During the course of it the King, so Baldwin later remarked, told a lie – the only one he ever did tell to Baldwin. He said he (the King) had no right to interfere in the affairs of Mrs Simpson just because she was his friend. He had of course been interfering like mad.

Only four days after this meeting with Baldwin, the King, walking in the garden at Fort Belvedere, broached the question of abdication with the man who was eventually to play the role of trusted go-between for Edward and the future George VI, Walter Monckton. The King had known Monckton since his brief spell in 1912 as an undergraduate at Magdalen, for Monckton had been president of the Oxford Union; and as Attorney General to the Duchy of Cornwall since 1932 Monckton was already well versed in the King's affairs.

The Simpsons' divorce proceedings went ahead as planned. The usual fabricated evidence necessary for a divorce those days was sworn to be true, and the judge, reluctantly, granted Wallis Simpson a decree nisi with costs against her technically innocent husband, his costs later being reimbursed, very probably with funds made available to Mrs Simpson by the King. That evening a triumphant Edward dined with Wallis, and gave her a £10,000 emerald ring, which he had already had inscribed at Cartier 'WE [Wallis and Edward] are ours now, 27 × 36.' As far as he was concerned, they were engaged.

Two days later Robert Bruce-Lockhart, who in 1930 had joined the *Evening Standard* to write the Londoner's Diary in collaboration with Harold Nicolson, and dined out a good deal with the King, the Simpsons and the reigning society hostesses, noted in his diary, 'Talk, as usual, mostly about the King and Mrs Simpson . . . Everyone . . . is convinced that the King will marry her.'[1] The only question to be settled was whether the King would abdicate in order to do so, or whether he would marry morganatically. 'One must conclude,' Michael Bloch has written, 'that the King in his heart knew what was coming – but that he did not wish to know.'[2] The King in fact knew he had to go, but was in no hurry to make the first move. On 3 November he opened parliament for the first and last time, driving in a Daimler instead of a coach because it was raining, although the coach did not leak. Harold Nicolson (like Churchill, an incorrigible romantic) told his wife the King looked like a boy of 18. Another bisexual onlooker, and an equally incorrigible snob, Chips Channon, knocked yet another year off the King's 42 years, describing him as 'looking exactly as he did in 1911, at the investiture [as Prince of Wales] at Caernarvon.'

There was a real dilemma facing the King. Mrs Simpson's decree would not be made absolute until April 1937. His coronation, with the Duke of York appointed chairman of the Coronation Commission, had been fixed for 12 May. That left perhaps three weeks in which to get married (practically an impossibility), or to go forward to his coronation without first revealing his matrimonial plans. Events continued to drift, until the King returned to Fort Belvedere on 13 November at the conclusion of his visit to the Home Fleet. His butler told him a letter had arrived from Major Hardinge (dated that day), who had telephoned to stress how important it was the King should read it immediately. It read as follows:

Sir,

 With my humble duty.

 As your Majesty's Private Secretary, I feel it my duty to bring to your notice the following facts which have come to my knowledge and which I *know* to be accurate.

(1) The silence of the British press on the subject of Your Majesty's friendship with Mrs Simpson is not going to be maintained. It is probably only a matter of days before the outburst begins. Judging from the letters from British subjects living in foreign countries where the Press has been outspoken, the effect will be calamitous.

(2) The Prime Minister and senior members of the Government are meeting today to discuss what action should be taken to deal with the serious situation which is developing. As Your Majesty no doubt knows, the resignation of the Government – an eventuality which can by no means be excluded – would result in Your Majesty having to find someone else capable of forming a government which would receive the support of the present House of Commons. I have reason to know that, in view of the feeling prevalent among members of the House of Commons of all parties, this is hardly within the bounds of possibility. The only alternative remaining is a dissolution and a General Election, in which Your Majesty's personal affairs would be the chief issue – and I cannot help feeling that even those who would sympathise with Your Majesty as an individual would deeply resent the damage which would inevitably be done to the Crown, the corner-stone on which the whole Empire rests.

If Your Majesty will permit me to say so, there is only one step which holds out any prospect of avoiding this dangerous situation, and that is for Mrs Simpson to go abroad *without further delay*, and I would beg Your Majesty to give this proposal your earnest consideration before the position becomes irretrievable. Owing to the changing attitude of the Press, the matter has become one of great urgency.

This letter has been criticised as unsympathetic, as too bold, and unlikely to achieve its objectives. The fact remains that Hardinge was acting quite properly in writing as he did, and it required some courage on his part to take the bull by the horns. The King had virtually forbidden anyone but the Prime Minister to approach him on the subject, and the letter came as a bombshell because it forced him to realise the game was up. Hardinge was intelligent but very traditional, and eventually even fell foul of George VI, who sacked him for incompetence in 1943. But for all his failings as a courtier, on this occasion he was merely the bearer of bad news, for which Edward VIII never forgave him. But the King was moved to action. He asked Walter Monckton to liaise between himself and the Prime Minister (this was of course the Private Secretary's prerogative) and then, without even acknowledging the letter, he asked Hardinge to arrange an audience with Baldwin. He wanted Baldwin to bring with him four other members of the cabinet. The Prime Minister declined. (One of those the King wanted to see at this stage was Duff Cooper.) In arranging to see Baldwin so soon he had immediately gone against the advice of Monckton, who had counselled patience. King Edward VIII was not the easiest man to serve.

After lunching with Baldwin on 15 November, the Australian High Commissioner confirmed by letter his belief that the Dominions would not accept Mrs Simpson as queen, that if the King insisted on marrying her he would have to abdicate, and that if he refused to abdicate the Government would have to resign. The Governor General of Canada had already sent a warning shot across Baldwin's bows. The Labour Party told him they did not object in principle to an American, but they would not accept Mrs Simpson. Privy Councillors were threatening to resign. Still the press remained silent, so that only those at the centre of affairs, in the heart of the capital, knew how close the nation was to political turmoil.

At his meeting with Baldwin at Buckingham Palace on 16 November, the King immediately broached the subject of a constitutional crisis. Baldwin left the King in no doubt that marriage to Mrs Simpson, whereby she would become queen, would be unacceptable to the country. But he also advised the King there would be no objection to Mrs Simpson becoming his mistress. The King said that was hypocrisy, and that he intended to abdicate and marry. It seems that this intention was immediately imparted, by Baldwin, to Alexander Hardinge, whose wife, presumably afraid a servant might peep at her diary, wrote that night, '*Le Premier Ministre a vu le roi ce soir – le souverain va partir.*'

By now Queen Mary was at least being kept informed of events by her 'poor silly son' (as she came to think of him when speaking to Harold Nicolson on 29 July 1952, the day he presented her with a copy of his life of George V).[3] David dined with her after seeing Baldwin, and she wrote to him the following morning to say, 'As your mother I must send you a line of true sympathy in the difficult position in which you are placed – I have been thinking of you all day, hoping you are making a wise decision for your future.' This kind and thoughtful letter should be read in conjunction with a letter the King, as Prince of Wales, had sent to Freda Dudley Ward on 18 October 1921: 'My mother is sweet to me & so sensible. There's really no rot about her although she is a martinet. But that is her upbringing and no fault of hers, and she really is a wonderful woman.' And both letters should be borne in mind when assessing the former King's comment to his wife when Queen Mary died: 'I'm afraid the fluids in her veins have always been as icy cold as they are now in death.'[4] Perhaps this last caustic complaint was activated by Queen Mary's steadfast refusal to accept that in abdicating Edward made the right decision, and her equally steadfast refusal ever to receive the Duchess of Windsor.

Although Queen Mary was not averse in widowhood to dancing the Hokey Cokey, both she and George V were reserved by nature, and both found it impossible to express physical affection. But in letters to one another, and to their children, they never disguised the depth of their true feelings. 'Most darling David,' Queen Mary would write to her eldest son, signing her letters, 'ever yr devoted Mother', and the King addressed the Prince of Wales as 'Dearest David' and signed off, 'Ever my dear boy, Yr most devoted Papa'. But Queen Mary was never in any doubt where Edward's duty lay. The concept of duty was the cornerstone of her own life. She had been coerced into an engagement with the second in line to the throne, the uncouth, dissolute Duke of Clarence & Avondale, and when, mercifully, he died she had not hesitated to fulfil her duty again by marrying his less than romantic younger brother. But her maternal sympathies in 1936 were fully engaged. Indeed, they were engaged twice over, for she realised that if Edward did abdicate, Bertie would have to take over, and the only thing to be said for that was that he had a supportive wife, and two children to succeed.

No one had ever regarded Bertie as being natural material for kingship. Edward himself thought nothing of calling on the Duke and Duchess of Kent for tea on 15 November, when we can hardly imagine they discussed the weather, before taking the trouble to inform his heir presumptive of his intentions. This he did on 17 November, having told his mother the night before.

Yet even at this stage the King had not decided irrevocably to abdicate. He asked the Government to consider two proposals, one reasonably practical, the other a virtual impossibility. The non-starter was an unconstitutional suggestion that he broadcast to the nation and then go abroad while 'the people' somehow came to a decision. This would have undermined the right of his ministers to proffer advice, and presupposed some overwhelming verdict in the country one way or the other. No one who had studied the Civil War could have countenanced the possibility of splitting the nation into two factions in a dispute concerning the King. The second suggestion was that he should have a morganatic marriage. This would have satisfied Mrs Simpson, for she had consistently tried to separate from the King so that he should not abdicate. A morganatic marriage in theory would have provided a face-saver all round. But this idea, too, was given short shrift. Edward told his mother apropos of Wallis, 'for me the question is not whether she is acceptable to me but whether I am worthy of her.'[5] He would never have contemplated his wife being saddled with an inferior status if he could avoid it – but this was precisely what happened in the end. A morganatic marriage would have automatically disinherited his children too, so that he would in effect have reigned as a caretaker king, the line of descent going eventually to his brothers and their children. This would have diminished his own standing and authority. There would have been no place for a morganatic wife on any official occasion – the state opening of parliament, for instance; she would always have stayed at home, a constant reminder that the King's wife was not the Queen.

The reason so many people in society had discussed the prospect of a morganatic marriage, and had spread rumours about Mrs Simpson being created Duchess of Edinburgh, was because no one ever seriously believed she would be queen. The King was the last to wake up to that. Baldwin has been reported as telling John Davidson, Chancellor of the Duchy of Lancaster, that the King wanted Mrs Simpson 'to be a Duchess – not to be royal, but less than royal, but rather better than an ordinary duchess'. Such a remark, if ever made, would have been jibberish. To be 'less than royal' is a state that doesn't exist. Either you are royal or you are not. And there is no way anyone can be 'better than an ordinary duchess' short of being a princess, and hence royal. It is small wonder the idea scarcely got off the ground. In any case, Baldwin did not believe the necessary legislation would be passed by parliament. And the whole matter of the King's marriage had to be settled one way or the other before the coronation, a vastly complex ceremony involving countless visitors from overseas, which could hardly be postponed indefinitely. When Edward eventually abdicated, time was so short that the original date was retained. Same Day, Different King became the watchword.

Queen Mary had twice asked to see Baldwin. On the first occasion, abandoning her usual rigid demeanour, she came 'trotting across the room', and, without even giving Baldwin time to bow, took his hand in both of hers and exclaimed, 'Well, Prime Minister, here's a pretty kettle of fish!' She was in communication with Hardinge, too, one of whose diplomatic tasks was to make sure Queen Mary did not drive up the Mall to see the King while Mrs Simpson was at Buckingham Palace. Queen Mary also discussed her son's affairs with the Archbishop of Canterbury, and of course with members of her family, in particular with the Princess Royal, but on no occasion could she bring herself to have a frank and friendly talk with the King himself.

The day after dining with his mother, Edward told the Duke of York of his intention to marry Wallis. The Duke and Duchess of York had many friends outside immediate Court circles – writers and intellectuals like Osbert Sitwell – but they never mixed as freely in café society as Edward had done. Hence they were less attuned to gossip, and the King's intentions came to Bertie as a shock. '[He] was so taken aback by my news that in his shy way he could not bring himself to express his innermost feelings at the time,' the Duke of Windsor recorded in his autobiography. 'This, after all, was not surprising, for next to myself Bertie had most at stake: it was he who would have to wear the crown if I left, and his genuine concern for me was mixed with the dread of having to assume the responsibilities of kingship.'

By 23 November the Duke of York pulled himself together sufficiently to send a charming letter to the brother he had always believed was going to be so successful on the throne:

> My dear David,
>
>   When you told me of your decision to marry Wallis the other evening, I do hope you did not think that I was unsympathetic about it. Since then I have been thinking a great deal about you, as I do *so* long for you to be happy with the one person you adore.
>
>   I, of all people, should understand your own personal feelings at this time, which I do indeed.
>
>   I do realise all your great difficulties, & I feel sure that whatever you decide to do will be in the best interests of the Country & Empire.
>
>   I feel I must send you this note, because when we were talking the other evening I am afraid I could not say what I really felt, as your news came as such a great surprise to me.
>
>   Do let me know when I can come & see you tomorrow.
>
>   Ever
>   Your very devoted
>   Bertie

The Duke saw his brother again on the evening of the 24th. Unknown to him, on the same day that he wrote that letter, the Duchess was picking up her pen to send a rather frantic note to her brother-in-law, which she headed PRIVATE. Taken with her opening sentence, '*Please* read this,' we may wonder whether she was uncertain about letters even from the family getting through the haphazard administration. 'Darling David,' she wrote,

Please read this.

Please be kind to Bertie when you see him, because he loves you and minds terribly all that happens to you. I wish that you could realise how loyal & true he is to you, and you have no idea how hard it has been for him lately.

I *know* that he is fonder of you than anybody else, & as his wife, I must write & tell you this. I am terrified for him – so Do help him.

And *for God's sake* don't tell him that I have written – we both uphold you always.

E.

We want you to be happy more than anything else, but it's awfully difficult for Bertie to say what he thinks. You know how shy he is – so do help him.

Never once did Edward see fit to ask Elizabeth if she minded awfully becoming Queen, with responsibility for training the heir to the throne and for holding the hand of a highly overwrought and nervous king. But then Edward did not even consult his Household. When his Assistant Private Secretary, Sir Godfrey Thomas, told the Duke of York he had 'been shut out of all discussion about the King's relationship with Mrs Simpson', the Duke replied, 'That is what we all have, myself included, and I feel it very much. I have tried to broach the subject many times this year but he has always turned a deaf ear to it.'

'Every day I pray to God that [the King] will see reason, and not abandon his people,' the Duchess wrote to Queen Mary, but her prayers were in vain. The King was living in a strange hyperactive world of his own. He had his Christmas card printed, an eighteenth-century watercolour of the Fort, which was sent to friends after the Abdication, as if he was still living there. He embarked on one last public engagement, a goodwill visit, conducted with unparalleled success, to the depressed mining areas of Wales. Within hours of his return, short of sleep and suffering from a heavy cold, he attended a dinner party as the guest of honour of Chips Channon, where he 'ate a lot, drank claret and laughed much'.[6] Mrs Simpson was there too. Victor Cazalet, Member of Parliament for Chippenham, noted that every few minutes the King gazed at her, a happiness and radiance filling his countenance 'such as makes you have a lump in your throat'.

On 30 November Harold Nicolson went to see Ramsay MacDonald, then Lord President of the Council, who said of the King, 'That man has done more harm to his country than any man in history.'[7] Nicolson gained the impression that the cabinet and privy council were now determined that Edward should abdicate. He noted that the King 'imagines that the country, the great warm heart of the people, are with him. I do not think so.' The problem with royalty, when they come to assess public opinion, is that they have never been in touch with it, because they have never been a part of it. Only three days later, just ten out of 400 people assembled for a literary evening in Islington were prepared to join in the singing of the national anthem. (In those days the national anthem was sung far more frequently than today; before the curtain went up at every theatrical performance, for instance.) Recording the literary evening on 3 December, Harold Nicolson wrote, 'I do not find people angry with Mrs Simpson. But I do find a deep and enraged fury against the King himself. In eight months he has destroyed the great structure of popularity which he had raised.' Nicolson had just learned that the cabinet had been in almost permanent session, that the King would be forced to abdicate, even that the name by which his brother would be known, George VI, had been settled – by the Duke, presumably. 'We are all staggered with shame and distress,' Nicolson recorded. 'I never dreamt it would come to this.'

Oliver Baldwin, the Prime Minister's son, told Harold Nicolson his father and the King 'walked round and round the garden at Fort Belvedere discussing the business, and then returned to the library having agreed that HM must abdicate,' by which stage Baldwin was feeling exhausted, asked for a whisky and soda, and when it was poured, 'S.B. raised his glass and said (rather foolishly to my mind), "Well, Sir, whatever happens my Mrs and I wish you happiness from the depth of our souls." At which the King burst into floods of tears. Then S.B. himself began to cry.'[8] No wonder Nicolson added, 'What a strange conversation-piece, these two blubbering together on a sofa!' But Nicolson had surely been taken for a ride by Baldwin's son – or the son by the father. Oliver Baldwin was not present, and his account, at best, was only second-hand. Would Baldwin have referred to his wife as his Mrs? It hardly seems likely. And the King, unlike the Duke of York, was not much given to crying.

On the first day of December the Bishop of Bradford, Alfred Blunt, addressing his diocesan conference, took the opportunity of saying he wished the King would give more positive signs of his awareness of the need of God's grace. The Bishop had just returned from a meeting at Lambeth Palace, and the general topic of conversation in London was not the frequency with which the Supreme Governor of the Church of England received communion at St George's Chapel but his desire to marry Mrs Simpson. 'It was,' writes Michael Bloch, 'unheard-of in recent times for a bishop to utter any criticism of the monarch.'[9] It still is. But in 1936 it was also rare for a newspaper to criticise the monarchy. Blunt's few but carefully chosen words released the press from their self-imposed silence. 'The King's Matter' was no longer the preserve of society and politicians, it was public property. On 2 December Baldwin reported to the King that plans for a morganatic marriage were unacceptable both at home and throughout most of the Empire, an Empire which at that time covered one-fifth of the world's surface. Once more, he urged the King to give up any idea of marrying Mrs Simpson. But 'To all arguments based on responsibility towards his people,' Mrs Baldwin, rather better informed than her son, wrote in her diary that evening, 'the King did not react.' Baldwin told his niece, Monica Baldwin, who at the age of 21 had become a Roman Catholic nun, the King seemed 'bewitched'.[10]

Between 29 November and 3 December the Duke and Duchess of York were away from London – in Edinburgh, where he was to be installed as Grand Master Mason of Scotland (all the royal brothers were Freemasons, as is the present Duke of Kent) and she was to receive the Freedom of the City. The Duke says he was kept fully informed of the situation, yet on his arrival at Euston Station on 3 December he was 'both surprised & horrified' to see billboards proclaiming 'in block letters "The King's Marriage"'.[11] He hastened to Queen Mary, to whose apron strings he was much attached, 'to tell her how surprised I was that the whole matter had been published.' Then he sped to Buckingham Palace, where he found his brother 'in a great state of excitement', babbling about plans to broadcast and to leave the country while the people decided what was to be done. Baldwin arrived for an audience late in the evening, having been involved in a car crash, and promised to consult the cabinet in the morning about the proposed broadcast. Not having seen Queen Mary for ten days, the King then drove to Marlborough House. 'A dreadful announcement' was how Bertie later recorded Edward's reiteration of his determination to marry Mrs Simpson. The King asked the Duke of York to see him at the Fort the next day, then postponed the appointment for 24 hours – and 24 hours later again put his brother off. On 4 December Princess Olgar of Yugoslavia, sister of the Duchess of Kent, wrote in her diary, 'The Yorks came for a wander, he mute and broken.' Two days later: 'Bertie in an awful state of worry as David won't see him or telephone.' That evening, 6 December, the Duke telephoned the Fort, and was told by a servant, 'The King has a

conference and will speak to you later.' His call was not returned. At
1.00pm the next day the Duke again telephoned the King, 'who told
me he might be able to see me that evening.'

Since the Hanoverian succession, only two heirs presumptive had
previously succeeded, William IV and Victoria, both without any
discussion in parliament. And not since Henry VIII had anyone
attempted to disinherit the lawful successor to the throne. Nowhere in
Edward VIII's Instrument of Abdication, which was to form the basis
of the Abdication Bill, was his successor named or nominated, for
short of a treasonable or revolutionary act his successor could be no
other than his heir presumptive. It has been suggested, however,
without a shred of evidence, that Bertie was excluded from discussions
at the Fort because of worries about his fitness to succeed, and the
burden he would lay, if he did accept the Crown (it was not his to
refuse; you can only abdicate after succeeding, not before), on Princess
Elizabeth. Not content with suggesting the Government were plotting
to bypass the rightful heir, those who subscribe to this theory have
gone on to suggest that the Duke of Gloucester too was being counted
out, and that serious consideration was being given to offering the
crown to the Duke of Kent, on the spurious grounds that he had a son.
He also had a drugs problem, and just happened to be fifth in line of
succession. The story gives little credit to the intelligence of Baldwin
and still less to the record of previous sovereigns who happen to have
been women.

On 3 December Mrs Simpson fled to the south of France, escorted
by Lord Brownlow, a lord-in-waiting, the car loaded with jewellery –
£100,000 worth of it according to Brownlow's estimate.[12] Her final act
of hauteur had been to walk out of the Fort without one word of
thanks to the staff who had befriended and waited on her. So much for
her later snide comments about the Duchess of York's 'famous charm'.
With Mrs Simpson out of the country but still the subject of
harassment, the King became agitated and profoundly depressed, too
concerned with his own passions to care tuppence whether he was
succeeded by the Duke of York, the Duke of Gloucester, the Duke of
Kent or a pet monkey. After driving Mrs Simpson to a villa near
Cannes, Brownlow returned to London, and on 8 December he wrote
from 16 Cumberland Terrace to Lady Diana Cooper to say, 'it is quite
impossible for her to leave the villa and even difficult to go into the
garden without being photographed by long-range cameras.

'When the history of these past ten days comes to be written there
will be much that the public should know about the attitude of Wallis

throughout the time of great sadness and controversy. No one has worked harder to sacrifice herself . . .

'I cannot tell you how good and patient she has been.'[13]

The King was in a terrible state. Following his late night visit to Marlborough House on 3 December, it was one o'clock the following morning by the time he set off for the Fort. A small crowd, gathered outside the Palace, gave him a cheer – and for one crazy moment he envisaged stopping the car, getting out and putting his case to them.

From now until the end of his inglorious reign he remained in seclusion at the Fort, without a properly constituted Household and isolated from his bewildered family.

By 4 December it was clear that a King's Party was forming in the capital. Banners even read 'God Save the King from Baldwin'. Most of the popular press were on the King's side, many of the papers expressing romantically inspired support for a morganatic marriage. Rumours began to fly around that a 'plane was on standby, and that the King proposed to broadcast and then leave the Government to clear up the mess. The cabinet rejected any proposed broadcast, but then Alan Lascelles sent a message to warn the cabinet that the King was 'engaged in secret consultations with Churchill and Beaverbrook and might be preparing flight or some other surprise move.'[14] This was quite untrue, but it was a measure of the panic people were in. Next Neville Chamberlain, Chancellor of the Exchequer, voiced the opinion that the crisis over the monarchy was paralysing foreign policy, and eventually Baldwin, although pressed to make a statement to the House of Commons there and then, agreed to ask the King to help to make a statement immediately after the weekend. It was time for the King to make up his mind. Even overseas royalty were in a state of alarm. The Archbishop of Canterbury lunched in London on 4 December with the Crown Prince of Sweden, and afterwards wrote in his diary, 'He was distressed for and by the King and said that this was a matter which affected not this Empire only, but all the countries where the Monarchy survived.'

The King summoned Sir Edward Peacock, Receiver General of the Duchy of Cornwall, to the Fort. He was keen to find out how abdication would affect his income from the Cornwall estates. With Baldwin's consent, he also invited a friend to dinner he had not seen all autumn, Winston Churchill. Churchill was both a virile critic of Baldwin's coalition government and a champion of the King. After many had turned towards the new Court, Churchill's adherence to Edward VIII could well have ruined him. When Neville Chamberlain, who succeeded Baldwin as Prime Minister in 1937, resigned while the country was at war, King George VI would have preferred Lord Halifax as Prime Minister, and it is a tribute to both Churchill and King George that, before long, they had established a mutual affection and admiration which transcended any memories the King might have harboured of Churchill's support for his brother only four years before.

Churchill counselled the King under no circumstances to go abroad, but to ask Baldwin for more time. He was also gravely alarmed at the King's mental condition, noticing that twice he lost the thread of what he was saying, and suggested retirement to Windsor Castle, accompanied by doctors. Churchill also offered the King false hope, by promising to draft a statement on his behalf for the Sunday papers, which would muster support for a King's Party. This was Churchill at his most mischievous and inept. In his memoirs the King tells us he then spent 'a night of soul-searching', which sounds dramatic but can hardly have been true. With the following disingenuous words he justified the decision he had taken: 'I reject the notion . . . that, faced with a choice between love and duty, I chose love. I certainly married because I chose the path of love. But I abdicated because I chose the path of duty. I did not value the Crown so lightly that I gave it away. I valued it so deeply that I surrendered it, rather than risk any impairment of its prestige.'

How close the country had come to some sort of civil war can be gauged from a letter the King received after his abdication from Colin Davidson, a friend and contemporary, whose father had served as an extra equerry to George V: 'When the history of this episode comes to be written it will be realised that your nobility in refusing even to test your popularity was a sign of true greatness, and probably saved the very existence of the Empire . . . I must humbly express my intense admiration for your obvious and inflexible determination not to encourage a "King's Party". It was within your power to create Civil War and chaos. You had only to lift a finger or even come to London and show yourself, to arouse millions in your support.'

From France Mrs Simpson wrote the King a frantic 15-page letter. It began, 'I am so anxious for you not to abdicate,' and went on to advise that if he did abdicate he should secure a proper financial settlement and discuss the matter of their titles – an indication perhaps that she had by now agreed to marry him one way or the other.

Edward approved a statement to be made to the House of Commons by Baldwin which referred to the 'risk of the gravest injury to National and Imperial Interests' should the present state of suspense and uncertainty continue. In the early hours of Monday 7 December the King decided to ask for his own recognition of that risk to be added to the statement, and personally telephoned Malcolm MacDonald, Secretary for the Dominions, who was responsible for distributing the text to overseas prime ministers. The King thought nothing of telephoning people at two o'clock in the morning. MacDonald happened to be in the bath. He advised his sovereign that the amendment would be acceptable while standing up stark naked.

Meanwhile, Churchill's declaration in support of the King had appeared in the Sunday papers. In the following Monday's *Daily Mail* Lord Rothermere, another bull in a china shop, delivered himself of the opinion that in no circumstances could the country afford to dispense with a king with 'such superlatively splendid qualities'. Chips Channon thought that people were weary of the crisis, but that the world was 'now divided into Cavaliers and Roundheads'.[15] But when Baldwin arrived at the House of Commons on the afternoon of 7 December he discovered unanimity and he was greeted in the chamber by cheers. He read the statement agreed with the King. When Churchill rose to interject he was howled down.

A last ditch plan was cooked up to send to Cannes Mrs Simpson's solicitor or the Chief Whip (her solicitor eventually went), to attempt to persuade her to renounce the King. Had she done so, and had the King accepted her decision, the country would have had for the next 36 years a king almost entirely incapacitated, in private and in public, by loneliness, boredom and frustration. But Edward forsook his 'sacred trust' on a double gamble; that Mrs Simpson would be granted a decree absolute, and that she would marry him. Neither proposition was a certainty when he left England, spurned by most of his servants but in jaunty mood. He telegraphed the new King, 'Have had good crossing. Glad to hear this morning's ceremony [George VI's Accession Council] went off so well. Hope Elizabeth better [the Queen had been suffering from influenza]. Best love and best of luck to you both. David.'

Meanwhile, Wallis issued a somewhat ambiguous statement: 'Mrs Simpson throughout the last few weeks has invariably wished to avoid any action or proposal which would hurt or damage His Majesty or the Throne. Today her attitude is unchanged, and she is willing, if such action would solve the problem, to withdraw from a situation which has become both unhappy and untenable.' This scarcely amounted to an unequivocal renunciation of the King, yet the result was that many people were lulled into a belief that the crisis was over.

On 8 December Ramsay MacDonald wrote in his diary, 'Knew this to be the decisive day & I had known the King too long to doubt what his decision would be. All his gifts, all his genius, all his opportunities would be submerged in his fascination [for Mrs Simpson]. Apart from her he was still promising to be a great King. His relations with his Ministers were admirable & so were his thoughts of his people & his Empire. His answer that he was to abdicate came today.' In fact, the King had seen the Duke of York the previous evening and told him of his definite decision to abdicate – without bothering to ascertain the feelings of the Duke or his wife. 'I am terrified for him' the Duchess had written to the King on 23 November. But at least later that night the two brothers did get down to discussing the disposition of family property and heirlooms. Edward had inherited Balmoral Castle and Sandringham House, both of which the new King would have to buy from him. The uncertainty and the tying up of loose ends could not have been made any more tolerable by a visit to the Fort the following day by the Duke of Kent, who spent hours trying to persuade the King to stay.

Baldwin also made one final appeal to the King, who was on the telephone to Mrs Simpson when he arrived. The King was alarmed to see that the Prime Minister had brought his suitcase with him. However, after dinner Baldwin was persuaded to return to London, but not before the King had told him his mind was made up and that he wished to be spared any further advice – and not before Baldwin, not in the least abashed, had returned to the charge with renewed vigour. There followed one of the strangest royal dinner parties ever assembled. The King placed Baldwin on his right, and the other guests included the Dukes of York and Kent. When, at 6.05pm, the King had telephoned the Royal Lodge to say, 'Come and see me after dinner', the Duke of York had decided to strike while the iron was hot. He jumped into his car, arriving at the Fort ten minutes later. 'The awful & ghastly suspense of waiting was over,' he recorded. 'I found him pacing up & down the room, & he told me his decision that he would go.' Now, at the dinner table, a general gloom descended upon everyone save the King. In fact, the Duke of York noted, 'my brother was the life and soul of the party, telling the PM things I am sure he had never heard before about unemployment centres etc.' The Duke, seated between the Prime Minister and Walter Monckton, at one stage whispered to Monckton, 'And this is the man we are going to lose.'

Next morning Baldwin told the cabinet the dinner party had been like a madhouse. Although convinced the King meant to go, Baldwin got the cabinet collectively to send one final message to the Fort. It read: 'Ministers are reluctant to believe that Your Majesty's resolve is irrevocable and still venture to hope that before Your Majesty pronounces any formal decision, Your Majesty may be pleased to reconsider an intention which must so deeply distress and vitally affect all Your Majesty's subjects.'

A reply was promptly despatched, in the King's own hand. 'His Majesty has given the matter his further consideration but regrets he is unable to alter his decision.' Another message arrived, at the Fort, from Mrs Simpson's solicitor, to say she was willing to instruct him to withdraw her petition for divorce 'and willing to do anything to prevent the King from abdicating.' The King was, he replied, already in the process of abdicating, and Mrs Simpson was advised not to withdraw her petition, as the King would then be sure to lose both his throne and the marriage he so desperately desired. Just two days before the Abdication, negotiations were still in a muddle concerning not only money but the King's wish to retain Fort Belvedere. This would have entailed a former king and his wife living just six miles from Windsor Castle, and no serious consideration was given at the time to the desirability of Edward returning to live in England at all. Financial arrangements were also left up in the air; so was the matter of any future title.

Events were moving with such shocking speed towards a kind of operatic climax that mistakes and misunderstandings were perhaps almost inevitable.

Queen Mary wrote in her diary on 9 December, 'Bertie arrived very late from Fort Belvedere and Mr W. Monckton brought him and me the paper drawn up for David's abdication of the Throne of this Empire because he wishes to marry Mrs Simpson!!!!! The whole affair has lasted since Novr. 16th and has been very painful – It is a terrible blow to us all & particularly to poor Bertie.' Poor Bertie had in fact, in his own words, broken down '& sobbed like a child'. 'In any other country there would have been riots,' Queen Mary wrote to her exiled son a week later, and followed this up two years later by telling him, 'I do not think you have ever realised the shock which the attitude you took up caused your family and the whole Nation. It seemed incredible to those who had made such sacrifices during the war that you, as their King, refused a lesser sacrifice.' Among those who had lost relatives was her daughter-in-law, the new Queen Elizabeth, four of whose brothers fought in the war. When, a few days after the Abdication, Lord Salisbury expressed sympathy for the departed King,

Queen Mary put him firmly in his place, saying it was only Bertie who deserved sympathy or who had made any sacrifice.

The 'paper drawn up for David's abdication' read as follows:

> I, Edward the Eighth, of Great Britain, Ireland and the British Dominions beyond the Seas, King, Emperor of India, do hereby declare my irrevocable determination to renounce the Throne for Myself and My descendants, and My desire that effect should be given to this Instrument of Abdication immediately.
>
> In token whereof I have hereunto set My hand this tenth day of December, nineteen hundred and thirty-six, in the presence of the witnesses whose signatures are subscribed.

It was signed at Fort Belvedere by the King on the morning of the 10th, and was witnessed by his three brothers. 'It was a dreadful moment', the Duke of York recalled in a memorandum on the whole business, '& one never to be forgotten by those present', who included Sir Edward Peacock, Walter Monckton (whose name King George consistently misspelt Monkton), Sir Ulick Alexander, Keeper of the Privy Purse, and George Allen, King Edward's solicitor. 'One or two curious incidents happened later re. the servants' the Duke added, and then, infuriatingly, failed to say what those curious incidents were. He remained at the Fort 'all the morning & afternoon' but found the tension unbearable so drove to his Windsor home, the Royal Lodge, where he then found he could not rest alone (the Duchess was ill in bed in London). At 5.45 pm he returned to the Fort. Next on the agenda was 'a terrible lawyer interview', which nevertheless 'terminated quietly and harmoniously'. After dining at the Royal Lodge, not alone but with Lord Wigram (Private Secretary to George V and later a Permanent Lord-in-Waiting to George VI) and Sir Edward Peacock, the Duke returned to London, where he found 'a large crowd outside my house cheering madly. I was overwhelmed.' Having presumably looked in to see how his wife was, the restless Duke then went to Marlborough House to see his mother.

During the afternoon a message from the King to the House of Commons had been read by the Speaker, and Baldwin opened a debate on the Abdication Bill. Harold Nicolson thought the speech 'Sophoclean and almost unbearable'. Clement Attlee, leader of the opposition, asked for an adjournment, and in the words of Nicolson, the Commons filed out 'broken in body and soul', conscious that they had heard 'the best speech that we shall ever hear in our lives. There was no question of applause. It was the silence of Gettysburg.'

In a corridor, Baldwin confided to Nicolson that he had had a success, adding, 'You see, the man is mad. *MAD*. He could see nothing but that woman. He did not realise that any other considerations avail. He lacks religion. I told his mother so. I said to her, "Ma'am, the King has no religious sense." I do not mean by that his atheism. I suppose you are either an atheist or an agnostic. But you have a religious sense. You realise that there is something more than the opportune. *He* doesn't realise that there is anything beyond. I told his mother so. The Duke of York has always been bothered about it. I love the man. But he must go.'[16] He went in fact at 1:52 pm the next day, the moment at which the Declaration of Abdication Bill became law. It had been rushed through its second reading, committee stage, report stage and third reading before lunch, and then had gone straight to the House of Lords, where it received assent on the King's behalf from three Lords Commissioners; for the King himself to have signed the Bill would have been tantamount to committing regal suicide, but the effect was the same. The moment the Commissioners indicated the royal assent, the Duke of York became king, but not before a number of speeches opposing the Bill had been made by Republicans, suggesting it would be better to abolish the monarchy altogether. Repair work regarding such sentiments awaited the next reign.

While all this was going on the departing monarch was entertaining Winston Churchill to lunch, and Churchill repaid the King's hospitality by contributing a few deft strokes to the speech that Edward intended delivering over the air that night, now that he was free of ministerial constraints. When G. M. Young was researching Baldwin's official biography he is said to have discovered that Edward VIII felt so free of ministerial constraints that he had begun the original draft of his farewell broadcast, 'I am now free to tell you how I was jockeyed out of the Throne,' and that Churchill made him put such an inflammatory remark on the fire.[17]

The first time it truly struck Bertie that he was King of England was when he arrived at the Fort on the evening of 11 December and Edward's servants called him Your Majesty. The new King gave what must have been an uncomfortable family dinner that night, at the Royal Lodge. Those present were Queen Mary, the Duke of Gloucester, the Duke of Kent, the Princess Royal, Princess Alice, Countess of Athlone and her husband, Queen Mary's brother the Earl of Athlone, and the former King Edward VIII. Missing was the Queen, who had that morning sent a note to Edward to say:

Darling David,

I am so miserable that I cannot come down to Royal Lodge owing to being ill in bed, as I wanted so much to see you before you go, and say 'God bless you' from my heart.

We are all overcome with misery, and can only pray that you will find happiness in your new life.

I often think of the old days & how you helped Bertie & I in the first years of our marriage – I shall always mention you in my prayers, & bless you.

Elizabeth

Edward's farewell message, delivered from the Augusta Tower at Windsor Castle in that hybrid American-Cockney Harold Nicolson thought 'really terrible',[18] deservedly has become a radio classic, and is reproduced as Appendix B. He was introduced as High Royal Highness Prince Edward. Then the listening millions heard the sound of a loud knock, and rumours circulating that Sir John Reith had flounced out of the room and slammed the door. As the Duke of Windsor explained in his memoirs, 'The noise, I believe, was actually caused by my banging my shoe against the table leg as I shifted my position to read.'

According to a little-known book called *Rat Week: An Essay on the Abdication*,[19] not published until 17 years after Osbert Sitwell's death, Lord Athlone told Sitwell that after Edward had left for the Castle, Bertie, 'dear old boy, fairly went for his brothers, saying, "If you two think that, now that I have taken this job on, you can go on behaving just as you like, you're very much mistaken! You two have got to pull yourselves together."'

When David returned to the Royal Lodge he said goodbye to his mother and sister, who were returning to London. As the family party began to break up, he was made painfully aware of his new status when none of his royal relatives curtsied to him and only the Earl of Athlone bowed. The Princess Royal and Princess Alice, after kissing Bertie goodnight, curtsied to him instead. Edward hung on until midnight, ensuring that the Naval Guard of Honour at Portsmouth would have to hang around too. Then, with only Walter Monckton and his cairn, Slipper (fatally bitten by a viper on Candé golf course the next year), he took the road to Hampshire. His brothers walked to the front door to see him off. Bertie and David kissed one another, and David bowed, saying, according to an account retailed to Henry Channon by Walter Monckton (although it may be doubted whether David called his brother Sir), 'God bless you, Sir. I hope you will be happier than your predecessor.' So saying, he 'disappeared into the night, leaving the Royal Family speechless.'[20] A new reign and a new era had at last begun.

3

Jacobite Blood

WHO WAS THIS WOMAN OF 36, lying in bed with influenza in a mansion at Hyde Park Corner? She had become Queen Consort of England and mother of the heiress presumptive. Her life was destined to span almost the entire twentieth century and her exceptional personality was to stamp itself on the hearts and minds of the nation. She was not exactly a stranger either to drama or to privilege, but while she seemed tailor-made to take on her new responsibilities, nothing connected with her early years, not even nebulous connections with Scottish monarchs, would have encouraged anyone other than a professional soothsayer to invest more than sixpence on her one day being crowned in Westminster Abbey.

Elizabeth Angela Marguerite Bowes-Lyon was born on 4 August 1900 (the First World War was to commence on her fourteenth birthday), the youngest daughter and ninth child (there were ten, but the eldest girl did not survive childhood) of Lord and Lady Glamis (pronounced Glarms).[1] We know that she was thus baptised at All Saints' Church, St Paul's Walden in Hertfordshire, on 23 September; what we do not seem to know for certain is where she was born. The generally accepted version of events is that her mother was staying in Belgrave Mansions, Grosvenor Gardens, the London home of her father-in-law, the 13th Earl of Strathmore & Kinghorne. It was six years since Nina-Cecilia Glamis had given birth to a baby, she was 38, and she decided to avail herself of the amenities of a maternity home (most babies were born at home in those days). But from this point, it is possible that mythology takes over.

The child arrived about a fortnight early. This is the charitable explanation for Claude Glamis's absence, playing cricket in Scotland, but conflicting timetables have been provided, and he may have been in London. Because the child was premature it has been conjectured that an ambulance was summoned. Some believe the future Queen Mother was born in the flat, some in the ambulance (horse drawn, presumably, which is the most romantic possibility), and some in the maternity home. Asked in 1993 if she knew anything about the Queen Mother being born in an ambulance, someone who had known her for 70 years, the Dowager Viscountess Hambleden, said, 'I'm sure she wasn't. I've never heard anything about it. That's quite a new one to me!'[2]

Seven weeks after his daughter's birth, wherever this mildly controversial event took place, Lord Glamis went to Hitchin, a few miles north of his Hertfordshire home, to register the birth. He alleged that Elizabeth had been born at St Paul's Walden, in a house bequeathed to his father by his paternal grandmother, where Elizabeth was to spend much of her childhood. Official credence was given in 1937, when Elizabeth unveiled a plaque commemorating her birth in the parish. She was, however, almost certainly born in London. Registering the birth of children was a legal formality the lower orders were expected to fulfil, and one which many of the aristocracy regularly ignored. Glamis had already been fined, in 1893, for taking 54 days to register the birth of his son Michael (he should have done it within 42 days). Yet it took 48 days before he got around to registering Elizabeth, and once again he had to fork out a penalty of seven shillings and sixpence, the equivalent today of 37p. By the time that David, his tenth and last child, was born (in 1902) he seems to have tired of the rigmarole altogether and did not register David's birth at all.

There is practically no documentary evidence relating to the childhood of Elizabeth Bowes-Lyon, but it is possible to imagine the atmosphere of a baronial castle, of a family steeped in wealth and surrounded by servants, of a great deal of dressing up which may have ignited the Queen Mother's love of house party games, especially charades, of a social world dictated by the seasons, of grouse shooting and yachting, London parties, nannies, governesses, ponies (the Queen Mother had one called Bobs), hoards of yapping dogs, handsome older brothers with moustaches, plus fours and immaculate manners, and with liberal attitudes limited to being considerate to retainers. The Queen Mother's childhood was also unclouded by financial worry (so that in later life extravagance came perfectly naturally to her) or uncertainty of any sort about the future (even when it came, the war was expected to last a few weeks). In Elizabeth's case it is safe to say too that her family was emotionally secure. At a time when contraception consisted of coitus interruptus and many women withdrew from sexual relations altogether in their mid-thirties for fear of unwanted pregnancies, it is obvious that Lord and Lady Glamis enjoyed a genuine marriage. Eight children appeared in 11 years, with a six-year gap between the eighth and ninth child. Realising Elizabeth would soon feel isolated from her older brothers and sisters, they obligingly produced a brother for her.

Her mother was an attractive and talented woman, from whom Elizabeth inherited her immaculate complexion, and who taught the children to read and write, to dance and draw, to play the piano, to speak French, and to appreciate the beautiful possessions that filled not only the Hertfordshire house but a vast London home, 20 St James's Square, later exchanged for 17 Bruton Street, a castle in County Durham (now demolished) and the family's principal residence for 600 years, Glamis Castle in Angus. As a very small child, Elizabeth had a taste of nursery school in London, and some elementary education was instilled at a 'select class for girls' in Kensington, but almost all her formal education was acquired through a succession of governesses, one of whom was German and taught Elizabeth to speak the language. These lessons were curtailed when war broke out and the governess, who remembered Elizabeth at the age of 13 as having 'a small, delicate figure, a sensitive, somewhat pale little face, dark hair and very beautiful violet-blue eyes,' reluctantly went home.

The Queen Anne house at St Paul's Walden, called the Bury, which was eventually inherited by David Bowes-Lyon (he conveniently became a banker), dates from the early eighteenth century. With its formal French gardens and statuary it would have supplied a sense of elegance. The London mansion would have prepared any future queen for the sort of opulence that tends to overwhelm the public rooms of royal palaces. And life at Glamis, with its myriad conical towers, battlements and obligatory ghosts, provided the perfect background for someone marrying into a family which had been, since Victoria's time, in love with Scotland and everything Scottish. The earldom of Strathmore, to which Elizabeth's father was heir, had been bestowed by Charles II in 1677, that of Kinghorne by James I in 1606. The family had entertained Mary Queen of Scots and become faithful if reckless Jacobites (the 5th Earl of Strathmore died fighting for the Old Pretender), retaining, when they became High Church Episcopalians, eight candles on the altar in their private chapel. In the eleventh century, Malcolm II died from wounds at Glamis; a sixteenth-century Lady Glamis was burnt as a witch. All these traditions, honours and houses were inherited by Elizabeth's father when she was three and a half.

On her mother's side Elizabeth Bowes-Lyon was descended from the 3rd Duke of Portland, twice prime minister under George III, and hence she has the slightly quirky distinction of having been a cousin of the eccentric Bloomsbury hostess Lady Ottoline Morrell, whose aunt, Louise Bentinck, was Elizabeth's grandmother. Louise too was not short of money or taste, with a house in Richmond, Surrey, a beautiful Renaissance palace, the Villa Capponi, in the hills overlooking Florence, another villa at Bordighera and an apartment in Rome. As a young girl, Elizabeth, like Lady Ottoline, paid visits to the Villa Capponi, and naturally excursions were made to the Uffizi.

Ottoline Morrell was not the only outré relative on the fringe of the family. In 1945 George VI was only too happy to appoint Professor Anthony Blunt as his Surveyor of the Pictures, for not only was he the world's leading expert on seventeenth-century French painting but a third cousin of the Queen. Blunt was reappointed Surveyor of the Queen's Pictures in 1952, and the new Queen Elizabeth II knighted him in 1956, but 23 years later cancelled and annulled the knighthood when Blunt was unmasked as a Russian spy. His funeral in 1983 was definitely one family gathering the Queen Mother had no intention of attending. Another skeleton was heard rattling in the family cupboard shortly after the Queen Mother's marriage, when a disowned second cousin once removed, Connie Bain, decided to prove that although born out of wedlock to a grandson of the 13th Earl of Strathmore, her parents had later married and hence she was legitimately Connie Bowes-Lyon. In 1924 the Court of Session agreed with her.

Far more embarrassing was the discovery in 1987 that two of the Queen Mother's Bowes-Lyon nieces, Katherine and Nerissa, both listed in *Burke's Peerage* as having died, were alive but living in a mental hospital; indeed, that both had a mental age of three or four, and having been sent as children to a special school in Hemel Hempstead were committed some time during the Second World War. They were the daughters of the Queen Mother's brother John, who had died in 1930. When the identity of the two poor women became known in 1982 the Queen Mother, patron of Mencap, sent a cheque to the hospital. Mental instability of a different sort occasioned a tragedy only weeks after the Queen Mother's wedding, when her 23-year-old nephew Angus committed suicide after his fiancée broke off their engagement. To some extent most blue-blooded aristocratic families inherit unstable genes, and the Bowes-Lyons even possess a family monster, a boy supposedly born on 18 October 1821, the great-great uncle of the Queen Mother, who also, supposedly, died the same day, but has come down in family folklore as having been so physically deformed that he was shut away in the darkest recesses of Glamis Castle, his younger brother Thomas eventually succeeding as the 12th Earl. The possible existence of a monster in her pedigree, however, remains one of the many private matters upon which the Queen Mother's lips remain firmly sealed.

As a young man, Elizabeth's father had been stationed in barracks at Windsor. Guard duties apart, the family were no strangers to royal functions and gratitude. The 14th Lord Strathmore was eventually appointed Lord Lieutenant of Forfarshire, and was made a Knight of the Garter, a Knight of the Thistle and a Knight Grand Cross of the Royal Victorian Order. To describe his youngest daughter as precocious sounds rude, for this is often taken to refer to a child who pushes herself forward and shows off in front of adults. But, in the sense that she developed early, Elizabeth was certainly precocious, learning to speak at a very early age and generally acquiring an interest in the adult world at a time when adolescent gaucheness might more commonly be in evidence. This is often the case with a girl who arrives late in a family dominated by older boys, who tend to make a fuss of her, treating her more like a young person than a child. It was natural, too, as the older children matured and left home, for Lady Strathmore to become particularly close to Elizabeth, sharing with her many of the household duties. Hence, although Elizabeth enjoyed a close childhood friendship with her young brother David (until he was sent away to boarding school), her world tended to revolve around adult conversation and activities. Furthermore, when she was 11 she had to cope with the unexpected, and largely unexplained, death of her 24-year-old brother Alexander, and a close personal experience of bereavement in childhood tends to hasten emotional development. If she had needed a further spur to maturity it occurred when she was 14 and war broke out. Glamis became a convalescent hospital. The dining room was turned into a 16-bed ward. Soldiers ate in the crypt. And Lady Elizabeth Bowes-Lyon was recruited as a sympathetic helper.

Within a week of one another, two of Elizabeth's brothers, Fergus and John, made a mad dash to the altar, John relieving his bride of an uncomfortable mouthful of maiden names (she was the Hon. Fenella Hepburn-Stuart-Forbes-Trefusis, daughter of Lord Clinton and eventually the mother of the two mentally retarded nieces), and Fergus marrying Lady Christian Dawson-Damer, daughter of the Earl of Portarlington. Both, together with Patrick, then left for the front, followed soon afterwards by Michael, who was eventually taken prisoner. By the time that Fergus returned home on leave, in 1915, he was the father of a two-month-old daughter. On his first day back in France, aged 26, he was killed, at Loos. When the news reached Glamis, Lady Strathmore, now having lost three of her children, collapsed, and became a semi-invalid. The steel had finally entered Elizabeth's soul. However much life on the surface was in the future to be seen as fun, the age of innocence was over, duty took hold of her, and a mask came down to hide from all but her most intimate family and friends any clues that might reveal the true depth of her private emotions.

London society was as close-knit as the Bowes-Lyon family itself, and once the London season had resumed its hectic round of dances after the war, royalty and their natural allies the aristocracy were pretty much thrown together. Elizabeth came out at the usual age of 18, and her mother gave a dance for her; the season of debutantes' coming-out dances was traditionally regarded by fond mamas as a kind of high-class marriage market, much parodied in *The Importance of Being Earnest*. But although a friend of the family, Lady Buxton, witnessed the dance and prophesied that Elizabeth was set to break a good many hearts, there is no evidence that she ever did. She was far too circumspect to become entangled in any relationship that would get too serious on the part of her many male admirers.

By the time that Elizabeth had attended the wedding of two brothers and her sister Rose there were few contacts she had not made among the families of the rich and well-known. The King's only daughter, Princess Mary, three years older than Elizabeth, soon became a firm friend, and in 1922 Elizabeth was a bridesmaid at the Princess's marriage in Westminster Abbey to Lord Lascelles. The exact date, 28 February, is an interesting one, for it marked the first occasion on which the Queen Mother rode in a royal procession. Lascelles was heir to the 5th Earl of Harewood, to whom George V offered a marquessate, declined on the superstitious grounds that marquesses died out more quickly than earls. Princess Mary's husband was dubbed Lucky Lascelles, in the belief that it was his good fortune to have secured such an eligible bride, after being turned down by Vita Sackville-West. As Lascelles was immensely wealthy and owned (or would when his father died) a very grand house full of art treasures, it was the King who should have been congratulating his daughter. Three years before the Lascelles wedding, Elizabeth Bowes-Lyon had stayed at Althorp in Northamptonshire when she was a bridesmaid to Lady Lavinia

Spencer. Sixty-two years later the same house and family were to provide a bride for the Queen Mother's eldest grandson.

But even before the Lascelles wedding, at which Elizabeth would have met any members of the Royal Family she did not by then already know, she had made the acquaintance of the King's second son, Prince Albert. She and Bertie actually met for the first time at a children's party, but her first presentation to him occurred thanks to the good offices of one of the most bizarre courtiers ever to haunt the corridors of Buckingham Palace. Had Horace Farquhar not existed it would have been necessary for a novelist like Evelyn Waugh to invent him. He began life in 1844 as the fifth son of a baronet, and became an intimate crony of Edward VII. George V continued the relationship, addressing him as 'My dear Horace' and signing letters 'Your sincere old friend, G.R.I.'. Farquhar made a great deal of money through banking, and gave a great deal of it to the Conservative Party. They in turn gave him a baronetcy. After just three years in the House of Commons, as MP for West Marylebone, he went upstairs to the House of Lords, having explained to one of Gladstone's secretaries that he had subscribed more than the 'accepted tariff'. He had gained access to royal circles through his friendship with the Earl of Fife (created a duke on his marriage to Edward VII's eldest daughter, Princess Louise), and was appointed Master of the Household, a privy counsellor and an extra lord-in-waiting to King Edward. By way of gratitude, he managed to involve several other members of the Royal Household in a financial scandal on the Stock Exchange, involving shares in a Siberian gold mine. The shares rocketed and then plummeted, leaving, it was alleged, Lord Farquhar £70,000 better off. Those who had lent their names to this venture included the King's private secretary.

Nevertheless Farquhar's career, along with his bank balance, continued to prosper. George V appointed him a lord-in-waiting, and in 1915 Asquith made him Lord Steward of the Household (this was, at the time, a political appointment). Farquhar managed to get his valet exempted from military service, and in 1917 he was made a viscount. Both during and after the war he spent money like water, ending up with a house in Grosvenor Square, a lease on White Lodge in Richmond Park and a sub-lease from the King on Castle Rising in Norfolk. In 1922, having been a viscount only five years, Lord Farquhar received the Grand Cross of the Order of the Bath and an earldom. He was, however, riding for a fall, and became exceedingly eccentric, engaging in the most childish and obstreperous contretemps at Court over matters of etiquette and precedence. When, in 1922, Lloyd George's coalition government fell (the Prime Minister had sold one honour too many) the Palace were glad to be rid of a meddlesome Lord Steward.

Lord Farquhar had been treasurer of the Conservative Party, and in 1923 it transpired that he had been diverting donations, and was unable to account for all the sums that had passed through his hands. Lord Lincolnshire, another personal friend of the King, who regarded Farquhar as 'semi-idiotic', had in fact got wind of Farquhar's involvement in the sale of honours. He survived into 1923, however, entertaining King George and Queen Mary to dinner in May, but dying some three months later. The saga of his will provided a fitting coda to a life of total make-believe. It ran for pages, and included bequests to the King and Queen, Queen Alexandra, the King's sisters, Princess Arthur, Duchess of Connaught, the daughters of Princess Louise and no fewer than 48 members of the aristocracy. The estate was initially sworn for probate at £400,000. The King had been left anything he wished to choose from the contents of Castle Rising, the Queen, an avid collector of antiques, the entire contents of White Lodge.

Alas, no one got a penny, for Lord Farquhar's will proved not to be worth the paper it was written on. Every stick of furniture was mortgaged, and the final value of the estate was nil. Even worse, he had acted as a trustee to the Fife estates (the Duke had died in 1912), and £80,000 from that quarter was now discovered to be missing. His innocent co-trustee, the Duke's widow, became liable for the debts. She was, so Lord Lincolnshire reported, 'open-mouthed in consequence'. Having regained her royal composure, Princess Louise began sending off family portraits to Christie's. Another picture, belonging to the Howard family, produced a disquieting postscript to the Farquhar story. On repossessing Castle Rising from the King, whose sub-tenant Farquhar had been, the owners noticed that a painting by Crome had been repositioned high on the wall. When it was brought down to be cleaned it was found to be a copy.

This then was the farcical Lord Farquhar who, in 1920, gave a dance at 7 Grosvenor Square, inviting both the newly created Duke of York (Prince Albert became Duke of York on 3 June 1920) and Lady Elizabeth Bowes-Lyon. While staying at Balmoral that autumn the Duke motored over to Glamis to renew his acquaintance with Lady Elizabeth, and he was back at the castle a year later. 'It is delightful here,' he reported to his mother, '& Elizabeth is very kind to me. The more I see of her the more I like her.' It would have been surprising had Elizabeth not been kind to her royal guest (she was kind by nature, and would have been especially drawn to someone shy and with a stammer, for her supportive instincts are strong) and even more suprising had the Duke not liked her. Everyone else did. It is often said of some women that they could have married anyone, and undoubtedly that was the case with Lady Elizabeth; there is no evidence that she ever seriously contemplated marrying anyone else, but one hint that she might be interested would have brought any number of suitors to her door. Perhaps she never looked elsewhere because she had a sense of destiny. But in 1921 she was still only 21, and although both men and women married far younger than they do now, her extreme youth must surely account, in part, for her reluctance, at first, to become engaged, even to Bertie.

If it was true that Elizabeth could have married anyone she wanted how much truer must it have been of the King's second son? It is impossible to imagine Elizabeth Bowes-Lyon marrying anyone of whose love she was not absolutely sure. 'She was touched by his persistence, really' in the opinion of Lady Hambleden, who knew the Queen Mother before her marriage.[3] Elizabeth needed to feel confident that she had not just been selected as a suitable royal bride, but that her husband to be was in love with her – which indeed he was. One can dismiss out of hand stories current at the time that Elizabeth was originally destined to marry the Prince of Wales. 'Elizabeth had many admirers but he was not one,' says Lady Hambleden. 'Edward was attractive, certainly, but the Queen Mother would never have married such a weak character!' On the other hand, in the opinion again of Lady Hambleden, who saw him for weeks at a stretch between 1937, when she was appointed a lady-of-the-bedchamber, until his death 15 years later, the Duke of York was both brave and stable. 'Edward VIII wasn't a very stable character' she recalls, with a degree of understatement. 'What Elizabeth Bowes-Lyon liked about the Duke of York was his very stable character. He was a courageous man, too. For instance, he couldn't bear heights, and he told me once that he had to go up a lighthouse. He thought, "I simply can't do this." Then he said to himself, "You've jolly well got to climb to the top." They both had noblesse oblige.'[4] What they also shared in common was a simple and sincere religious conviction. 'The Queen Mother is deeply religious' in the judgement of one of her closest friends. 'She couldn't imagine life without religious observance.'[5] In the way George VI thought that people who poached and those who didn't shoot birds were equally stupid it was beyond his comprehension that anyone could be an atheist or an agnostic.

'The clubs are in gloom', Chips Channon recorded in his diary when he 'almost fell out of bed' on reading of Elizabeth's engagement to the Duke of York (the papers had run a rumour on 5 January 1923 that she was to marry the Prince of Wales). He thought her 'more gentle, lovely and exquisite than any woman alive'. He and Elizabeth had been staying at Firle Place in Sussex with Lord Gage at the time he expressed this opinion, and he added, 'I longed to tell her I would die for her, although I am not in love with her. Poor Gage is desperately fond of her – in vain, for he is far too heavy, too Tudor and squirearchal for so rare and patrician a creature as Elizabeth.' When confirmation that she was to marry York appeared in the papers Chips wrote, 'We have all hoped, waited, so long for this romance to prosper, that we had begun to despair that she would ever accept him. He has been the most ardent of wooers . . . He is the luckiest of men, and there's not a man in England today that doesn't envy him.' Certainly the Queen Mother brought out – she still does – the chivalrous instinct in men, particularly perhaps in homosexuals, for she is the sort of woman in whom a sexually ambivalent man like Chips Channon might feel able to confide without intruding on her own sexuality.

It was true, as Channon recorded, that Bertie had been the most ardent of lovers, despite which it had begun to seem as though Elizabeth would never accept him. But whenever his royal duties, not in those days particularly arduous, allowed, Bertie was to be found at the same country house parties or dances as Elizabeth, on one occasion taking to the floor at the Forfar Masonic Hall in a tartan kilt and dancing a highland reel with Elizabeth, who, according to the *Forfar Herald*, 'presented a dainty picture in her simple mid-Victorian gown of fuchsia hyatanne taffeta'. She continued to dance highland reels well into her eighties. It was during the Duke's protracted courtship that Elizabeth took what was perhaps going to be her last opportunity to go on holiday as a private person. She paid a visit to Paris, where the ambassador was Lord Hardinge, the father of a close friend, Diamond Hardinge. Diamond's brother, Alexander, had been appointed Assistant Private Secretary to George V in 1920; it was Alexander Hardinge's early friendship with Elizabeth that was to give him easy access to her home in Piccadilly during the Abdication crisis.

It was not just to Elizabeth that the Duke of York had been attracted. His own home life had been rigorously geared to the observance of strict Court etiquette, little changed since his great-grandmother's reign, and to the deference he paid to his parents (Queen Mary constantly reminded the boys that their father was also their sovereign). But at Glamis he experienced a far more relaxed atmosphere, and he may well have yearned for a wife who would create in his married home a lightness of touch that stemmed from an informality he positively envied. As well as going to Glamis the Duke of York got to know Elizabeth Bowes-Lyon by paying visits to the Bury at St Paul's Walden, a house so unlike his own gruesome childhood home, York Cottage, that he must have longed to take up permanent residence. It was in fact at the Bury that he finally persuaded Elizabeth to marry him.

Under the Royal Marriages Act of 1772 he required the King's consent, which was officially granted on 12 February 1923, the engagement having already been announced in the Court Circular on 16 January. That the King's consent appears to have been a formality should not detract from the fact that for a prince to marry a commoner was still a rare occurrence (the illegal marriages of George III's irresponsible offspring did not count), if not indeed, in modern times, a unique one. James II, also as Duke of York, married, as his first wife, a commoner, Lady Anne Hyde, but she died before he came to the throne, and one has to go back to the reign of Henry VIII to find commoners (four in fact: Anne Boleyn, Jane Seymour, Catherine Howard and the twice widowed Catherine Latimer) who became queen consort before Elizabeth Bowes-Lyon was to do so in 1936. 'You & Papa were both so charming to me yesterday about my engagement,' Bertie wrote to Queen Mary, '& I can never really thank you properly for giving your consent to it. I am very happy & can only hope that Elizabeth feels the same as I do.'

By the time Elizabeth decided she was grown up enough to marry into the Royal Family, and to forsake those freedoms we all take for granted – to step out of doors when we want, go shopping, get on a bus, sunbathe at Blackpool – she had endured the death of two brothers, she had nursed and entertained wounded soldiers, and had helped to put out a fire at Glamis. Perhaps most importantly of all, she had passed muster with Queen Mary, who went over to Glamis herself to vet her first prospective daughter-in-law, and expressed satisfaction afterwards at the way the young Lady Elizabeth had deputised for her mother, who was ill. For Elizabeth to be on good terms with her father-in-law, and especially her mother-in-law, was going to prove critical in the years ahead, but it would have been almost impossible for George V not to have fallen a little in love with her himself. A martinet about time, he was charmed into waiting lunch for Elizabeth, and she was invited to call him Papa, as his own children did.

To one of Queen Mary's ladies-in-waiting, the Countess of Airlie, the Duke of York wrote in reply to a letter congratulating him on his engagement, 'How can I thank you enough for your charming letter about the wonderful happening in my life which has come to pass, and my dream which has at last been realised. It seems marvellous to me to know that my darling Elizabeth will one day be my wife. I owe so much to you, and can only bless you for all you did.' What Lady Airlie had done was engineer a succession of meetings between Bertie and Elizabeth at her Scottish home, Cortachy Castle.

We can safely assume that neither the Duke of York nor Lady Elizabeth Bowes-Lyon took exception to *The Times*'s remarking, 'There is one wedding to which the people look forward with still deeper interest – the wedding which will give a wife to the Heir to the Throne.' On the morning of the wedding itself, the paper commented, 'In the public mind Lady Elizabeth Bowes-Lyon is probably all the more welcome an addition to the Royal Family because the public knows practically nothing about her.' All *The Times* seemed to know was that she was 'small, dark, and piquante', which according to Longman's *Dictionary of the English Language* means 'agreeably stimulating to the palate', 'engagingly provocative' and 'having a lively arch charm'. Readers were also informed that she was a 'very keen and accomplished dancer', 'good at lawn tennis' and did not hunt much yet 'but hopes to do so more in the future'. Bertie hunted, but the Queen Mother has never, since a small child, been seen to sit astride a horse.

The bride brought into the relationship a host of personal friends, while the bridegroom seems to have had very few close friends. Unlike Elizabeth, Bertie knew no one in the world of the arts, but he was later to adapt surprisingly easily to the company of the Queen Mother's more racy acquaintances – people like Osbert Sitwell and Maggie Greville. It has been suggested that Group Captain Sir Louis Greig, who had served with the Duke on the *Malaya* in 1917, accompanied him to Cambridge as an equerry and was appointed Comptroller in 1920, an appointment he held until 1923, was the only close friend the Duke of York ever made. For friends, therefore, the Duke became heavily reliant on his wife. What especial attribute had he to offer her? Elizabeth's father, to whom she may to some extent owe her longevity (he was 89 when he died in 1944), was already 45 when she was born. By the time she came out he was approaching old age. Patrician, self-assured and genially authoritarian, Lord Strathmore represented continuity but had never manifested physical paternal affection. Perhaps what Elizabeth had been seeking, and why she showed no interest in the run-of-the-mill 'debs' delights' she met at balls and in country houses, was a father figure – not necessarily someone older than herself but a replacement for her father in terms of a man born to an hereditary position of power and influence, someone in fact upon whom she could lean; not someone to replace her father, whom she loved, but someone to mirror his status in the only world she knew, that of the unquestioned social hierarchy. In that respect, as a prince of the blood, the Duke of York, for all his shyness and deference to his older brother, fitted the bill to perfection.

Elizabeth had certainly led a very sheltered life, and there were aspects of her new role she still knew little about. Hence she gave a ready welcome to a reporter from the *Star*. Innocuous though it was, it was to be her first and last press interview, and the occasion for her one and only rap over the knuckles from George V. As the world moved into a more liberal frame of mind on many social issues, it was just as well the future Queen Mother learned to keep the press, who nevertheless adore her, at arm's length, confining her remarks, when asked, for example, to comment on a grandson's engagement, to 'It's lovely, isn't it!' For one thing both she and Bertie had in common was an inbred reactionary attitude where politics and social values were concerned. Summing up the Queen Mother's character in the 1960s, Noël Coward recorded in his diary that she had 'irrepressible humour, divine manners and a kind heart'. But her kind heart and divine manners have sometimes had to work overtime. According to one member of her Household, 'She's very, very right-wing, and has often had to disguise her natural inclinations. For example, she used to be very good at dancing with black students when she was Chancellor of London University. She always made a very good effort, but she doesn't really like black people, although of course she would never show it. She just thinks they are different.'[6]

'The trouble with the Royal Family is they're not educated, they're not graduates,' was how the donnish and liberal Lord Ramsey, when Archbishop of Canterbury, used to excuse the Queen Mother's eccentric foible of referring in his presence to millions of her daughter's subjects as 'blackamoors'. The Queen Mother was once at a charity concert at the Royal Academy of Music, of which she was patron, and said to the conductor, Sir Neville Marriner, 'I thought the blackamoor on the drums was awfully good.' These racial gaffes she commits quite unselfconsciously; they are the result of her accident of birth – both its timing and its privileged and sheltered nature. And of course no one has ever dared correct or educate her. Another academic, at Eton, who has met her on a number of private occasions, over a drink, says, 'Oh, behind closed doors it all just comes out!'[7] The Queen Mother is entirely her own woman. In 1931, as Duchess of York, she went so far as to break with protocol by despatching a busload of servants to London to help Duff Cooper, the official Conservative candidate, fight a by-election. The Independent Conservative candidate was Sir Ernest Petter, whose manifesto she threw in the wastepaper basket. No wonder the Chancellor of the Exchequer, Hugh Gaitskell, after staying at Windsor Castle in 1951, noted in his diary, 'The King and Queen are extremely conservative in their views, the Queen particularly so.' On the question of colour, the Royal Family's general attitude remains a mystery. They for ever pay lip service to the Commonwealth but no member of the Royal Family has ever employed a black member of the Commonwealth in their Household, even in the humble capacity of an equerry.

In January 1923 Elizabeth and her parents spent a weekend at Sandringham, still occupied by the deaf 79-year-old Queen Alexandra. 'Elizabeth is charming, so pretty & engaging & natural' Queen Mary recorded in her diary. The King, too, thought her 'pretty and charming' and regarded Bertie as 'a very lucky fellow'. Elizabeth, who quite fearlessly stood up for the King's sons when they were in trouble, reciprocated his feelings. When he died she wrote, 'I miss him dreadfully. Unlike his own children, I was never afraid of him, and in all the twelve years of having me as a daughter-in-law he never spoke one unkind or abrupt word to me, and was always ready to listen and give advice on one's own silly little affairs. He was so kind and dependable. And when he was in the mood, he could be deliciously funny too!'[8]

It was strange that the first prince to be married in Westminster Abbey for 541 years (the last had been Richard II, in 1382) should have been the one to return there under such traumatic circumstances 14 years later, to be crowned. The wedding took place on 26 April 1923. Plans to broadcast the service were shelved when it dawned on the Dean and Chapter that the service might be listened to by men in public houses wearing cloth caps – but such was the world in which the Yorks began their 29 years of happy married life. One of the stewards was a crook by the name of Maundy Gregory – none other than Lloyd George's notorious honours broker; for his services the Duke presented him with a gold cigarette case. And just as odd, the first house in which the royal couple lived after their itinerant honeymoon was White Lodge – graciously lent to them by another crook, Lord Farquhar.

The honeymoon began in Surrey, at Polesden Lacey. Once a Regency villa visited by Sheridan, this was the much remodelled home near Dorking of Margaret Greville, a rich, flamboyant snob, better known to her society friends as the Hon. Mrs Ronald Greville. Here the couple stayed, in rooms once occupied by Edward VII, until 7 May, while Mrs Greville camped out at her Mayfair residence, 16 Charles Street. Many who enjoyed her hospitality felt they could afford to be exceedingly rude about her. Cecil Beaton found her a 'galumphing, greedy, snobbish old toad who watered at her chops at the sight of royalty'. To Harold Nicolson she was 'a fat slug filled with venom'. But Mrs Greville, who collected a DBE, could afford to ignore insults and also to entertain in a grand manner. She provided an unpredictable atmosphere, aided by a couple of butlers who were seldom if ever sober, which must have appealed to the fun-loving side of Queen Elizabeth's nature. Elizabeth was in any case, like Queen Victoria, no stranger to intoxicated servants. One of the butlers at Glamis was reputed often to be the worse for wear. After a dinner party at Polesden Lacey in 1935, attended by Osbert Sitwell (to whom Mrs Greville left £10,000), Sitwell reported to his boyfriend, David Horner, 'It was like jazz night at the Palladium. All the butlers were drunk – since Maggie was ill – bobbing up every minute during dinner to offer the Duchess of York whisky.'

When Mrs Greville died, on 15 September 1942, at the Dorchester, the Queen Mother gave Osbert Sitwell a graphic obituary of her own. 'I shall miss her very much,' she wrote to him. 'She was so shrewd, so kind and so amusingly *un*kind, so sharp, such fun, so naughty.' It has been said that Mrs Greville once declared her intention of leaving her money to the deserving rich, and indeed Princess Margaret did receive a legacy of £20,000. But in *George VI*[9] Patrick Howarth is many miles wide of the mark when he asserts that she left to the Queen Mother £1.5 million. Her total estate was sworn for probate at £1,623,191, the bulk of which, together with Polesden Lacey, went to the National Trust. What the Queen Mother received, with Mrs Greville's 'loving thoughts', were all her 'jewels and jewellery', a magnificent bequest, in fact, for her jewellery included a diamond necklace once owned by Marie Antoinette.

Another part of the Duke and Duchess of York's honeymoon was spent at Glamis, where the Duchess developed whooping-cough. Was she under stress? It is interesting to note that almost all the recorded times when the Queen Mother, who normally enjoys the rudest of health, has been ill have been at times of emotional crisis. During a tour of New Zealand in 1927, having left her first baby, not yet a year old, in England, she developed tonsillitis. As George V approached death she contracted pneumonia, and as the Abdication crisis reached its climax a year later she was bedridden with influenza. Normally, however, she has scarcely known what infirmity is. At 90 she was still perfectly capable of walking after a good lunch, on St George's Day, from the Upper Ward of Windsor Castle to the Lower, for the annual Garter Service in St George's Chapel, chatting amicably to whoever happened to be beside her (the King of Spain or the Prince of Wales), waving to her fans, and ascending the steps to the West Door without a stick or taking anybody's arm. Impervious to the cold, she will cheerfully picnic in the north of Scotland in October, when normal people are huddled round a log fire. Even in the heat of the West Indies she once thought nothing of motoring 80 miles out of her way to attend a private lunch party, arriving on time, eating curry and leaving late.

It could hardly be said that the Duke of York enjoyed an uproariously happy youth. What the Duchess did was to instil into the House of Windsor the idea that it was possible to lighten the royal touch without any loss of dignity, something neither Queen Mary, nor her daughter the Princess Royal, found at all easy. Both were shy, Queen Mary painfully so (in recent years she has been incongruously compared to Lady Bracknell; no description could be less appropriate), and apart from the Queen and the Princess Royal, there were no female members of the Royal Family taking any serious part in public life. Various granddaughters of Queen Victoria, staunch and admirable ladies like Princess Alice and Princess Marie Louise (the Duke of York's first cousins once removed), took part in charitable enterprises, but they were hardly known to a wide circle of the population. There was even a daughter of Queen Victoria, Princess Henry of Battenberg, who lived until 1944, but all she had ever done was act as companion to her mother. The three somewhat catty sisters of George V had taken scant interest in royal duties (one married a Scottish earl, one the future King of Norway, and the unmarried sister, Victoria, 'a bitch of the first order' according to the Duke of Windsor,[10] remained cloistered at Sandringham, her one excitement of the day being to telephone her brother).

There were few criteria by which the new, young and inexperienced Duchess could gauge what was expected of her or how formal or light-hearted she was meant to be. In point of fact, in 1923 the position of a British princess had hardly altered from the time when Queen Victoria's daughters dutifully opened the odd hospital and drove round Windsor Great Park beside their mother. (The Queen's third daughter, Princess Helena, who died six weeks after the Duchess of York's wedding, founded the Helena Club at 82 Lancaster Gate, for Ladies from Good Families with Modest Means who are Obliged to Pursue an Occupation in London. This became the May of Teck Club in Murial Spark's novel *The Girls of Slender Means*.[11])

Although the Princess Royal was fifth in succession to the throne, by courtesy of her marriage the Duchess of York found herself, after Queen Mary, the second most senior female member of the Royal Family, and eventually the mother of two princesses with only a bachelor uncle between their father and the crown.

4

Married to a Hanoverian

NOT ONLY DID ELIZABETH Bowes-Lyon have to weigh up the privileges and restrictions of marrying into the Royal Family, she had also to assess the character of that family itself, so closely interrelated that almost all of them were to some extent tainted with unstable Hanoverian blood. (Queen Mary was the great-granddaughter of George III and therefore her husband's first cousin once removed.) It is commonly assumed that in the clinical sense George III was mad; he suffered in fact from an hereditary disease called porphyria, which can be traced back to Mary, Queen of Scots and forwards to two of her contemporary descendants.[1] Four of George III's sons, and his granddaughter, Princess Charlotte, were sufferers.[2] George IV came firmly to believe he had led a charge at Salamanca and had fought at the Battle of Waterloo. William IV made gabbling, sometimes almost incoherent, speeches designed to turn any foreign minister's hair white with worry. His brother, the Duke of Cumberland, who for three and a half terrifying years was Queen Victoria's heir presumptive, was undoubtedly deranged. Victoria herself not infrequently feared for her own reason, and much of her behaviour, especially after the death of the Prince Consort, was wildly neurotic. The most charitable thing one can say for her grandson, the Duke of Clarence & Avondale, heir to the throne after his father the Prince of Wales, was that he was educationally subnormal. His solitary service to the nation was performed by dying.

Hanoverian instability on a pretty impressive scale was the inheritance of the British Royal Family, and, as if to cleanse some of the tainted blood for the benefit of future generations, the Queen Mother brought as part of her dowry inheritance from such staunch English stock as the earls of Oxford, Devon, Northumberland, Shrewsbury, Stanley and Salisbury, not to mention the dukedoms of Norfolk, Bedford and Devonshire. Charles Darwin and even, it is believed,

Shakespeare became cousins to the Royal Family. And from Ireland the Queen Mother was to bequeath to her Hanoverian descendants their most distinguished Irish blood, that of the dynasties of Munster and of the Ui Neill high kings.

The immediate family with which Lady Elizabeth Bowes-Lyon made an alliance had itself been severely damaged by parents neither of whom had the remotest rapport with children, least of all their own. After the murder in 1917 of the Tsar of Russia, the Tsar's sister, the Grand Duchess Xenia, was given the use of Frogmore Cottage in the grounds of Windsor Castle. Queen Mary called one day, and reported to the Prince of Wales that the children were having 'great bicycle rides & making a good deal of noise, of course the poor things did not know I was in the house, but all the same it is a decided bore.' None of the King and Queen's sons could be said to be 'normal'. All four who survived childhood (the life and death of the epileptic Prince John have been shrouded in secrecy) were only redeemed by their wives. David was seriously prone to depression. Henry, Duke of Gloucester, was virtually a nonentity. In his youth he had made a passable professional soldier, even though it was said he had difficulty remembering the names of members of his own regiment, but when a dippy member of parliament, Sir John Wardlaw-Milne, suggested during a censure debate in July 1942 that British fortunes would be improved if the Duke was appointed Commander-in-Chief, the House of Commons was reduced to gales of helpless laughter. (With his penchant for inventing nicknames for his family, the Duke of Windsor had already aptly dubbed Harry the Unknown Soldier.) The following year he was despatched to Australia as Governor General, a post originally earmarked for his more glamorous younger brother, the Duke of Kent, who was killed in 1942. Not a great deal can be said for the talents of George, Duke of Kent, however, for he had so few; he played the piano rather well, but much of his early life was simply spent in night clubs.

Had Bertie not had the perspicacity as well as the perseverance to pursue Elizabeth Bowes-Lyon it is unlikely he would have survived the Abdication as he did. 'By nature a shy, nervous and affectionate child, easily frightened and somewhat prone to tears' is how his official biographer, Sir John Wheeler-Bennett, succinctly summed up the young prince.[3] He was just the kind of boy who would develop both a terror and a respect for a father who was not only king but a rough and ready sailor, the type of man who thinks that if you shout loud enough foreigners will understand – especially necessary in the case of George V himself, whose ineptitude at French made even his wife wince. Bertie acquired an inferiority complex very early, by being compared, unfavourably, with an exuberant older brother and a pretty young sister. As a result, he slid silently into the background. Even there he was unable to escape from birthday messages like the one he received from his father in 1900. 'Now that you are five years old I hope you will always try to be obedient & do at once what you are told, as you will find it will come much easier to you the sooner you begin. I always tried to do this when I was your age & found it made me much happier.' Bertie tried to gain attention and affection, but there was no more chance of his parents understanding him and his needs than there was of Queen Victoria doing cartwheels.

At least Bertie had indulgent grandparents close at hand, and when his father returned from an eight-month visit to Australia he discovered both Bertie and David had developed a taste for fun and games. So he handed them over to a general factotum, Frederick Finch, who acted as nursemaid and chastiser, and to a tutor, Henry Hansell, a dour bachelor schoolmaster. If ever two young boys would have benefited from day school they were David and Bertie, but the idea of princes rubbing shoulders with commoners was regarded as out of the question. As a result, Bertie's formal education lacked breadth, imagination and the guidance of even a born teacher. Sir John Wheeler-Bennett has said that Henry Hansell 'might, in fact, have stepped straight out of the pages of one of Dean Farrer's great school romances. His was the muscular Christianity of *St Winifred's*, and this might not have occasioned too great a difficulty had he not expected his pupils to be equally imbued with the characteristics of *Eric, or Little by Little*.'[4] In 1953 the Duke of Windsor told Harold Nicolson that Hansell never taught them anything (he certainly didn't teach them to spell; the Duke thought 'understand' was two words), and indeed, at the age of seven and a half Bertie was still incapable of dividing by two.

He was also left-handed, and Mr Hansell was not one to let such an 'abnormality' slip past. Bertie was made to use his right hand. It was also noticed, in particular by his father, that he was knock-kneed. That was no problem, either. By day and by night he was forced to wear splints. Alexander Hardinge once remarked it was a mystery why George V, 'who was such a kind man', was 'such a brute to his children'. The frustrations, brought on partly by hereditary traits of character, partly through environmental circumstances, led to Bertie developing a stammer. In adult life only one person proved capable of calming him down, the Queen Mother. Peter Townsend has recalled how 'The steady regard of his blue eyes only changed – and then, to an alarming glare – when he was irked, or rattled. Then, he would start to rant noisily, and the Queen would mollify him with a soothing word or gesture; once she held his pulse and, with a wistful smile, began to count – tick, tick, tick – which made him laugh, and the storm subsided.'⁵ 'The King certainly did have a temper,' Lady Hambleden confirms, 'but it didn't last very long, because the Queen was so marvellous with him.'⁶

When Bertie was ten he was again separated from his demanding parents, who spent almost six months on a visit to India. But time and distance were no protection from paternal reproof. 'You & David seem to have misunderstood that we wanted you both to write to Mama & I every alternate week, as Mary does,' the Prince of Wales wrote to Bertie from Delhi. 'David ought to have written last week instead of this week to me, & you ought to have written to me this week. I don't know how the confusion has come.' A separate letter went off to Mr Hansell. 'The two boys ought to write to the Princess & I each week alternately so that they both write each week,' he was instructed. In the Sandringham schoolroom, the boys were made to play at being at school. When David went to the Royal Naval College, Bertie was promoted 'head-boy' and Prince Henry took 'the second boy's place'. By 20 December 1907 a sadly uncomprehending Mr Hansell was reporting to the Prince of Wales, 'I should say that Prince Albert has failed to appreciate his position as "captain".' Prince Albert was probably too intelligent to want to have anything to do with such nonsense.

Bertie's most serious problem remained an almost congenital inability to master mathematics, a disadvantage – although a minor one in their case – inherited by the Queen and Prince Charles. 'You must really give up losing your temper when you make a mistake with a sum,' his father wrote to Bertie. 'We all make mistakes sometimes, remember now you are nearly 12 years old & ought no longer to behave like a little child of 6.' At 11 the Prince was in fact at the very age when boys long for adult male companionship, and preferably for a father, or a surrogate father, they can clamber all over. George V did kiss his boys goodnight, but never once did he or Queen Mary pick them up when they were children and give them a cuddle. Letters were their favourite form of communication, because they were the safest. The King, in fact, was permanently buttoned up. On the return of the Duke and Duchess of York from an Australian tour in 1927 the King, due to meet them at Victoria Station, told his son, 'We will not embrace at the station before so many people.' And just in case anything else should go wrong, he added, 'When you kiss Mama take yr hat off.'

It seems almost incredible that at the age of 12 Prince Albert was accepted on his own merits for training as a naval cadet. Mr Hansell, never one to boast of his own achievements, described the boy as scatter-brained. But he did add, in his final report on Bertie to the Prince of Wales, 'I have always found him a very straight and honourable boy, very kind hearted and generous; he is sure to be popular with the other boys.' By the time he left Dartmouth in 1912 (he was nearly 17) he had become a smart and charming-looking lad, and by the time he was photographed in 1918, in Air Force uniform, he was every bit as handsome and engaging as David. He still had a stammer, he suffered from digestive disorder, but he had gained an official pilot's certificate in the days when flying was still a hazardous occupation and, after some reluctance on the part of his father to allow him to stay so long, he managed to enjoy a year of study and freedom at Trinity College, Cambridge. Here, at the age of 24, he buried his head in Dicey's *Law of the Constitution*. He also read what the journalist Walter Bagehot had to say about the British Constitution, and in particular the role to be played within it of monarchs and princes. The idea that in 1936 he came to the throne totally unprepared is completely unfounded.

That the future King always seemed to be setting himself Everests to conquer may seem a romanticised notion, but it bears examination: naval lessons and training at 12, front line service at 19, learning to fly, making public speeches while handicapped by a stammer, desperately trying to propitiate frigid parents and to emulate a wildly popular older brother, and striving to become a tennis player fit to play at Wimbledon, which he did in the men's doubles in 1926, were not the achievements of a man incapable of responding to encouragement. Unfortunately, by the time he was at Cambridge he had succumbed irresistibly to the pleasures of tobacco. From then on, as Lady Hambleden has correctly observed, 'he smoked like a chimney.'[7] Almost anyone who has served in the armed forces learns to smoke when young, and the generation that survived the First World War became notoriously heavy smokers. The young Prince of Wales was seldom photographed on informal occasions without a cigarette dangling between his lips, and the era of the night club saw men and women swirling the night away enveloped in clouds of smoke. Smoking was extremely fashionable, heavily encouraged by Craven A advertisements, and indulged in without the faintest suspicion about the consequences. It was a folly for which both David and Bertie would pay a heavy price; Bertie developed cancer and David died of it.

The Duke and Duchess of York were married three years before their first child, named after her mother, was born – at the London home of her maternal grandparents. Even now the Yorks still had no settled London place of their own. It was an odd honour to have befallen the Strathmores, for both the Queen Mother and Elizabeth II to have been born in their premises, and they pulled off a hat trick four years later when the Duchess travelled to Glamis for the birth of her second child, Princess Margaret. When a neglected town house, 145 Piccadilly, four doors away from Apsley House at Hyde Park Corner, was ready, the Yorks moved in to what was to be their first real home Thanks to the dotty Lord Farquhar they had lived originally at White Lodge, where for a short time they tolerated something the Queen Mother never contemplated again, the services of a poor cook. 'I had better warn you,' the Duke wrote to his mother, having invited his parents to lunch on 28 June 1923, 'that our cook is not very good, but she can do the plain dishes well, & I know you like that sort.' Indeed, the King and Queen could not be said to have been gourmets. One day, thinking to give his father a pleasant surprise, the Prince of Wales produced an avocado pear. 'What in heaven's name is this!' the King exclaimed. They were essentially an unsophisticated couple, and in that respect they could not have differed more markedly from their new daughter-in-law.

White Lodge is a Palladian revival mansion built by George II, and an influential stream of statesmen and national heroes have processed through its portals: Lord Bute; Henry Addington (who was educated at Cheam, England's oldest preparatory school, where the Duchess of York's eldest grandson, Prince Charles, was destined to be sent as a boarder in 1957); Lord Nelson. It had been the childhood home of Queen Mary and the birthplace of the future Edward VIII, and is now the home of the Royal Ballet School. In 1923 the cook was to prove the least of the problems for the Duke and Duchess of York when they took up residence. There was scarcely any central heating, the rooms were freezing cold, the electric lighting was unsafe and the plumbing insanitary. After a year the Duke and Duchess were complaining that it cost them £11,000 a year to live in the house, which also had no privacy. 'Whereas in former days, Richmond Park was practically in the country,' Sir Frederick Ponsonby reminded Sir Lionel Earle of the Ministry of Works in a letter written on 10 November 1924, 'it has been brought very near London by charabancs and motor cars; the result is that on Saturdays and Sundays the crowd round the house is so great that they hardly dare put their noses outside, and on weekdays there is also a certain number of people always waiting to see them come out and go in.' Sir Frederick was instructed to try and find them some London accommodation.

'I knew from the very start, when White Lodge was allocated to them, that this young couple would never be satisfied and happy there,' Sir Lionel wrote to Sir Warren Fisher of the Treasury the following day. 'They are both passionately fond of dancing, and naturally wish to come to London practically every day for this purpose.' Indeed, the newly married Yorks did not hurry to take on public duties, and were extremely cross while relaxing at Holwick Hall in County Durham, one of the Strathmores' spare country houses, to learn that at short notice they had been deputed by the Foreign Secretary, Lord Curzon, to attend the christening of the infant son of King Alexander of Yugoslavia, and the wedding of the King's cousin, Prince Paul, to Princess Olga of Greece. The Duke told Louis Greig he thought Lord Curzon should be drowned: 'He must know things are different now.' In other words, the Duke was no longer free to dash across Europe at a moment's notice; he had a wife who would need to shop for clothes first.

The christening proved a rather alarming initiation into royal duties for the Duchess. The baby nearly drowned, when it slipped into an enormous font and had to be fished out by the Duke, who was standing by as a godfather. Serbian hospitality left something to be desired, too. 'We were quite a large family party,' Bertie reported to his father, 'and how we all lived in the palace is a mystery. We were not too comfortable and there was no hot water!' The Duchess kept her end up at all events. 'They were all enchanted with Elizabeth, especially Cousin Missy,' Bertie wrote home. 'She was wonderful with all of them and they were all strangers except two, Paul and Olga.' Cousin Missy was Queen Marie of Rumania, the eldest daughter of Queen Victoria's second son, Alfred, Duke of Edinburgh.

Another method of avoiding the rigours of life at White Lodge was devised in December 1924 when the Yorks set sail for Kenya. Their ultimate destination? The game reserves, where, in time-honoured royal tradition, they proceeded to slaughter the wild life. Lions, oryx, rhino, crocodile all emerged to pay their respects, only to fall prey to a seemingly irresistible urge on the part of royalty to fire guns. Harold Nicolson, who wrote George V's biography, famously remarked that before becoming king he had done nothing but kill animals and stick in stamps, and George must have been delighted to hear that in Uganda Bertie had shot his first elephant.

It was not until 1926 that a lease was taken on 145 Piccadilly, and then it could not be made ready until after the Duke and Duchess returned from Australia the following year. Ponsonby informed Sir Lionel Earle on 15 October 1926 he had arranged for the Duke's 'personal knick-knacks, his clothes and also all the Duchess' dresses, etc., to be locked up in Buckingham Palace, whilst the servants are to go on board wages.' 145 Piccadilly was a late eighteenth-century Adam mansion which had been defaced by the Department of Woods and Forests. For a time the two Princesses were able to play in Hyde Park itself, but sightseers need not trouble searching for 145 Piccadilly today. It received a direct hit in 1940, and is no more. One can take with a pinch of salt Marion Crawford's description of 145 Piccadilly as 'neither large nor splendid'. 'It might,' she wrote in *The Little Princesses*,[8] 'have been the home of any moderately well-to-do young couple starting life.'

In 1931 the King made the Royal Lodge in Windsor Great Park, with 90 acres, available to the Yorks as a weekend retreat, and this, with its marvellous cedars, rhododendrons and azaleas, remains the Windsor home of the Queen Mother today. The Royal Lodge was once the home of Thomas Sandby, deputy ranger of the Great Park. His, and his brother Paul's, drawings and watercolours in the Royal Collection is the finest collection of their work in existence. Later the Prince Regent lived at the Royal Lodge, and the house owes its present appearance (its salmon pink walls can be glimpsed from one of the public walks) to his principal Windsor architect, Sir Jeffry Wyatville.

With the Prince of Wales showing no inclination to marry, the Duchess of York set about grooming her daughters for stardom. At any rate, stardom was soon thrust upon them. From the start they were the subject of admiration and affection. Hardly had Princess Elizabeth been born than the Duke was writing from Brisbane to his mother to tell her, 'It is extraordinary how her arrival is so popular out here. Wherever we go cheers are given for her as well & the children write to us about her.' When, in 1929, the Yorks went into official residence at the Palace of Holyroodhouse in Edinburgh, the Duke having been appointed Lord High Commissioner, the Duchess wrote to Queen Mary, 'The only thing I regret is that we have not got Lillibet here. I fear that it has been a very great disappointment to the people. . . . It almost frightens me that the people should love her so much. I

73

suppose that it is a good thing, and I hope that she will be worthy of it, poor little darling.' Those last words almost have a ring of clairvoyance about them.

She and her children had the field to themselves. Princess Mary had produced a son, only eighth in succession to the throne, in the year of Princess Elizabeth's birth, and until the Duke of Kent was persuaded to cease sowing wild oats and settle down with a penniless but elegant Greek princess in 1934, and the Duke of Gloucester, 12 months later, married the retiring daughter of the Duke of Buccleuch & Queensberry, the Duchess of York was the only young female attraction. It was also becoming increasingly obvious to politicians and courtiers that Bertie, with his faultless duchess by his side and a pair of demure, well-scrubbed and well-behaved little girls, was the only son of George V fit to succeed. Fond as they may have been of dancing, the Yorks were never seen cavorting on the beach at Sandwich, as was the Prince of Wales, not with a wife but in the company of his mistress, Mrs Dudley Ward, and *her* two daughters. Neither were they ever encountered in sleazy night clubs in the company of Prince George, whose liaisons swung between equally unacceptable men and women, one of his homosexual escapades resulting in an attempted blackmail.

Dutiful work now became the order of the day at 145 Piccadilly, where the Duchess began to take on the patronage of charitable institutions, some of which have rather a comical sound to them today: the Mothercraft Training Centre, for example. But she must have enjoyed going to Finsbury Town Hall for the Costermongers' Ball. 'She lays a foundation stone as though she had just discovered a new and delightful way of spending an afternoon,' according to *The Times*. Following visits paid to industrial cities by the King and Queen at the instigation of the Archbishop of Canterbury, the Duke increasingly interested himself in the welfare of young men and boys from industry, and he became president of the Industrial Welfare Society. He took an interest in Dr Barnardo's Homes and the National Playing Fields Association, and at New Romsey he established annual holiday camps for boys from rich and poor homes alike to meet. He and the Duchess used to join in community singing, their favourite number, accompanied by light-hearted tapping of knees and other extremities, being 'Under the Spreading Chestnut Tree'.

Royal diaries were nothing like so booked up in advance as they are today, and it is interesting to note that in 1926 the Duchess of York's engagements were so relatively scant that no coy announcement was made when she became pregnant, to the effect that Her Royal

Highness would be carrying out no further duties after such and such a date; when she quietly withdrew from public view no one noticed. Even in 1931 Elgar contrived to get the Duke and Duchess to a studio to attend a recording of the *Nursery Suite* at just four days' notice. Elgar had dedicated this piece to the Duchess and her daughters, and she asked Elgar to play the fifth movement, 'The Wagon Passes', a second time.

A royal industry was in the process of being created, seemingly with untutored professional flair. Even the Duke's stammer was taken in hand. Persuaded by the Duchess to make one last effort to seek at least a partial cure, on 19 October 1926 the Duke arrived at 146 Harley Street for his first consultation with an Australian speech therapist, Lionel Logue, who had been practising in London for a couple of years. Logue, one of the founders of the British Society of Speech Therapists, made a note of what was an historic occasion: 'He entered my consulting room at three o'clock in the afternoon, a slim, quiet man with tired eyes and all the outward symptoms of the man upon whom habitual speech defect had begun to set the sign. When he left at five o'clock, you could see that there was hope once more in his heart.' Almost daily for ten weeks the Duke went to see Logue, where he was taught, most importantly, to control his breathing. Terrified in case his father should regard him as unable to fulfil major royal duties, the Duke wrote to King George V to say, 'I have been seeing Logue every day, & I have noticed a great improvement in my talking, & also in making speeches which I did this week. I am sure I am going to get quite all right in time, but 24 years of talking in the wrong way cannot be cured in a month.

'I wish I could have found him before, as now I know the right way to breathe my fear of talking will vanish.'

In 1903 Admiral Lord Fisher of Kilverstone was at Balmoral, and noted 'The two little princes [David and Bertie] are splendid little boys and chattered away the whole of their lunch-time, not the faintest shyness.' It may have been that Fisher tuned in to an early love both boys were to develop for the sea, and there is no reason to imagine that Bertie's shyness or stammer were on permanent display; they probably always related to the company he was in. But the Duke's reference, in 1926, to '24 years of talking the wrong way' pinpoints the onset of his stammer to the age of seven. Clearly he was not born to stammer; seven was about the age at which he was made to write with his right hand. Before long the Duke was writing to Logue himself to say, 'I must send you a line to tell you how grateful I am to you for all that you have done in helping me with my speech defect. I really do think you have given me a real good start in the way of getting over it & I am sure if I carry on your exercises and instructions that I shall not go back. I am full of confidence.'

As king, Bertie never entirely lost what he now described as his 'speech defect', but it certainly ceased to be a stammer. In 1945 Harold Nicolson reported to his younger son it was 'almost intolerably painful to listen to him. It is as if one read a fine piece of prose written on a typewriter the keys of which stick from time to time and mat the beauty of the whole. It makes him stress the wrong word.'[9] By contrast, on VE Day that year James Lees-Milne listened to the King's broadcast, and noted in his diary, 'It was perfect.'[10] There were times during his wartime broadcasts when the King did hesitate rather unnervingly before a particular word, and he never entirely lost his dislike of the microphone. He dreaded his Christmas Day broadcast in particular, which until almost the end of his life, when he was very ill, was live. But by 1945 he had received much personal encouragement from Logue, who often remained with him while he broadcast. He was with him in the air raid shelter at Buckingham Palace on 23 September 1940 when the King announced the creation of the George Cross. 'Despite the unpleasant conditions [the All Clear could actually he heard during the broadcast] he spoke splendidly,' Logue later recalled. 'A stout effort.' He had been present too when the King broadcast, to Lees-Milne's approval, on 5 May 1945. So had the Queen. 'We both stand rigid for the first two sentences,' Logue again recalled, 'but the King's voice is gathering strength and power and we glance at one another and smile, and so we stand until the end. I know the Queen was praying. I was too.' Afterwards, 'his wife quietly kisses him, and says, "Well done, Bertie!"'

In contrast to the Duke's evenly modulated, rather 'manly' voice, quite devoid of the guttural tones of his father, the Duchess's voice was unmistakably, and fashionably, upper class, but was described by Osbert Sitwell as 'musical and appealing' with a 'peculiarly emotional quality'.[11] She pronounced (and still does) gone as gorn and off as orff, and could never in a million years have been mistaken for a shop girl. Indeed, there was a measure of Mayfair in her voice that might well have cracked a champagne glass. Both her daughters acquired their mother's upper-crust accent, although the Queen modified hers considerably in the light of criticism early in her reign. The acquisition of accents by the Queen's children in a much more egalitarian age is more a matter for amusement than serious speculation; the Princess

Royal sounds like a bossy prefect, the Duke of York like an equally bossy naval officer (which he is), whilst for reasons best known to himself the Prince of Wales appears to have reinvented the English language entirely, and sounds as if he has lost his way in a peasoup fog.

In the last years of George V's life it was becoming increasingly obvious to politicians and courtiers that the throne might be in safer hands than those of the Prince of Wales. It was also becoming increasingly obvious to the King that his second son was the obedient, dutiful sort, in marked contrast to his eldest. The King's attitude towards Bertie had relaxed thanks to Elizabeth's insistence on speech therapy. A visit by Bertie to Balmoral in the autumn of 1926 resulted in a letter to Lionel Logue in which Bertie reported that he had been 'talking a lot with the King, & I have had no trouble at all. Also I can make him listen & I don't have to repeat everything over again.' In his turn, the King reported to Queen Mary, 'Delighted to have Bertie with me . . . have had several talks with him & find him very sensible, very different to D.'

Back in 1920, when Bertie heard he was to be created Duke of York, he had told his father he hoped he would live up to the title in every way, receiving the welcome assurance that 'this splendid old title will be safe in your hands & that you will never do anything which could in any way tarnish it.' The King expressed the hope that Bertie would always look upon him as his best friend '& always tell me everything'. On his honeymoon, the Duke received the final seal of approbation. 'You have always been so sensible & easy to work with & you have always been ready to listen to any advice & to agree with my opinions about people & things, that I feel that we have always got on very well together (very different to dear David).' The King added, prophetically, 'I am quite certain that Elizabeth will be a splendid partner in your work & share with you & help you in all you have to do.'

Only the next year, from Northern Ireland, Bertie confirmed his father's predictions. He wrote to George V to say, 'Elizabeth has been marvellous as usual & the people simply love her already. I am very lucky indeed to have her to help me as she knows exactly what to do & say to all the people we meet.'

By the age of 27, Elizabeth was already the subject of the first of a good many sycophantic biographies, *The Duchess of York*, by Lady Cynthia Asquith.[12] This purported to be 'an intimate and authentic life-story including many details hitherto unpublished, told with the personal approval of Her Royal Highness.' (It appears that the only biography which has not met with the Queen Mother's approval was

Queen Elizabeth: A Life of the Queen Mother by the novelist Penelope Mortimer, but that was hardly intended to be sycophantic.[13]) Lady Cynthia was correct to note that after her marriage to the Duke of York, Elizabeth had shown 'an intelligent understanding of what may be called the profession of being royal'.

Officially, of course, the prospects for the Duchess of York remained relatively modest; a town house, a country retreat, the patronage of various innocuous charities, visits to shipyards and hospitals, and the occasional overseas tour. Her children, but not her grandchildren (unless her daughters married royalty), would be royal. She herself would never be short of money or beautiful possessions, but then, as Lady Elizabeth she had hardly been brought up a pauper. Had she not married a prince she would in all probability have become the wife of a peer or a wealthy landowner, probably both. But with the increasingly erratic behaviour of the Prince of Wales, and the fatal collapse of the King's precarious health (like his father Edward VII, George V was a heavy smoker and prone to bronchitis), the Duchess's prospects began to acquire wider horizons. And only 11 months after the death of George V they blossomed into regal magnificence – a king for a husband, four houses instead of two, one of them a palace and two of them castles, as well as luxury and adulation beyond the wildest dreams of those ordinary everyday folk with whom she was about to enter into a lifetime's unblemished love affair.

5

The Letters Patent

THE SHOCK TO THE nation of the sudden departure of King Edward VIII was enormous. One minute he was there, the next, gone. It is inconceivable today that every man, woman and child in the land would not have received a blow-by-blow account from the press. But in 1936 most people were either too busy working or looking for work to involve themselves in more than a very superficial way in the private lives of politicians, royals or the denizens of café society. Even though the King's private affairs were intimately connected with his public responsibilities, the idea of ordinary people prying into conversations held in Buckingham Palace would have been regarded not only as preposterous but impossible.

There were courtiers like Hardinge and Lascelles who cordially disliked and distrusted King Edward, but to the man in the street, who knew nothing of his dereliction of duties, his unpunctuality and his inconsiderateness, the King was a hero. He was seen as a veteran of the trenches and, they imagined, some sort of champion of the down-and-out, as well as being an agreeably informal apologist for the age of the cocktail and the Charleston. This was an era that had begun with the signing of the Armistice in 1919, an era that saw a relative leavening of social status, a diminution of the vast wealth of the aristocracy and a greater opportunity for enjoying holidays and entertainment, in particular the cinema, where love and lovers were glamorised. Moral values were shifting – away from the hypocrisy of Victorian England towards a more laissez-faire attitude. Women had worked in munitions factories, the chaperone had been put out to grass, people were beginning to make their own decisions about their lives. Yet the King, it appeared, had not been allowed to marry for love.

Although the aristocracy had welcomed wealthy American women into their ranks in order to shore up the fabric of stately homes, when it came to accepting an American on the throne there seemed to the

Establishment to be a distinct difference between foreign consorts imported from France or Germany, Spain or Denmark and one from the United States; Americans on the whole were thought to be brash and vulgar, and Mrs Simpson was held to be a prize example of the species. The fact that she had her Christian name embossed in blue script diagonally across the left-hand corner of her writing paper was *not* considered a promising augury for future regal conduct. Her 'Hollywood' track record of marital failures told against her even more. What if her third marriage should end in divorce? Henry II had married a divorcée, Henry VIII had been granted annulments, George I was divorced before he came to the throne and George IV was separated, but these were seen as historical aberrations. There may have been no strict constitutional impediment to Mrs Simpson becoming queen. Even the allegation, as has now been made by numerous biographers, that Wallis was born 17 months before the marriage of her parents could not in law have been held against her. It was enough, for the Establishment, that governments throughout the Empire had given her the thumbs down.

So prejudice prevailed and the King had gone. Unfortunately for himself, for his future wife and for the reputation of the new King and Queen, he left in such a hurry (he told his closest friend, Major Edward Metcalfe, he didn't know until about an hour before he left England where he was heading for[1]) that hardly any consideration was given as to what he would be called, what he would do, where he would live or what he would live on. Magna Carta makes it plain that, whereas the state has the right to forbid entry, no Englishman born and bred can be exiled, even by the sovereign. Yet clearly it would have been improper for Edward to have taken up residence in the country whose throne he had just vacated. For any king to have his predecessor breathing down his neck is an untenable position. Yet while Edward had been happy to sell Sandringham and Balmoral to his brother, he rather fancied retaining the grace and favour residence, Fort Belvedere. In his naivety, when he sailed for France he never imagined he would be destined to live abroad for the rest of his life.

He had money saved up – a considerable amount of money, as it transpired – from his revenues as Duke of Cornwall. He foolishly declined to reveal the amount to George VI, but the moment he abdicated he ceased to receive Duchy of Cornwall revenue or an allowance from the Civil List as king.[2] Obviously it would have been undignified for a former monarch not to maintain an appropriate standard of living, and, before Edward left, he negotiated (or thought he had negotiated) a personal allowance of £25,000 a year from his brother in the event of parliament declining to include him in the new Civil List. (It was a measure of inflation-proof incomes that parliament only normally reviewed the Civil List at the start of each new reign.) The allowance was to be contingent also on George VI taking possession of Sandringham and Balmoral. It was never a generous arrangement but it seemed straightforward, £25,000 a year being the sum voted in 1911 by parliament to meet the official expenses of the Dukes of Gloucester and Kent.

It was also in order to regularise Edward's position, as though he were a younger brother, that as the first act of his reign King George VI announced, at his Accession Council, that he intended to confer upon him a dukedom, the title chosen being Windsor. It all sounded very appropriate. Already the new King had given clear-sighted instructions that, when Edward broadcast from Windsor Castle, he should be announced as His Royal Highness Prince Edward. And, in addressing the Privy Council, he said, '[my brother] will henceforth be known as His Royal Highness the Duke of Windsor.' This was actually a technical slip on the part of the King, whose intentions were perfectly clear. Strictly speaking, Prince Edward would not be entitled to use his peerage until publication of the Letters Patent, delayed, in Edward's case, until 8 March the following year. Meanwhile he was indubitably His Royal Highness Prince Edward. Sir Claud Schuster, Clerk of the Crown and Permanent Secretary to the Lord Chancellor, got a wigging from the Duke of York when, on 11 December, realising that Sir John Reith was about to make a fool of himself by introducing the former King as Mr Edward Windsor, Bertie said, 'That is quite wrong. Before going any further I would ask what he has given up on his abdication.' To this, the luckless Schuster had said he was not sure. Nervously irritable and out of patience with everyone at this time, the Duke of York snapped, 'It would be quite a good thing to find out before coming to see me.' One reason Bertie was appalled at the prospect of his brother being hailed as a commoner (which clearly he was not) was that if he *was* a commoner he would be able to return to England and get elected to parliament.[3] Equally clearly, Schuster's advice was that, on abdicating, the King was only giving up the Crown, not the royal status with which he was born. King George recognised from the start that, as the son of a monarch, Edward remained both a prince and a Royal Highness.

In his broadcast, the former King made contradictory statements about what he planned to do with himself. 'I now quit altogether public affairs . . . and if at any time in the future I can be found of service to His Majesty in a private station I shall not fail.' In what private station he imagined he would be invited to serve it is hard to imagine; not, surely, as his brother's valet? Within three years the Duke of Windsor was, in fact, pestering Churchill for a job, and ended up as Governor of the Bahamas. He also said, 'It may be some time before I return to my native land,' a remark which no doubt sent further shivers down the spine of the new Queen, shivering as she already was with influenza. What did he mean? Return for a holiday? Return to live?

While waiting in Austria for his dukedom to be gazetted, Prince Edward was at first wretched with worries that superseded any concern over his future titles, income or place of abode. What concerned him more than anything was that Wallis should receive her decree absolute. So stringent were the divorce laws at that time that he and she did not even dare live in the same country. (Another reason for the Prince and Mrs Simpson to keep apart was because he had undertaken not to see her until the Civil List was settled.) Had the King's Proctor successfully intervened and shown any cause why the decree absolute should not be granted, Edward's fate would have been of Graeco-tragic proportions. In the event, Mrs Simpson's divorce was finalised on 3 May, when she reverted to her maiden name of Warfield, the name by which she married the Duke. But by the time that day of relief arrived the harmonious atmosphere in which King George VI and the former Edward VIII had kissed and parted at the Royal Lodge had been sadly dented.

Wallis Simpson had no doubts (although she never revealed her evidence) where the fault lay. There had in fact been an investigation into the divorce petition, which needless to say had driven Prince Edward and Mrs Simpson nearly frantic with worry. 'I blame it all on the wife – who hates us both,' Mrs Simpson wrote to the Prince in February 1937, referring of course to Queen Elizabeth. Earlier, in December 1936, by which time the Duchess of York had become queen, a fact that had not yet registered with Mrs Simpson, Wallis had written to the Prince to say, 'Really David the pleased expression on the Duchess of York's face is funny to see. How she is loving it all. There will be no support there.' As it had been some months since Mrs Simpson could possibly have seen the Queen, whether as Duchess of York or otherwise, she was presumably relying on newspaper photographs for information about the Queen's demeanour. The note of jealousy as well as anxiety is perhaps indicative of the fact that Wallis would have liked to have been in the Queen's shoes. No one, least of all the Duchess of York, had done anything other than try to persuade King Edward to stay on the throne. On the other hand, the Duchess of York had never suggested he could do so and marry Wallis as well. Undoubtedly Elizabeth was enjoying being queen, but it was not a position she had ever engineered for herself; David had done that, with single-minded determination.

Mrs Simpson's frame of mind is starkly revealed in a letter she wrote to Prince Edward on 3 January 1937, in which she referred to King George as a puppet placed on the throne by politicians. She was fretting about having her marriage announced in the Court Circular (she was still married to Ernest Simpson, and would remain so for another four months!), and was expressing concern in case she was not accorded the title of Royal Highness. 'I loathe being undignified,' she told the Prince, with unconscious irony, 'and also of joining the countless titles that roam around Europe meaning nothing. To set off on our journey with a proper backing would mean so much.' She told him, 'Up to the present, the only person who has made a big gesture is you.' No remark could more precisely clarify the gap in comprehension between Wallis Simpson and those in London whom she despised. 'Frankly I am disgusted with them all,' she informed Prince Edward, who had indeed made a big gesture, by which it is reasonable to suppose that Mrs Simpson really meant a big sacrifice. In the eyes of the Court, he had made no sacrifice at all, he had absconded from a sacred trust.

There was no need for the Queen to waste energy hating Prince Edward and Mrs Simpson, and had Mrs Simpson seen the Queen's letter of 11 December 1936, addressed to 'Darling David' and praying that he would find happiness in his new life, she would have known that, far from hating her brother-in-law, the Queen had been genuinely fond of him. As for the 'big gesture', the Queen had written (again, of course, unknown to Wallis), 'I don't think we could ever imagine a more incredible tragedy, and the agony of it all has been beyond words. And the melancholy fact remains still at the present moment, that he for whom we agonised is the one person it did not touch.'[4]

What the Queen was now faced with was round two of a public relations exercise she had first embarked upon in 1923. She and the King had taken over a parliament, a nation and a vast empire profoundly shaken by the very possibility of abdication. The Queen herself now had to care for a mother-in-law who in one year had buried her husband, been displaced from much of her regal eminence, been compelled to move house, and whose eldest son had committed an act which to her was so incomprehensible as almost to amount to treachery. Writing to the Duke of Windsor in 1938, Queen Mary was to remind him how she had implored him 'for your sake and the sake of the country' not to abdicate, yet he had not seemed able to take in any point of view but his own. At Christmas 1937, at Sandringham, she collapsed physically and emotionally, and remained in her room for a whole week. '[The Abdication] very nearly killed poor Queen Mary,' Queen Elizabeth reported to Victor Cazalet. 'There is indeed such a thing as a broken heart.'[5]

The kind of moral support the Queen found herself having to offer to Bertie's family can be gauged from Osbert Sitwell's recollections of the Abdication. He was bold enough to mention Mrs Simpson to the Queen on several occasions, and always the Queen 'spoke of her without venom'. What she told Sitwell had most saddened her was the sorrow of other members of the Royal Family, 'because each member of it – more especially Queen Mary and the Princess Royal – had regarded King Edward with a particular affection and taken a particular pride in him.' The Queen told Sitwell in 1937 that Queen Mary, 'though one might not guess it from her demeanour', was very emotional, and what the Queen could not forgive was the fact that Mrs Simpson had induced the Duke of Windsor 'to take up an attitude of coldness, and sometimes of rudeness', to his mother. The Queen even found herself having to comfort George V's old aunt, Princess Beatrice. When Sitwell ventured to say to Princess Beatrice one day at Kensington Palace, 'How painful all this business about Mrs Simpson must have been for you, Ma'am,' Queen Victoria's youngest daughter replied, 'I cannot tell you: I feel besmirched!'[6]

To some extent Mrs Simpson remained the scapegoat for Queen Mary's feelings of grief and guilt regarding her son's behaviour. In order to reassure both matriarch and monarch, it was essential to create as speedily as possible an impression of a stable and well-loved substitute for the errant David. This became Elizabeth's first priority. It was not an easy task. George felt betrayed by his brother. When writing his memorandum on the Abdication he could not even bring himself to pen that scapegoat's name. Mrs Simpson quite simply became a dash, although he did once manage to refer to her as 'she'. Even after Mrs Simpson had become Duchess of Windsor, the Queen abbreviated her name, in a letter to Queen Mary, to 'Mrs S'.[7] But in conversation the Queen more commonly referred simply to 'that woman', an expression which found its way into *Time* magazine, much to the indignation of the Duke of Windsor.

The King was deeply insecure and his nervousness was easily encouraged. The Queen's greatest fear was that her husband would never replace David in the affections of the nation, and that in the event of some new constitutional crisis the King would be found wanting. The last thing she needed was a rival Court established down the road at Fort Belvedere. Even if the former King's English home were only to be retained as a domestic haven, the possibility of having to entertain and be entertained by the Duchess of Windsor on terms identical to the Duchess of Gloucester or the Duchess of Kent was an emotional chore the Queen could not contemplate. What were they supposed to talk about all evening, the rhododendrons?

In 1939, perhaps egged on by his intemperate wife, the Duke of Windsor, in a letter to Queen Mary, referred to Elizabeth as 'that common little woman'.[8] He would have cause to regret this description, for Queen Mary was bound to show the letter to the King.

When he scanned the 1937 New Year Honours List, Prince Edward was disappointed to discover he had not been appointed a personal aide de camp to the new King, who had nevertheless – and quite needlessly – reappointed him a Knight of the Garter. (Edward was to complain later that only he, not his wife, received the Coronation Medal.) A more significant appointment to the Most Noble Order of the Garter, founded in 1348 by Edward III and England's most prestigious order of chivalry (but not the oldest; Knights Bachelor date from about 1220), had been made just three days after Bertie became King. 'He had discovered that Papa gave it to you on his, Papa's birthday, June 3rd,' the Queen wrote to Queen Mary, 'and the coincidence was so charming that he has now followed suit, & given it to me on his own birthday.' Queen Philippa, wife of Edward III, and other ladies of her time were admitted to the Order of the Garter as Dames de la Fraternité de St George, but until Queen Elizabeth II opened the Garter to women in 1990, appointing the first commoner, Lavinia, Duchess of Norfolk, as a lady companion, the only women in this country to slip in as Ladies of the Garter before the Queen Mother were Queen Alexandra and Queen Mary. (Queens Regnant are ex officio members as Sovereign of the Order.) The Queen has since given the Garter to Princess Juliana of the Netherlands, the Queen of Denmark, the Queen of the Netherlands and the Princess Royal.

Exiled in Austria and no longer the Fountain of Honour, Prince Edward contented himself with skiing by day and playing poker at night. Other Viennese diversions included Turkish baths, shopping, and Embassy cocktail parties. Despite the lack of official duties it had still not quite sunk in that he was no longer king. One evening, during dinner, the real King telephoned and was given a message that he should ring back at 10 pm. Edward, in turn, was informed that the King was too busy, and would ring back at 6:45pm the following day. 'It was,' Edward Metcalfe reported to his wife, 'pathetic to see HRH's face. He couldn't believe it! He's been used to having everything done as he wishes. I'm afraid he's going to have many more shocks like this.'

Unknown to anyone except Prince Edward's small entourage, who made sure he did not see them, the Prince was receiving up to 300 letters of abuse a day, from all parts of the world. What the Prince was more concerned about was his financial situation. 'He won't pay for anything' Major Metcalfe told his wife on 27 January. 'It's become a mania with him.' Edward also had time, having been invited to the British Embassy on 3 February, to make 'a great fuss over decorations. He has sent for all his orders etc to put on. He says he must keep up his dignity.'[9]

On 8 March the Prince's dukedom of Windsor was gazetted, but without the customary addition of any courtesy titles. It was unprecedented for a peerage in the rank of duke, marquess or earl to be created without at least one, and usually two courtesy titles, to be held by the eldest son and possibly grandson. The heirs to a dozen dukedoms are currently marquesses and six are earls. Even in the case of royal dukes, whose sons would rank as princes, the dukedom is invariably accompanied by an earldom and a barony. King George VI had himself been created Duke of York, Earl of Inverness and Baron Killarney. Prince Henry had received the dukedom of Gloucester together with the earldom of Ulster and the barony of Culloden, and Prince George became Duke of Kent, Earl of St Andrews and Baron Downpatrick. On the eve of his daughter Princess Elizabeth's marriage, King George was to create her fiancé Duke of Edinburgh, Earl of Merioneth and Baron Greenwich.

The lack of any courtesy titles for the Duke of Windsor can scarcely be explained away as an oversight by the King or the patent office, the Lord Chamberlain or anyone else. Extensive research in the Royal Archives by Sir Kenneth Scott, Deputy Private Secretary to the Queen, has failed 'to show why the Letters Patent of March 1937, which conferred the title of Duke of Windsor, did not add any other courtesy titles.'[10] The slight was clearly intended as a preliminary shot in the battle to reduce the status of the former King, and any heirs he might have.

The Queen first sat for Cecil Beaton, at Buckingham Palace, in July 1939, wearing one of her Norman Hartnell creations. Posing in profile to obscure the rounded features already so apparent full-face, she set about creating an aura of glittering fantasy.

The Queen Mother's love of party games and dressing up was established at Glamis. Aged nine, she poses with her favourite brother, David.

A prematurely aged King George VI with the sturdy consort – Cookie, as the Duke of Windsor nicknamed her – from whom he drew constant strength and support.

In 1924, the recently wed Duchess of York drove with her mother, the Countess of Strathmore & Kinghorne, to the opening of the British Empire Exhibition at Wembley. Opposite Lady Strathmore sits the Duke of York.

A photograph of the youthful 'Prince Charming', Edward VIII, published as a postcard in 1936, when he was 42.

Below: Even before the Abdication, constant public appearances by the Duchess of York with her well-scrubbed neatly dressed children, pointed up the Prince of Wales's lack of family life. In 1935 she arrives at the Royal Tournament followed by Princess Margaret Rose, cheerfully taking precedence over her elder sister, Princess Elizabeth.

Above: After Buckingham Palace had been bombed, the Queen said she felt she could look the East End in the face. Surrounded by animated but undernourished Cockney urchins, her furs and jewellry made a startling contrast with the endemic poverty of wartime working-class life.

At King's Cross, on a bleak February day in 1952, the Queen Mother, widowed at 51, watches her husband's coffin carried from the train. With her are her elder daughter Elizabeth 11, her son-in-law the Duke of Edinburgh and her brother-in-law the Duke of Gloucester.

Left: In 1946, in the Mall, the King, with the Queen, Queen Mary and the two princesses, took the salute at the Victory Parade. Before she died in 1953 Queen Mary was to experience the loss of three of her children, Prince John, the Duke of Kent and the King himself.

The Queen Mother has always delighted in her grandchildren. With her in the garden at Clarence House in August 1960 are the 11-year-old Prince Charles, Princess Anne and the baby Prince Andrew. In attendance: a ubiquitous corgie.

Putting a brave face on their mutual antipathy, the Queen Mother and the Duchess of Windsor meet, only for the second time since the Abdication, at the funeral of the Duke of Windsor at Windsor Castle in 1972.

Above: At Ascot in 1966, Queen
Elizabeth, who has since clocked up
over 400 winners, gives her horse
Oedipe a consoling pat. He had
only come in third, but he still represented a satisfying source of
income, pleasure and pride.

Relieved of the royal handbag by her
Page, William Tallon, Her Majesty
Queen Elizabeth the Queen Mother
is free to receive birthday gifts with
both hands outside Clarence House
on 4 August 1993. As old as the
century, she seems all set to see it
out.

The popular and affectionate image of the Queen Mother is of a mildly inebriated gambler. Although she certainly enjoys a drink she is in fact never the worse for wear; nor does she ever place a bet. It was the Princess of Wales, seen above at Ascot with the Queen Mother in 1987, who is said to have been discovered, by Queen Elizabeth, at the foot of the stairs at Sandringham.

There was also a muddle over the financial provisions for the Duke. Some wanted him included in the new Civil List; others thought it better to increase the King's provision so as to enable the King to pay his brother a kind of secret pension. While the squabbles continued not only were funds not being made available for the Duke, no member of the Royal Family could be in receipt of their Civil List monies. This included the Queen herself, who was busy setting up her new establishments at Buckingham Palace and Windsor Castle. She had additional ladies-in-waiting to appoint, secretaries to hire, clothes to order.

The legacy of the Duke's departure was becoming very tiresome, particularly when Sir Warren Fisher, Permanent Secretary to the Treasury, brought his civil servant's brain to bear on the matter, and declared the Agreement signed by the King and the Duke to be invalid because the Duke had not disclosed the extent of his private means. Whereas the Duke had told the King, before leaving England, that he 'did not think he had £5,000 a year',[11] it transpired he had amassed a personal fortune from the Duchy of Cornwall revenues, variously estimated at between £800,000 and £1.1 million.[12]

On 11 February the King wrote to his brother to say he was very disturbed that the Fort Belvedere Agreement had got into the hands of the Government and the press, which threatened to complicate the forthcoming discussions of the Select Committee on the Civil List. He thought they would insist on a full disclosure of the Duke's private means, and might try to reduce the Civil List by any sum the King proposed to pay him, as they were still 'a little sore with you for having given up being King'. It was, he said, all very difficult and complicated, but he hoped 'for both our sakes' that when Walter Monckton, still playing the role of honest broker, went out to Austria 'to explain things', he and David would 'hit on a solution'.[13]

'I have kept my side of the bargain [by which he meant he had not seen Mrs Simpson] and I am sure you will keep yours,' the Duke wrote to the King on 21 February. He proposed, in fact, a new agreement; that they forget about the allowance, in exchange for which the Duke should receive £25,000 a year by way of rent for Sandringham and Balmoral. In addition, he offered to pay £4,000 a year towards pensions granted by their father. 'It seems quite unnecessary that there should be a disagreement between us,' the Duke told the King, 'but I must tell you quite frankly that I am relying on you to honour your promise.'

The King, for his part, replied that the whole matter had been a great worry, and it would be 'a great pity' if the Duke could not agree with *him* – agree that it was best to tear up the Fort Belvedere Agreement. 'You know the last thing I want is a family row' the Duke told his solicitor, George Allen, on 13 March, 'but they are heading the right way for the finest ever.'

One reason for keeping the Duke of Windsor out of the Civil List was to prevent any discussion about him in parliament so soon after the Abdication when the List was debated. The less the King and Queen heard any mention of the Duke in public the better they were pleased. They were only just getting to grips with their new situation, they had the Coronation in May to prepare for, they were anxious for some sort of return to the good old days. Only the day after the Duke's farewell broadcast the Archbishop of Canterbury had been invited to 145 Piccadilly, where he found the new King and Queen 'as they have always been, most kind and cordial'. He talked with them for about an hour about 'the crisis', about 'the poor Duke of Windsor' and then about arrangements for the Coronation. Remembering 'the strained and wilful ways' of 'the late King', Lang breathed a sigh of relief when writing up his diary; he recalled that at 145 Piccadilly he had found 'an atmosphere of intimate friendship'. He had been looking forward to Edward's coronation 'as a sort of nightmare'. Now he was sure that 'to the solemn words of the coronation there would be a sincere response'. Lang was assured of a continuity with the past when at Christmas he received a letter of seasonal greetings from the King, and noted that in the handwriting of George VI, and especially in his signature, it would be difficult to see any difference from that of his father. 'Prosit omen!' he wrote.

While solicitors, Members of Parliament and of course the two royal brothers had been debating royal finance, George VI had finally been appraised, by the Keeper of the Privy Purse, Ulick Alexander, and Edward Peacock, the Duke of Windsor's principal financial advisor when he was Prince of Wales, of the extent of the Duke's private means. Following a night spent at Windsor Castle by the Foreign Secretary, Anthony Eden, Eden's colleague, Oliver Harvey, noted in his diary on 21 April that Eden had found the King 'much incensed against the Duke of Windsor who was trying to get more money out of him, although he had gone off with something near a million £! When he abdicated it had not been known that he had this sum representing apparently savings in his private account and King George had undertaken to get him a parliamentary grant or to make him an allowance. When this had been discovered there was great indignation, and it was felt that Edward had put in some very sharp practice. These savings out of the Prince of Wales's revenues would normally be used by the King when he came to the throne, and of course this King is deprived of these into the bargain. Incidentally Edward has already settled the larger part of the interest on this sum on Mrs Simpson.'

Over dinner Eden and the King and Queen had also discussed a question that lay at the core of their scheme to keep Edward out of England, the denial to his wife of royal status. 'There was also indignation,' Harvey recounts, 'over Edward's wish to make Mrs S HRH when they marry as King George feels that he cannot expect his subjects to curtsey to her. It appears, however, that according to Sir J. Simon [John Simon, the Home Secretary] as the D. of Windsor is HRH, the moment she marries him she must become HRH automatically and there is no stopping it except by special Act of Parliament.

'Finally the D of W wishes to come back again and this King George is most anxious to prevent as although he is sure his brother would not want to intrigue he feels certain she would make him.'

On the question of money, the Duke's solicitor now sprang into action. If parliament made no provision in the Civil List for the Duke, and the King defaulted on his promise of a pension, then, George Allen suggested, the Duke would go back on the Agreement too and retain Balmoral and Sandringham. As late as 2 July, clearly delighted to have the upper hand for once, the Duke was writing to Allen to say, 'I shall be very glad when you are back in London [Allen was in Newfoundland], and able to deal with Buckingham Palace who are really behaving abominably.' He had heard that the valuations of Sandringham and Balmoral were still not completed and he believed that his brother was 'trying to wriggle out of the Agreement, which I am absolutely determined he shall not.' The Duke wished Allen 'to inform the King that, if he does not fulfil his part of the bargain by the end of July, I shall take steps to prevent "the Court" moving to Balmoral in August.'

The new Civil List had finally been approved on 24 May. The King would receive £410,000 per annum, the Duke nothing. In July the King offered an allowance of £20,000, to be paid only during the King's lifetime and contingent on neither the Duke nor his wife returning to England without the King's consent. For months the lawyers argued. Churchill cautioned the King's Private Secretary that de facto exile was unconstitutional. And on 22 December 1937 the Duke wrote to Neville Chamberlain, Prime Minister since 28 May, to say 'the treatment which has been meted out to my wife and myself since last December, both by the Royal Family and the Government, has caused us acute pain.' By Royal Family the Duke could only have meant the King, the Queen and Queen Mary. The financial wrangles were to drag on until February 1938, when eventually the combined market value of Balmoral and Sandringham was settled at £300,000, which sum the King paid over to trustees, providing an income of £10,000 a year for the Duke. The King agreed to pay a further £11,000 a year as a voluntary allowance, but retained the right to cease payment if the Duke ever set foot in England against the advice of the Government. It is highly probable that it was in order to finance the Duke of Windsor that George VI asked the Inland Revenue whether he needed to pay income tax, and was told he did not; this arrangement lasted until 1992, by which time Queen Elizabeth II had amassed a fortune. The sums involved were not generous and the terms pretty insulting, but at least the Duke and Duchess were now able to lease a couple of properties in France, at Cap d'Antibes, where the Duke referred to his sitting room as the Belvedere, and at Versailles, where they were dogged by servant problems; one member of their staff turned out to be a thief and another a Communist!

'No one will ever really understand the story of the King's life . . . who does not appreciate . . . the intensity and depth of his devotion to Mrs Simpson,' Sir Walter Monckton wrote. 'To him she was the perfect woman.'[14] Ironically, his mother had written to David on 27 June 1915, four days after his 21st birthday, 'I hope some day you will find the woman who will make you happy!' When he did, she refused to receive her. A measure of Edward's dependence on Wallis is clear from the way he managed to drag her name into a letter to Diana Cooper, thanking her, on 21 January 1936, for a letter of sympathy on the death of his father: 'She gives me the courage to carry on.'[15]

Now he planned to marry the perfect woman just as soon as she was free, and he had no doubt at all that this was to be a royal wedding. His cousin, Lord Louis Mountbatten, stayed with him during March 1937 and twice offered to act as best man. That was kind of him, the Duke said, but there was no need; his two younger brothers would come over as supporters.[16] Perhaps he had been misled about the family's readiness to be involved in his wedding. The previous month he had enjoyed a visit, lasting almost a week, from his sister and her husband, now Earl of Harewood, and another lasting '5 hectic days' from the Duke of Kent. But, by royal standards, the nuptials degenerated into a very shoddy affair, with a congregation of only 11, Major Metcalfe acting as best man. The service was not even held in a church (the makeshift altar was a chest), and the priest who officiated was a volunteer from Darlington ('a large-nosed red-faced little man' according to Lady Alexandra Metcalfe). Lang described him as 'a seeker of notoriety', and he did indeed embark on a lecture tour in the United States immediately after the wedding.

The day chosen by the Duke of Windsor for his marriage to the perfect woman, 3 June, was hardly the perfect day; it was the anniversary of King George V's birthday. Nevertheless Queen Mary braced herself to send a telegram. But wedding present came there none. 'I was bitterly hurt and disappointed that you virtually ignored the most important event of my life,' the Duke wrote in mid-June; he was so upset he failed to date his letter, which went on to claim that Bertie had consistently humiliated him ever since the Abdication.

The King and Queen also telegraphed good wishes, but the King had sent Monckton ahead with a letter, which tried to explain, and apologise for, Letters Patent dated 27 May purported to bestow upon the Duke 'the title, style or attribute of Royal Highness' while withholding such title, style or attribute not only from his wife but his descendants. The King told his brother he had been obliged to consult the British and Dominion prime ministers, but these were not the only gentlemen whose opinions he had sought, in the hope that they would coincide with his own. Lord Wigram, a former Private Secretary to George V and the new King's Permanent Lord-in-Waiting, told an official at the Office of the Parliamentary Council, Granville Ram, that the King was 'certainly of the opinion' that the title Royal Highness for the Duchess of Windsor required his consent, and when Ram reminded him that the Duchess of York's titles had stemmed directly from her marriage, Wigram countered by pointing out that 'as the Duke of Windsor does not come under the Royal Marriages Act, perhaps the Home Secretary might see fit to advise another course.' His argument was that only princes in the line of succession were entitled by right to the title Royal Highness.

The King's personal views and prejudices were made crystal clear on 4 May 1937 in a letter to Baldwin. 'Is she a fit and proper person to become a Royal Highness after what she has done in this country?' he asked. 'And would the country understand it if she became one automatically on marriage?' As things turned out, the country was to question why she did not. 'I and my family and Queen Mary all feel that it would be a great mistake to acknowledge Mrs Simpson as a suitable person to become Royal,' King George told his Prime Minister. 'The Monarchy has been degraded quite enough already.'

How, so soon into a reign begun so traumatically, could any prime minister be expected to ignore such an urgent request for support from his sovereign? The King had not consulted the Prime Minister, he had told him what he wanted. By 'family' the King unquestionably included his wife, and possibly the Dukes of Gloucester and Kent, but distant relatives were not slow in offering their opinions. The King's first cousin once removed, the Duke of Connaught, let it be known it would be 'awful' if Mrs Simpson automatically became a Royal Highness.

Lord Wigram told the Home Secretary, Sir John Simon, 'HM hopes you will find some way to avoid this title being conferred,' but it was a tall order. Simon, who had served as Solicitor General from 1910 to 1913 and as Attorney General from 1913 to 1915, and was one of the greatest lawyers of his time, considered, but rejected, the possibility of depriving the Duke of his title Royal Highness. Then he tried to oblige by suggesting that only princes within the succession were intended by Queen Victoria to be Royal Highnesses. Certainly there was no precedent for a former king being so styled, for although Richard II had been deposed (in 1399), as had Henry VI (in 1461) and James II (in 1688), no monarch had ever before voluntarily renounced the throne. But the lack of precedent did not dispose of the fact that the Duke of Windsor remained the son of a sovereign. Maurice Gwyer of the Parliamentary Council warned Wigram it would be impossible to imagine a more public or deadly slight than to 'deprive the Duke's wife of the title of HRH'. When Simon appeared to concur, Wigram, obviously briefed by the King, gave the game away by saying the marriage was unlikely to last long. Indeed, it was the Royal Family's firm conviction that a trail of divorced Royal Highnesses would imperil the dignity of the monarchy far more seriously than would one disgruntled Duke and a slighted wife for whom, they believed, there was little popular support. Had they hired the services of a competent fortune-teller they would have been staggered to learn that the marriage of which they all despaired would last for 35 years.

When eventually the King settled upon a totally spurious pretext for the Letters Patent – the alleged need to re-create the Duke a Royal Highness – Neville Chamberlain noted in his diary on 30 May, two days after taking over from Baldwin as Prime Minister, 'The King evidently found it a great relief to be able to tell his brother that so far from taking anything away, what he had done was to give him a title from which he would otherwise have been debarred.'

The Duke of Windsor lost no time, through his solicitor, in seeking the opinion of a King's Counsel, Sir William Jowitt (later Earl Jowitt, Attorney General from 1929 to 1932 and appointed Lord Chancellor in 1945), and another brilliant barrister, Patrick Devlin (later appointed a judge). They were unanimous in their view that the Letters Patent had 'no effect upon the rank and precedence to be accorded to the Duchess of Windsor'. Jowitt tended to switch political allegiance in order to gain power (he was successively a Liberal, a member of the Labour Party, a member of the National Labour Party and again a member of the Labour Party), and once in office as Lord Chancellor he reneged on his original opinion to the extent of saying the law was irrelevant. But this was merely an attempt to ingratiate himself with the new Establishment, and in no way invalidated his original opinion, published as Appendix C.

'The bitterness is there all right,' Lady Alexandra Metcalfe recorded on the day of the Windsors' wedding. 'He had an outburst to Fruity [her husband] while dressing for dinner. The family he is through with.' Wallis also told Lady Alexandra there was no insult 'they' hadn't tried to heap on her. There is no question that from the start the Duke saw in the Letters Patent not the hand of nimble-witted politicians but of aggrieved and scheming relatives. He had not yet grasped the true reason for trying to foist upon him the very thing he had been denied as king, a morganatic marriage. It was to keep him out of England as much as possible and his wife out for good, for the Queen and Queen Mary reckoned that so long as the Duchess of Windsor was a morganatic wife they had no call to receive her. Had she been a princess they could not have avoided the obligation. Knowing the Duke's extreme sensitivity, they had also calculated that, without his wife by his side, publicly acknowledged as his equal, he would not attempt to take part in any public engagements in England.

The Duke had good reason to feel bitter. When he investigated the possibility of a morganatic marriage before he abdicated he had been assured that an Act of Parliament would be necessary, there being no general recognition of a morganatic marriage in English law. On the contrary, under common law every wife, unless she happens to be a peeress in her own right, automatically enjoys the status of her husband (or in the case of the daughter of a peer marrying beneath herself in the order of precedence, retains her own courtesy title). Wallis Warfield married a prince; hence she automatically became a princess, and by custom she was entitled, as was her husband, to be addressed as Your Royal Highness (or Ma'am) and to receive from men a bow and from women a curtsey. But, as we have gleaned from

Oliver Harvey's diary, the King did not feel he could 'expect his subjects to curtsey to her'.

At the time of the King's own marriage, readers of *The Times*, house organ of the Establishment, were informed, 'It is officially announced that, in accordance with the settled general rule that a wife takes the status of her husband, Lady Elizabeth Bowes-Lyon on her marriage has become Her Royal Highness the Duchess of York, with the status of a Princess.' Two hundred divorces and the habit of stirring one's tea with a kipper could not alter that 'settled rule'. What the Royal Family had done, by instigating the Letters Patent (in law, not worth the velum they were written on), was to move the goalposts. The King had been in no doubt, when he gave instructions for Edward VIII to be introduced over the air as His Royal Highness, that far from abdicating his royal status all he had given up was the throne. When he informed his Accession Council that he intended to confer upon Edward a dukedom he said he would henceforth be known as His Royal Highness the Duke of Windsor. And when he had Letters Patent drawn up to create the dukedom they were inscribed HRH the Duke of Windsor.

But now it was alleged that Queen Victoria's Letters Patent of 1864 conferred the title Royal Highness only upon persons in line of succession to the throne. Having abdicated, the Duke of Windsor was no longer in line of succession. In fact what the Letters Patent of 1864 actually did was to confirm the attribute of Royal Highness upon the sons, and sons of sons, of a sovereign. Hence, although Edward had renounced the throne for his descendants, as the grandchildren of a sovereign his sons would still have been princes. But the Letters Patent of 1937 even purported to strip any children of the marriage of their rights. Had the King 'and his family' wanted to throw a proverbial spanner into the Windsors' marriage they could not have dreamed up a more destructive tool than the Letters Patent, which pretended to restore to the Duke a royal status he had never relinquished. All that the Letters Patent in effect achieved was to deny to the Duchess her lawful status, and by attempting to interfere with common law the King had acted unconstitutionally.

Once the wretched Letters were published they became a recipe for social embarrassment. Were people to extend to the Duchess the normal courtesies reserved for royalty, thus antagonising the Court in London, or were they to follow the dictates of the King and thus infuriate the Duke? Two ambassadresses to Paris, Lady Diana Cooper and Lady Dixon, opted to curtsey, and it became common knowledge that for many years the Duke himself referred to his wife as Her Royal Highness and gave instructions to the staff that they should do likewise. Before a dinner party at Cap Ferrat in 1938 Somerset Maugham warned his guests that the Duke got cross if the Duchess wasn't treated with respect. 'You won't get me curtseying,' said Lady Colefax. The scene was set for social friction of a high order, and fortunately Harold Nicolson was on hand to record it. When cocktails were produced 'we stood round the fireplace. There was a pause.

' "Oim sorry we were a little loite," said the Duke, "but her Royal Highness wouldn't drag herself away from the Amurrican orficers." He had said it. The three words fell into the circle like three stones into a pond. Her (gasp) Royal (shudder) Highness (and not one eye dared to meet another).'[17]

For years the Duke battled for formal acknowledgement of his wife's status, and pleaded with his mother and the King to receive her. They never did. 'None of us can relish the thought or contemplate the idea of those two persons living in this country even for a few months in the year without some misgivings,' King George wrote to Queen Mary on 23 September 1945. This was hardly surprising. The King had told Churchill on 9 December 1942 'quite honestly . . . I do not trust the Duchess's loyalty.'

And as far as the Letters Patent were concerned, the final hammer blow fell in 1949, by which time, worn out with his brother's importunings, the King's mind had parted with reality altogether. 'You must remember,' he told the Duke of Windsor, 'that I made your wife a Duchess despite what happened in December 1936. You should be grateful to me for this. But you are not.' The King had no more made Mrs Warfield a duchess than he had made Herr Hitler a Knight of the Garter; she became a duchess by marrying a duke.

In July 1937 the King had his brother's personal possessions removed from Fort Belvedere and stored at Frogmore, the early nineteenth-century house standing in the Home Park not far to the south of Windsor Castle, once the home of Queen Charlotte, wife of George III, and later the home of the Duchess of Kent, Queen Victoria's mother, and the birthplace of Queen Mary. He had no intention of keeping the Fort vacant for the benefit of an abdicated king. It was far too close to the Castle for comfort, and, as Frogmore at that time was uninhabitable (it is now open to the public), it is reasonable to assume the King hoped that the Duke would soon realise he was not expected to return, and would have his furniture shipped over to France. But perhaps the King had forgotten that during the debate on the Abdication Bill the Attorney General, obviously briefed by the cabinet, had stated there would be no obligation on the former King to live outside the British Dominions. Hence on 16 December 1936 Churchill had written to Prince Edward to say, 'I earnestly hope that it will not be many months before I shall be paying my respects to you at the Fort.' Lady Diana Cooper also fondly imagined the gay, inconsequential, carefree and ill-disciplined weekends would shortly resume. She told the Prince she was praying 'for the day you return to those who love you so and to the Fort you so love.'

In the autumn of 1936, at Balmoral, the British Ambassador to Washington, Sir Ronald Lindsay, came to the conclusion that the King 'did not feel safe on the throne,' that he was like 'the medieval monarch who has a hated rival claimant living in exile'.[18] Lindsay found the King, Queen, Hardinge and Lascelles 'almost hysterical on the subject of the Duke', believing he was trying to stage a comeback, and although Lindsay was doubtful whether, as the Royal Family seemed to believe, 'the Duke was a pawn in the hands of a scheming and ambitious wife', he nevertheless 'found himself won over by the Queen', who 'spoke in terms of acute pain and distress'. Lindsay recalled that all her feelings were lacerated by what she and the King were being made to go through, and that 'for all her charity she had not a word to say for "that woman".'

Within less than a year of the Abdication, the Duke and Duchess of Windsor decided to pay a visit, from 11 to 23 October 1937, to Germany. Hitler had risen to power as Chancellor via a bloodbath, and it was just this desire on the part of the Duke, so recently a Head of State, to strut around on the world stage as some sort of plenipotentiary that so unnerved the Queen. (Much to the consternation of the King and Queen, he was planning a visit to Washington too, but this was cancelled.) If anyone was to fraternise with foreigners, whether the French (to whom the King and Queen made their first state visit), the Americans, or the Germans it was the prerogative of Bertie. Everyone knew the Nazis were past masters at propaganda (they had invented the word, after all), and the conduct of the Duke in careering off to meet Hitler, who was photographed bowing over the Duchess's hand, was tantamount to proffering British royal approval of a regime backed by stormtroopers and a secret police.

The Duke of Windsor announced he was interested in studying German industrial relations, but to what use he planned to put his new-found knowledge it is hard to imagine. Sir Robert Vansittart, Permanent Under-Secretary at the Foreign Office, wrote a postcard to

Hardinge on 1 October to say, 'Personally, I think these tours, prearranged without a word to us, are a bit too much. And I hope our minions abroad will be instructed to have as little as possible to do with them.' Hardinge replied, 'I entirely agree with what you say about these tours, & I feel strongly that nothing should be done to make them appear other than what they are ie private stunts for publicity purposes – they can obviously bring no benefits to the workers themselves.'

The Windsors arrived in Berlin to discover the British ambassador had mysteriously been called away on urgent business, and the Chargé d'Affaires had been told to have nothing to do with the visit. This information was imparted on the railway platform by the Third Secretary. Any other royal duke greeted by a Third Secretary would have got straight back on the train. But not the Duke of Windsor, who submitted himself and his wife to the hospitality of the Nazis. They had tea with Field Marshal Göring, during which the Duke spotted a map on the wall that depicted Austria as part of Germany. Apparently this only mildly surprised him. Then they met Himmler, Hess and Goebbels, and were entertained to dinner by the Duke's first cousin once removed, Queen Victoria's grandson, the Duke of Saxe-Coburg & Gotha. He too was a Nazi.

During a visit to England the previous year, the Duke of Coburg had enjoyed several conversations with King Edward. He had taken tea with Queen Mary, and had reported to Hitler that for King Edward a British-German alliance was 'an urgent necessity', if possible in collaboration with France. He also informed the Reichschanceller that the King believed the League of Nations was a farce, and that he was resolved to 'concentrate the business of government on himself'. According to Hitler's emissary, King Edward wished to go over the head of Baldwin by talking personally to the Führer, either in England or in Germany.

The climax to the Duke's German visit was the acceptance of an invitation to visit Hitler at Berchtesgaden. The Führer kept them waiting an hour, which they did not seem to mind. And, after they had left, according to Hitler's interpreter, Hitler remarked, apropos the Duchess, 'She would have made a good queen.' There were many Nazis who also thought the Duke would have made a good king. Hitler, it also appears, referred to Queen Elizabeth as the most dangerous woman in Europe, perhaps one of the greatest compliments she has ever been paid!

Instructions from the Foreign Office to the British Embassy to boycott the visit did not preclude the Embassy relaying back details of the peregrinations of the semi-royal couple. In turn, these details were passed on to the King and Queen via the Foreign Secretary, the Prime Minister and the King's Private Secretary.

On 23 October the *New York Times* did not mince its words. 'The Duke's decision to see for himself the Third Reich's industries and social institutions and his gestures [he had actually raised his arm on several occasions in the notorious Heil Hitler salute, perhaps believing it was a friendly thing to do] and remarks during the last two weeks have demonstrated adequately that the Abdication did rob Germany of a firm friend, if not a devoted admirer, on the British throne. He has lent himself, perhaps unconsciously but easily, to National Socialist propaganda. There can be no doubt that his tour has strengthened the regime's hold on the working classes.' It was a damning indictment of a foolish and potentially very dangerous couple.

When in 1962 the British press finally revealed that the Duke of Windsor had hobnobbed with Hitler, Noël Coward contented himself with the following diary entry: 'Poor dear, what a monumental ass he has always been!'[19] But it was no wonder that, after only a year on the throne, the Queen saw many bridges waiting to be mended. If one brother could up sticks, abdicate and go abroad, cause trouble over money, property and titles, then visit Nazi Germany, why not one of the other brothers? Why not Bertie, if he found his stammer too much of a bother, or Henry, or George? What if the throne had passed to Edward's cousin, Princess Alexandra, 2nd Duchess of Fife? It had all been too easy. A precedent had been set, and the Queen's duty now was clear. It was vital to restore not only the public's confidence in the monarchy but to build up her husband's self-esteem. Like Queen Mary, Bertie felt personally tainted by the Abdication, as though a member of his family had produced an illegitimate child or had gone to prison for shoplifting. And the disgrace brought upon the monarchy was there for all the world to see. 'Degrading and horrible publicity' was only one of hundreds of reactions by British subjects to the American press coverage.[20] Now a former commoner, born, as sheer luck would have it, with inate royal professionalism, was poised to blot out the degradation.

6

Cookie Doesn't Crumble

'IF THE WORST HAPPENS and I have to take over, you can be assured that I will do my best to clear up the inevitable mess, if the whole fabric does not crumble under the shock and strain of it all,' King George VI had written to Edward VIII's Assistant Private Secretary, Sir Godfrey Thomas, during the Abdication crisis. The fabric didn't crumble, but that was largely thanks to Cookie. This was the nickname the Duke of Windsor and his wife bestowed on the Queen. They also referred to the royal couple as Mr and Mrs Temple, for they had dubbed Princess Elizabeth Shirley Temple. Kitted out in shiny leather shoes and little white socks, smartly tailored coats and perky berets, the two Princesses, two paces behind their energetic mother, were catapulted on to the nation as the epitome of wholesome family life. Pathé and Gaumont newsreels became willing allies in round three of the Queen's public relations exercise. No week passed without the Gloucesters or the Kents, and especially the King, Queen and the Princesses, being recorded at fashion shows, launching (or 'larnching' as the Queen would say) ships, expressing interest and concern, smiling, waving, being royal but human – above all, being a happy royal family.

To the exiled Duke of Windsor the King wrote on 3 July 1937, 'How do you think I liked taking on a rocking throne, and trying to make it steady again? It has not been a pleasant task, and it is not finished yet.' Before Bertie had taken over, Edward had blithely assured him, 'You are not going to find this a difficult job at all.'[1]

After a visit to Windsor in April 1937, Anthony Eden told Oliver Harvey the Queen had 'great character and common sense and encourages the King'.[2] Unlike her husband, the Queen Mother has always enjoyed an extraordinarily high boredom threshold, so high it could not have been sustained for 90 years at an artificial level. And unlike the King, she was never short of small talk, one of the banes of royal life. Whereas Queen Mary always walked behind George V, Bertie insisted, except on the most formal occasions, on the Queen walking ahead of him. In this way she was able to assess any situation, make the first greeting, and then encourage the King to join in the conversation.

In the early years of her public appearances the Queen walked almost on tiptoe, bouncing along at a fairly rapid pace, a characteristic acquired from her long strides on the moors in Scotland. In middle age she learned to move much more slowly, partly because, as Queen, she realised the need to allow the public to see her for as long as possible. Greatly influenced by her mother in so many ways, Princess Margaret early on imitated the Queen Mother's bounce on the balls of her feet. Osbert Sitwell thought no photograph could ever do justice to the natural beauty of the Queen's walk and carriage. 'Just as in a crowd waiting to greet her, every single man in it was convinced that he was the only person she had looked at, whose cheering she had acknowledged, so Her Majesty's entrance into a room, in palace, private house or city hall, at once imparted a notable liveliness to the gathering and heightened its temperature.'[3]

Sitwell first met the Queen a few months after her marriage, at a lunch party given by Mrs Ronald Cubitt. He had been told the Duchess was remarkably charming and intelligent, but admitted to secret cynical doubts. He was instantly bowled over, and came to believe that just as no photograph could do justice to the Queen's walk and carriage, so no photograph could ever do justice 'to her grace and beauty, which depended on colouring, on expression and inner light'. Sitwell raved equally enthusiastically about the 'peculiarly emotional quality' of the Queen's voice, 'which made her few broadcast speeches so memorable'.

He was one of the first to realise that 'in any station of life the Duchess of York, now Queen Elizabeth, would have been a remarkable and fascinating woman.' He thought she possessed more tact and charm than anyone he had ever met. In addition she was 'kind, wise, witty, good – above all, good, full of humour, comprehension, and heart; and a compassionate understanding of men and women, which, always valuable and rare, is never more needed than at a court.'

An instance of the Queen's gift for repartee occurred one day at Sitwell's Derbyshire home, Renishaw. Sitwell told the Queen how, after he had on a previous occasion presented his butler and his wife, Susan, Susan had remarked to her husband, 'Now we can die happy!' 'Yes,' said the Queen. 'It seems to take people in different ways.'

While in public the King was learning to relax, and to stand aside while the Queen put people at their ease, in private the quirks of ministers, and eventually the worry of the war, could drive him to frenzies of irritation. Although 'when not beset by cares,' Osbert Sitwell remembered, 'he had a delightful gaiety about him.' 'The Queen could always calm him when he was irate,' a former courtier recalls. 'There was some extraordinary communication between them.'[4] This ability of the Queen Mother, always to appear serene and at her ease, disguises the fact that she too has problems to deal with and human failings in her personality. At a luncheon party at Buckingham Palace in 1955 she told Vita Sackville-West she had never got over being shy when she entered a room. Asked what she thought the Queen Mother did with her anger, a psychoanalyst who has met her on a number of occasions said, 'It is a very neat kind of anger, very pat. It just flashes out. When it happens it can be very unnerving for the person who has displeased her, because the withdrawal of warmth is so unexpected. Princess Margaret has inherited this kind of anger, but she doesn't do it so nicely!'[5]

From being the mistress of a town house and the Royal Lodge, the new Queen now found herself running Buckingham Palace, Windsor Castle, Sandringham House and Balmoral Castle. Even with the Queen's innate good taste and legendary extravagance she would have been hard pressed to turn any of these properties into what most people would regard as a home, a place specially created to display the occupants's personality and interests.

Buckingham Palace, in particular, is essentially a showcase, a stage set for major royal occasions like state banquets. It is also a very grand office, where the ebb and flow of courtiers, politicians, privy councillors, diplomats and churchmen is almost constant. Nash's west front, looking over the 40-acre garden and lake, is more elegant and restful (although still rather uniform in design) than the heavy east front which confronts the public. Told in 1900 by her granddaughter Princess Thora that her dog didn't like Buckingham Palace, Queen Victoria replied, 'I can *quite* understand that!' Buckhouse Prison was how Edward VIII referred to the place.

The Palace takes its name from John Sheffield, who was created Duke of Buckingham in 1703 and built a house for himself which he called Buckingham House. It possessed royal connections from the start, for the Duke was married to an illegitimate daughter of James II. Always on the lookout for what he regarded as homely retreats from life at St James's Palace, George III purchased the property, renamed it The Queen's House, and added an impressive library. When George IV got his hands on the place, Nash was called in, to help the spendthrift monarch spend £200,000 on alterations. It was Nash who was responsible for the imposing state apartments, 'Frenchified' in 1902 by Edward VII. William IV, as mad as his father, had plans to turn the palace into a barracks, but Victoria, who in her youth was devoted to dancing, had other ideas. She built the ballroom, in which today investitures are held, before going off the place altogether. Perhaps one reason Victoria had no great love for Buckingham Palace was because her eldest son and heir was born there. Strangely enough, Edward VII remains the only sovereign to have died at Buckingham Palace. What he would think about his great-granddaughter letting in the public to pay for repairs to Windsor Castle is best left to the imagination.

Windsor Castle, which dates from the reign of William the Conqueror, and by 1263 was already being described as the most magnificent palace in Europe, is far more romantic. But again, thanks to George IV, and another of his architects, Jeffry Wyatville, the apartments of the Royal Family overlooking the east terrace, which until the catastrophic fire of 1992 contained a suite of three superb drawing rooms, one of which, the Crimson Drawing Room, was destroyed, give little scope for innovation by succeeding monarchs or their wives.

George VI and Queen Elizabeth followed the seasonal pattern set by George V and Queen Mary, moving to the Castle for Royal Ascot week, and to Sandringham for Christmas. When the Second World War caused disruption to daily life they took up permanent residence in the Castle, driving to Buckingham Palace and back every day. But, until then, their style of living was very traditional. 'The Queen liked the regimen,' a retired courtier has observed, 'and very much left it as it was. At Balmoral you could safely say the dinner menu from Monday to Saturday would be grouse roti Anglais every night, with venison or roast beef on Sunday.' Clearly not a superstitious man, at Windsor the King took over the Blue Room for his sitting room. It was here that in 1861 Prince Albert had died, in 1837 William IV also, and in 1830 George IV, starting from his chair and calling out to his page, as he clasped his hand, 'My boy, this is death.'

One of the Queen's earliest guests at Windsor was Edward VIII's boon companion, Lady Diana Cooper. Duff Cooper was a member of the Government (in 1937 he was First Lord of the Admiralty), and it was incumbent on the King and Queen to entertain both him and his wife, but Lady Diana became one of the Queen Mother's favourite guests and also one of her favourite hostesses. A cynic might rejoin that Lady Diana possessed beauty, money, a sense of fun to match the Queen Mother's, an exotic house and an excellent cook. Even so, such a staunch friend and supporter of Edward VIII might well have been cast aside had the Queen Mother's reputation for harbouring grudges been entirely deserved.

When Lady Diana stayed at the Castle on 16 April 1937 she left an illuminating account of events in her diary. She and Duff had been warned 'by the Comptroller's minion' to present themselves at the Castle 'at 6 or thereabouts, and that knee-breeches would be worn'. They arrived at about 6.30 pm at what looked to Lady Diana 'like the servants' entrance'. She says she then heard 'an impatient telephone-voice brawling "Trousers, trousers, I've said trousers four times"'' as they passed down 'a many-doored musty passage' which led to their suite. This consisted of 'a sitting room with piano and good fire, evening papers, two well-stocked writing tables and thirteen oil paintings of Royalty'. She counted 'about a hundred plaques, miniatures, intaglios, wax profiles etc. of the family in two Empire vitrines, and two bronze statuettes of King Edward VII in yachting get-up and another Prince in Hussar uniform'.

Communicating, she wrote, with 'this bower' was 'Duff's very frigid room with tapless long bath, enclosed and lidded in mahogany. Through this again is my throttlingly-stuffy bedroom with nine "oils" of the family and a bed for three hung with embroidered silk.'

The Master of the Household, Sir Hill Child, appeared, to explain that the King had changed his mind and trousers were to be worn; fortunately Duff had brought a pair with him. Before dinner Duff was required to see the King, leaving Diana 'to paint her face and go on wishing she could have a cocktail'. Dinner was eventually served at 8.30 pm. As far as the rest of the itinerary was concerned, Lady Diana was warned by the recently knighted Alexander Hardinge to 'leave dining room with gentlemen at 9.30, but gentlemen don't stop, they walk straight through us to the loo and talk and drink. Girls gossip until 10.15 when the men reappear flushed but relieved, and at 10.30 it's "Good night".'

After the King and Queen had duly 'said goodnight to the cringing company' Duff vanished. 'At last,' Lady Diana recalled, 'I'm down to a butler who replies with an inscrutable face: "He is with the Queen."' They drank tea for an hour, while the Queen 'put her feet up on a sofa and talked of Kingship and "the intolerable honour" but not of the crisis.' During dinner Lady Diana had thought she detected 'an inferior make of loud gramophone playing airs from *Our Miss Gibbs* and *The Bing Boys*' but 'from seeing a red uniformed band playing after dinner I suppose it was them muffled.'

Exactly a year to the day, on 16 April 1938, Sir John Reith was at the Castle to dine, and found the same muddle going on over clothes. 'The invitation said I was to bring knee-breeches and trousers,' he recalled in his diary, 'so I phoned Hill Child and he said it was a mistake. I had enquired if one were meant to turn up in pants with both alternatives ready; if not which would he tip. At 7.45 I suddenly thought that, with ordinary breeches, buckles wouldn't be worn on pumps. Phone up – told yes. Much relief. A few minutes later phoned back – bows. Much consternation.' The very fact that every man invited to Windsor Castle before the Second World War was expected to own knee-breeches shows how restricted was the guest list.

With the exception of the present Duke of Gloucester's father, who purchased the Elizabethan Barnwell Manor near Oundle in 1938, it is only in recent years that members of the Royal Family like the Prince of Wales, the Princess Royal and Prince Michael of Kent have opted to create private residences in period houses. The Edwardians had little taste anyway, preferring opulence to beauty. When Edward VII purchased Sandringham House in Norfolk his wife's lady-in-waiting, Lady Macclesfield, commented that it would have been difficult to find 'a more ugly or desolate looking place'. By the time the Queen took over its management in 1936 she was well aware that her father-in-law had worshipped the property. In time, George VI came to love Sandringham more than anywhere else in the world. The house has no architectural merit, for Edward VII knocked down the original nineteenth-century building and put in its place a mock Jacobean monstrosity. But here the King and Queen felt able to ape the manners of the county squirearchy, shooting birds and hares to their hearts' content.

Having married into the Royal Family, the Queen was also obliged to acclimatise herself to Balmoral if she was not to fall foul of the spirit of her husband's formidable great-grandmother Queen Victoria. This house, purchased by Victoria and Prince Albert, was sacred to his memory. Here they had tramped around the countryside, on foot and on pony, virtually incognito. Here they had talked with strangers who may not have known who they were. At least Balmoral was situated in an area already dear to Queen Elizabeth, and soon she too was taking guests and Household on elaborate picnics, often in the misty Scottish drizzle.

Before Queen Victoria fell in love with the Highlands, Balmoral had faint royal connections. A hunting lodge belonging to Robert II, who reigned from 1371 to 1390, once stood on the site. When, in 1852, Victoria received a large and unexpected legacy from an eccentric admirer called John Neild, she paid £31,500 for the 17,400-acre property, and Albert, who fancied himself as an architect, demolished the 'pretty little castle in the old Scotch style' that had first appealed to Victoria and built in its place a many-turreted and much castellated monument to the Romantic Movement. The royal couple went so Scots mad that Albert even designed a Balmoral tartan, of black, red and lavender on a grey background, large quantities of which were manufactured with the object of draping the house in it. (At Balmoral, even Queen Mary sported a tartan skirt.) Lord Rosebery remarked that having seen the drawing room at Osborne, Victoria's Italianate house on the Isle of Wight, he thought he had seen the ugliest drawing room in the world until he saw the one at Balmoral.

One of the Queen's first weekend guests at Balmoral, in September 1937 – and the choice was typical of her eclectic taste in friends – was the painter Rex Whistler, later killed in the war. He told Cecil Beaton, who had yet to meet the Queen, Balmoral 'all seemed a blazing brightness of colour.' He found hundreds of vases containing Victorian bouquets of flowers 'freshly and brilliantly arranged'. The gardens struck him as 'peculiarly fantastic', for the new King and Queen had inherited Victoria's over-abundance of statues, of dogs, deer and stags. Terrified of being late for meals, Whistler had borrowed a wristwatch for the occasion, but he found that an equerry would invariably tap on his door and say, 'It'll be all right if you come down in five minutes' time.' It was three o'clock in the morning before the Ghillies Ball came to a halt, at which 'the King and Queen jigged with great abandon.' Old Princess Marie Louise was staying too, and 'twinkled her toes by the hour'.

In the drawing room at Balmoral, as in those at Sandringham and Windsor, Queen Elizabeth initiated a tradition of after dinner games. 'Even in Ascot week, guests were roped into charades,' Lady Hambleden recalls. 'And the Queen Mother is very keen on racing demon. She's extremely good at it.'[6] On one occasion, at Windsor Castle, Eleanor Roosevelt, widow of the former American President, was dragooned into a game of charades, master-minded by the Queen, who wore a beard. But Winston Churchill, who was also present, refused point-blank to assist the Queen in her choice of words to be mimed. According to Mrs Roosevelt, he regarded charades as 'inane and a waste of time for adults', and remained in a corner, smoking his cigar and looking glum. His wife, however, knew her p's and q's and on 7 April 1948 she wrote to the Queen, 'I can truthfully say that I have not enjoyed a week-end Party so much for what seems an immeasurable space of time. After "Clumps", which I had not played for forty years (or more), & then in a much more sedate fashion, I felt nearly forty years younger.'

A young army officer was invited once to stay at Balmoral and declined to join the Queen in a game of canasta. 'I got one of her piercing looks out of those piercing blue eyes. I have never forgotten it and I do not wish to receive another!'[7] During the war, officer cadets from Mons Barracks at Aldershot were bussed over to Windsor Castle to provide dancing partners for the Princesses. One such, in May 1944, was John Gale, who became a distinguished journalist on the *Observer*. He recalled the Queen dancing 'Hands, Knees, and Boomps-a-Daisy' and later sitting on the edge of a chair, 'laughing constantly'.[8] Things reached a pretty farcical level at Sandringham one evening when the Queen made a young cleric dress up as a bishop (he actually became one some years later) and had the King march up and down as his chaplain, holding an umbrella as a crozier.

A week after Duff and Diana Cooper's visit to Windsor, Osbert Sitwell was invited to stay for a couple of nights. But over the Queen's attempts to create in her fortress homes an ambience of relaxation for her overwrought husband hung the menacing shadow of Edward, Duke of Windsor. In August 1938 Walter Monckton was staying at Balmoral, and said he felt quite plainly that the Queen believed 'it was undesirable to give the Duke any effective sphere of work. I felt then, as always, that she naturally thought she must be on her guard against the Duke of Windsor.' The reason was that David 'was an attractive, vital creature who might be the rallying point for any who might be critical of the new King who was less superficially endowed with the arts and graces that please.'[9]

This fear of the Duke of Windsor somehow usurping the adulation due to her husband was to become stronger once war had broken out and the King became the natural rallying point for a country fighting for its survival. First however there were old scores to be settled and new friends to be cultivated. Some had the sense to build bridges. Churchill wrote a smooth letter to the new King, and received, by hand, the following reply from the Royal Lodge dated 18 May 1937:

My dear Mr Churchill,

I am writing to thank you for your very nice letter to me. I know how devoted you have been, and still are, to my dear brother, and I feel touched beyond words by your sympathy and understanding in the very difficult problems that have arisen since he left us in December. I fully realise the great responsibilities and cares that I have taken on as King, and I feel most encouraged to receive your good wishes, as one of our great statesmen, and from one who has served his country so faithfully. I can only hope and trust that the good feeling and hope that exists in the Country and Empire now will prove a good example to other Nations in the world.

Believe me,
Yours very sincerely,
George R.I.

Others, including Lord Brownlow, the lord-in-waiting who had escorted Mrs Simpson to the south of France, got their marching orders. Brownlow's seventeenth-century family home, Belton House, was in Lincolnshire, and the King dubbed him 'the Lincolnshire Handicap'. Brownlow had been identified as one of those friends of King Edward whom the Archbishop of Canterbury had attacked in his ill-judged sermon. On his return to England, having helped settle his former monarch into his Viennese hideaway, he wrote a letter of complaint to the Archbishop. He was granted an interview at Lambeth Palace on 21 December, when, according to Chips Channon's diary entry for that day, he found Dr Lang 'unctuous, adamant, tearful and angry'. Lord Brownlow was due to go into Waiting (it is normal for all Household appointments to be continued for six months into a new reign). He even received 'his usual card of warning which he acknowledged'. The next day Brownlow read that Lord Dufferin & Ava had gone into Waiting, and when he telephoned Buckingham Palace for an explanation he was told his name would never appear in the Court Circular again. When he demanded to speak to Lord Cromer, the Lord Chamberlain, an inveterate critic of Edward and Mrs Simpson, he was told his resignation had been accepted, even though Brownlow had never tendered it. 'Am I to be turned away like a dishonest servant,' Brownlow wanted to know, 'with no notice, no warning, no thanks, when all I did was to obey my Master, the late King?' 'Yes,' replied Cromer. Channon wrote that he could not believe it was Queen Elizabeth's doing. 'She is not so foolish. It is those old courtiers, Wigram & Co. and above all Alec Hardinge.' Later, both Cromer and Wigram telephoned Lord Brownlow to admit it had not been the King who had dismissed him.

Lady Cunard, who according to Sir Peter Quennell 'regarded the new sovereign as the epitome of the domestic virtues that she considered most distasteful,'[10] found herself cut because it was believed she had encouraged Mrs Simpson in her ambitions to become queen. Shortly after deciding she couldn't face Christmas, Queen Mary headed a letter to Prince Paul of Yugoslavia 'Please Burn,' and informed him that 'The other day in my presence Bertie told George [the Duke of Kent] he wished him and Marina never to see Lady Cunard again and George said he would not do so. I fear she has done David a great deal of harm as there is no doubt she was friends with Mrs S at one time and generally made a great fuss of her. Under the circumstances I feel none of us, in fact people in society, should meet her.'

Those still regarded as persona grata, however, were invited by the Queen to large dinner parties at Buckingham Palace, where the food did not always meet with approval. A menu of soup, fish, quail, ham, chicken, ice and savoury had been 'unwisely selected', in the opinion of Harold Nicolson, who was invited to a grand display of 'gold candelabra and scarlet tulips' on 17 March 1937. The wine, however, he found excellent, and the port superb. After dinner, Nicolson noted, the Queen 'went the rounds' wearing on her face 'a faint smile indicative of how much she would have liked her dinner party, were it not for the fact that she was Queen of England'. He was full of admiration for the charm and dignity she displayed, and he found he could not help reflecting, as indeed it may reasonably be assumed the Queen did too, 'what a mess poor Mrs Simpson would have made of such an occasion.' The Queen's conduct 'demonstrated to us more than anything else how wholly impossible that marriage would have been.' The Queen took the opportunity, while doing her rounds, of teasing Nicolson about his 'pink' views, never having made any secret in private of her own politically right-wing opinions.[11]

On 27 May 1937 Ramsay MacDonald was received by the King, when he was offered an earldom which he declined. He also saw the Queen. When he told her how magnificently the King had come on since his accession, the Queen was obviously pleased but immediately enquired, 'And am I doing all right?' Ramsay MacDonald simply replied by a broad sweep of his arm, as much as to say the success of the Queen's own performance could be taken for granted.[12]

It was very much as partners in some great enterprise that the King and Queen had prepared for their coronation, attending two out of eight rehearsals. The Queen saw this occasion of unsurpassed state pageantry as containing true religious significance. It was also an opportunity to exploit popular public sentiment for a monarchy only recently besmirched by scandal and desertion. Dr Lang had originally tried to interest Edward VIII in the details of the coronation service, only to find the King anxious to have the service shortened. Edward, Lang noted in his diary, had seemed 'strangely detached from the whole matter'. After the Abdication, Lang did not bother to wait until the new King and Queen were installed in Buckingham Palace before discussing arrangements for the coronation on a visit to 145 Piccadilly. 'It was indeed like waking after a nightmare to find the sun shining,' he intoned. 'No words can describe my relief, my burden, like Christian's,[13] falling from my back.' At Easter 1937, at Windsor Castle, Lang took the King and Queen step by step through the service, and was gratified to find them 'most appreciative and fully conscious of its solemnity.' Three days before the grand event, King George and Queen Elizabeth were again submitted to the ministrations of this prattling old prelate, who called on them in the evening at Buckingham Palace. They knelt for his blessing, and when they rose, according to Lang, there were tears in their eyes.

The King and Queen were awake at 3 am. The King, foolishly, ate no breakfast, for he had 'a sinking feeling inside'. A Presbyterian chaplain fainting in the Abbey caused the Queen's procession to be held up, but when 'the little Queen', as the Archbishop of Canterbury disparagingly called her, did set off down the nave she 'advanced with a real poetry of motion'. The King, as he recorded in a memorandum that night, felt he had been kept waiting for hours. Then the Dean of Westminster nearly got the King to don a vestment called the Colobium Sindonis inside out. But the King knew better. When he came to make his Coronation Oath, the Archbishop covered the words with his thumb. The Lord Great Chamberlain's hands 'fumbled and shook' so much the King had to fix his own sword belt (he later told his daughter he wouldn't have employed him as a valet). And a piece of red cotton attached to the crown, indicating which way round it should be placed on the King's head, had been removed, so that the Archbishop had to do some impromptu juggling. The King said he never did know 'whether it was right or not'. One of the bishops trod on his robe and the King had to tell him 'to get off it pretty sharply as I nearly fell down'. The King managed to mistake two of the peers who did homage, confusing the Marquess of Huntley with the Marquess of Winchester and Lord Mowbray with Lady De Ros! But, as he told Ramsay Macdonald two weeks later, 'for long periods at the Coronation ceremony he was unaware of what was happening.'[14]

'There is no doubt that they have entered upon this task with a real religious sense,' Harold Nicolson noted.[15] The following day they tested the temperature of public approbation, and found it very warm indeed. A drive in an open carriage through the streets of London drew a spontaneous roar of approval. A Naval Review at Spithead followed on 20 May, greatly enlivened for listeners at home by Commander Thomas Woodrooffe's inebriated commentary: 'The Fleet's lit up, we're all lit up' he repeated a good many times. Empire Day, four days later, was celebrated by a Service of Thanksgiving at St Paul's. Ex-servicemen were reviewed in Hyde Park, and in July, during a visit to Scotland, the King invested the Queen with the Most Ancient and Most Noble Order of the Thistle: motto, No one provokes me with impunity – as Mrs Simpson had already discovered.

By January 1936 Hitler had established his National Socialist Party. Within two years, Austria had been annexed, and on 4 February 1938 Hitler took command of the German army. Edward VIII had never been against the occupation of the demilitarised Rhineland, and the King and Queen could hardly have been described as ardent re-armers. Indeed, they approved a policy of appeasement until the last minute. Nevertheless, within a very short time of the accession they realised they were even more desperately in need of friends overseas than at home. In 1938, the King and Queen embarked on their first state visit, to Paris. A show of solidarity with France was now essential – so essential that the visit took place while the Queen was in mourning for her mother. However, the President, Albert Lebrun, did agree to alter the dates to 19–22 July, Lady Strathmore having died at Glamis on 23 June.

'A swish young dress designer', as *Time* magazine described the young and ambitious Norman Hartnell, had been recruited to enhance the public appearances of the new Queen. This he did largely by reproducing crinolines from Winterhalter's portraits of the youthful Queen Victoria. With the untimely death of Lady Strathmore, Hartnell seized a golden opportunity to dazzle Paris and ensure his future career as royal dressmaker. At breakneck speed he ran up an entire new wardrobe in white. 'As usual,' the Prime Minister told the King afterwards, the Queen's smile 'took every place by storm'. This verdict was echoed by the President on a return state visit, when he said, at Dover, the French people had been conquered 'by the grace and charm of Her Majesty the Queen'. On this occasion, however,

Hartnell's romantic outfits had as much to do with her success as the Queen's by now famous smile.

The only snag about Paris as a showcase for Britain's new King and Queen was that Britain's former King and his wife were living a dozen miles to the south-west, at Versailles. Accordingly, plans were made to bundle the Windsors out of their temporary rented accommodation for the duration of the state visit. The Duke, naive and optimistic as ever, had hoped the King and Queen would not only call on him, but arrange for both him and Wallis to be invited to an official reception.[16] In the event, they were entertained to dinner by the British ambassador before retreating to the south of France, 'to leave the field clear for you in Paris', as the Duke explained to the King on 20 April. They left for their 12-acre rented estate at Antibes seething with indignation. 'The King thinks it would make him too nervous to see the Duke, charming little cad that he has shown himself,' the Duchess wrote on 9 May.[17]

The visit to Paris was far from a formality, and gave the Queen her first major experience of exposure to danger. Anarchist bombers were expected to strike by attacking the royal train. It was only four years since King Alexander of Yugoslavia had been assassinated in Paris, and the police were taking no chances. Sightseeing from roofs was prohibited, and an extra 9,000 reservists were called in to supplement the normal police force. Some 20,000 troops lined the streets. No expense was spared, either, to emphasise the political importance of Anglo-French accord. A railway station at the Bois de Boulogne was specially constructed, from which 10,000 pigeons were released. And the apartments at the Foreign Ministry where the King and Queen were to stay had been renovated at a cost of 12 million francs. At a luncheon in the Galerie des Glaces at the Palace of Versailles, 13 vintage wines were served.

Hartnell's success in creating a regal appearance for the Queen was complemented by another ambitious young man, Cecil Beaton, who had already been invited to photograph the Duchess of Kent. The Queen first sat for him, draped in her Hartnell creations and flanked by cupids and bowers of flowers, in July 1939. Beaton noted in his diary how inexplicable it was that he could ever have felt 'it was dreary and dowdy to have the Yorks on the throne.' Now he decided that 'no one could have done the job as well as she.' When Beaton first met the Queen he thought her face 'looked very dazzling, white and pink and the complexion flawless'. He noted too her 'effortless intelligence'. The Palace he found 'a happy combination of Regency and Edwardian', seemingly in a permanent state of repair. 'After every party we find someone has slashed a sofa with his sword!' the superintendent told him.

When the Deputy Master of the Household appeared he said to Beaton, 'Uh-huh-Her Majesty wanted to see you-uh-huh- about-uh-huh- choosing the dresses for this afternoon's pictures. I'll try and get you in quickly, because as a matter of fact I know the Queen- uh-huh-has got the- uh-huh- hairdresser at eleven.' By the time Beaton was 'at last bidden into the presence' he had lost any self-confidence he ever possessed. 'It is a great happiness for me, Ma'am,' he managed to stutter. 'It is very exciting for me,' said the Queen. She suggested an evening dress of tulle, and a tiara, and when Beaton asked if she could wear as much jewellery as possible, the Queen 'smiled apologetically and said, "The choice isn't very great, you know!"'

Beaton had been led to understand he would be given the statutory 20 minutes. By the time he had photographed the Queen in numerous different rooms, in doorways, on sofas, beside a priceless Louis Quinze desk, on the terrace and even by the lake he had taken up at least four hours of royal time. In the morning the Queen had been wearing a pale grey dress with long, fur-edged sleeves. She arrived after lunch in a ruby-encrusted crinoline of gold and silver. 'It is so hard to know when *not* to smile,' she commented, and disappeared to change into a spangled tulle 'like a fairy doll', with 'two rows of diamonds almost as big as walnuts', a coronation gift from the King. Later she draped herself in three rows of enormous pearls. So much for the lack of choice! 'Are three rows too much?' the Queen asked Beaton, and later removed one.

For the photographic session out of doors the Queen changed yet again, into a champagne-coloured lace garden party dress, and carried a parasol. 'Can you do a lot afterwards?' the Queen asked Beaton, as they sauntered around on the lawn. The answer was Yes. Over many years every photograph of the Queen Mother taken by Beaton and chosen for publication was retouched. This is why those taken at this memorable session in 1939, when the Queen was almost 39 years of age, seem to reveal the face of a woman of 30 at the most. At one moment the Queen enquired, 'Will my parasol obliterate the Palace?' Beaton reassured her that it was a very big palace. Obviously enjoying herself, the Queen posed beside a giant stone vase, in a summer house and under the trees. But eventually, with the sun beginning to wane, they walked back to the Palace 'where tired and baffled officials clustered by the door'.

Before he left, Beaton secreted in his pocket a handkerchief, scented with tuberoses and gardenias, which the Queen had tucked behind the cushion of a chair. Whether or not the Queen Mother missed the handkerchief, her loyalty to Beaton, as to Hartnell, lasted a lifetime. Beaton was summoned to photograph her on her 50th and her 70th birthdays (by which time Beaton was himself 66). And in 1963, when his collection of royal portraits was published, the Queen Mother wrote to him to say, 'I feel that, as a family, we must be deeply grateful to you for producing us as really quite nice and *real* people.'

On 14 September 1938 the King received a letter from Neville Chamberlain informing him that Hitler had made up his mind to attack 'Czecho-Slovakia', and 'then to proceed further East'. Chamberlain was 'considering the possibility of a sudden and dramatic step which might change the whole situation.' He was planning to go over to Germany to see Hitler, and sort the whole thing out. Hence he was writing to request the King's permission to leave the country 'in a last attempt to save the peace of Europe'.

The King said Yes over the telephone, and Chamberlain took off for Berchtesgaden. Meanwhile, the King toyed with the idea of writing to Hitler, as 'one ex-serviceman to another', and put the suggestion tentatively to the Foreign Secretary, Lord Halifax. It was not pursued. Chamberlain returned to London Airport to be handed a letter from the King telling him how much he admired his 'courage & wisdom' in going to see Hitler in person.

By 25 September cellars were being transformed into air raid shelters. And the King decided to remain in London instead of going with the Queen and the two Princesses to Clydeside for the launching of the 45,000-ton liner *The Queen Elizabeth*. 'I have a message for you from the King,' the Queen said. 'He bids the people of this country to be of good cheer, in spite of the dark clouds hanging over them, and indeed over the whole world. He knows well that, as ever before in critical times, they will keep cool heads and brave hearts. He knows too that they will place entire confidence in their leaders who, under God's providence, are striving their utmost to find a just and peaceful solution of the grave problems which confront them.'

At that moment, the darkest clouds were hanging over the people of Czechoslovakia. His Majesty's first minister, in collusion with the French, was about to announce that England would not go to war for the sake of a quarrel 'in a far-away country between people of whom we know nothing'. But his greatest hour was yet to come. Hitler decided to convene a peace conference. Once again Chamberlain flew to Germany, returning to Heston to wave his fluttering slip of paper in the breeze and to announce the arrival of peace in our time. His namesake, the Lord Chamberlain, was there to welcome him back on behalf of the King and to invite him to drive immediately to Buckingham Palace, so that the King could express to him personally his 'most heartfelt congratulations on the success of your visit to Munich'.

Next day (having escorted Chamberlain on to the Palace balcony, together with the Queen, to receive the cheers of the public) the King told Queen Mary, 'The Prime Minister was delighted with the result of his mission, as we all are, & he had a great ovation when he came here.' He and the Queen returned to Balmoral to resume their summer holiday. Chamberlain, meanwhile, hastened to assure the Archbishop of Canterbury 'that some day the Czechs will see that what we did was to save them for a happier future . . . And I sincerely hope' he added, 'that we have opened the way to that general appeasement which alone can save the world from chaos.'

Chamberlain then concentrated on building up friendly relations with Mussolini. Talking with the Duce, Chamberlain told the King in January 1939, was 'a much pleasanter affair than with Hitler. You feel you are dealing with a reasonable man, not a fanatic, and he struck us both [he and Lord Halifax] as straightforward and sincere in what he said. Moreover he has a sense of humour which occasionally breaks out in an attractive smile, whereas it would take a long surgical operation to get a joke into Hitler's head.'[18] The King was shooting game at Sandringham when he received this reassuring note. The Queen was doubtless organising a game of charades.

On the one occasion he had opened Parliament, Edward VIII announced his intention of visiting India after his coronation. At first, King George seems to have been keen to undertake a strenuous Durbar too; when a postponement to an indefinite future date was announced on 9 February it was assumed in some quarters that considerations of health had been paramount. The *News Chronicle* went so far as to suggest the King's health was 'causing grave concern to the Cabinet'. And 'a malicious whispering campaign in Britain directed against the King' was so virulent among 'famous Mayfair hosts and hostesses, prominent stockbrokers and some politicians' that every effort had to be made by the Queen to parade her husband in public as a fit and proper monarch. The stamina he displayed throughout a hectic schedule in Paris did much to dispel these rumours. Now, with the menace of war making Dominion goodwill more vital than ever, plans were made for a visit to Canada in May 1939. President Roosevelt wrote to the King to say it would be an excellent thing for Anglo-American relations if he also paid a visit to the United States. He assured the King that if he brought with him 'either or both of the children' he would try to organise 'one or two Roosevelts of approximately the same age' to play with them.[19] But the King told Roosevelt he would not be taking the children to Canada, as they were 'much too young for such a strenuous tour'. The visit, originally suggested as an informal one to the President's country house, Hyde Park, snowballed into a state visit, with Washington and New York on the itinerary.

In December 1936, when a news film was shown about the Abdication at the Embassy Cinema in Times Square, *Time* magazine reported that appearances by Edward and Mrs Simpson were greeted with cheers, particularly the scenes of them bathing in the Mediterranean. On the other hand, the Archbishop of Canterbury, 'Crown Princess' Elizabeth, and the new King and Queen elicited boos. And Stanley Baldwin received prolonged catcalls *and* boos!

As the date for departure grew nearer the King's qualms at leaving the country increased. This was not because he feared a difficult reception from starry-eyed partisans of the Windsors, but because Hitler had repudiated the Munich Agreement. He finally salved his conscience by scrapping plans to sail in a battle-cruiser, *Repulse*, which might be needed in action at any moment. *Repulse* eventually escorted the sovereign halfway across the Atlantic, the King and Queen having transferred to a hastily chartered Canadian Pacific liner, *Empress of Australia*. They promptly sailed into fog, then into an ice field, 'unable to see a foot either way' the King reported to his mother on 17 May. 'We very nearly hit a berg the day before yesterday, and the poor Captain was nearly demented because some kind cheerful people kept on reminding him that it was about here the Titanic was struck, & *just* about the same date!'

It would not have escaped the Queen that it was in Canada that as Prince of Wales, Edward VIII had 'won all hearts', when 'people seemed to go quite mad.' Fortunately for her self-esteem, the people proceeded to go quite mad again. Any talk of isolationism evaporated. 'Our Monarchs are most remarkable young people,' the Governor General, Lord Tweedsmuir, wrote to a friend in Scotland. The Queen, he said, had 'a perfect genius for the right kind of publicity. The unrehearsed episodes here are marvellous. For example,' he continued:

when she laid the foundation stone at the new Judicative Building I heard the masons talking and realised that some of them were Scots, and she made me take her and the King up to them, and they spent at least ten minutes in Scottish reminiscences, in full view of 70,000 people, who went mad! Then at the unveiling of the War Memorial, where we had some 10,000 veterans, she asked me if it was not possible to get a little closer to them. I suggested that we went right down among them, if they were prepared to take the risk, which they gladly did. It was an amazing sight, for we were simply swallowed up. The faces of the Scotland Yard detectives were things I shall never forget! But the veterans made a perfect bodyguard. It was wonderful to see old fellows weeping, and crying, 'Ay, man, if Hitler could just see this.' The American correspondents were simply staggered. They said that no American President would ever have dared to do that. It was a wonderful example of what true democracy means, and a people's king.

George VI had been the first King of Canada to visit that country as sovereign. On 9 June 1939, after dining at the General Brock Hotel at Niagara Falls, he entered the United States of America, again the first reigning British sovereign ever to do so. For some reason the King waited until the royal train had crossed the American border before investing his Assistant Private Secretary, Alan Lascelles, with the KCVO. This, as pedants were quick to note, was the first occasion (which was hardly surprising) that a knighthood had been conferred by a British sovereign on American soil.

Much of the American tour was predictably chaotic, and on one occasion the Queen nearly fainted in the heat. They were only too glad to relax at home with the Roosevelts. While staying at Hyde Park the royal couple attended the Episcopal parish church, where, to her surprise, the Queen found the service '*exactly* the same as ours down to every word, & they even had prayers for the King & the Royal Family. I could not help,' she wrote to Queen Mary on 11 June, 'thinking how curious it sounded, & yet how natural.' One reason George and Elizabeth enjoyed their visit to Hyde Park was because, again as the Queen told Queen Mary, 'They are such a charming & united family.' The King was deeply affected by the rapport he and the President established; indeed, he was moved by the entire tour. They returned to Canada, sailing home from Halifax in the *Empress of Britain*. 'I nearly cried at the end of my last speech in Canada,' the King later recalled. 'Everyone round me was crying.'

As the King's official biographer has written, 'The North American tour was indeed a climacteric in the King's life. It had taken him out of himself, had opened up for him wider horizons and introduced him to new ideas. It marked the end of his apprenticeship as a monarch, and gave him self-confidence and assurance.' Without the Queen taking a lead (she was 'the perfect Queen,' in the opinion of *Life*, 'eyes a snappy blue, chin tilted confidently . . . fingers raised in a greeting as girlish as it was regal'), initiating spontaneous gestures and laughing when things went wrong, as they frequently did (an entire sideboard laden with china crashed to the floor during dinner at Hyde Park), it is highly questionable, however, whether he would have returned to quite such a triumphant welcome at the Guildhall. His audience was surprised at his new-found mastery of public speaking, the result, in very large measure, of having had the sense to marry Cookie – one tough Scottish bun that had no intention of obliging the Duke and Duchess of Windsor by crumbling.

7

'The Most Marvellous Person in the World'

ENGLAND ENTERED THE SECOND World War, on 3 September 1939, unprepared and in a strange, trancelike state. In July, with the Queen and both Princesses, the King had paid a sentimental return visit to Dartmouth College. Most of the cadets had gone down either with mumps or chickenpox, and it deluged with rain. The King, however, lightened the occasion by reading out his own past misdemeanours from the Punishment Book. When the rain eventually eased off and the sun came out the Princesses played croquet with a group of hand-picked senior cadets – those declared free from infection. One was an 18-year-old Cadet Captain, Prince Philip of Greece. That evening Prince Philip was invited on board the royal yacht, the *Victoria and Albert*, for a dinner party. There is no earthly reason to suppose that his third cousin, the 13-year-old Princess Elizabeth, imagined she had just met her future husband. The idea may, however, have occurred to Lord Louis Mountbatten, Prince Philip's uncle, who was also present.

The Queen made time to read Hitler's manifesto, *Mein Kampf* (although between October 1933 and October 1938 it had been reprinted 22 times, she was one of the few English people to trouble to do so), and even sent a copy to Lord Halifax in case he hadn't seen it. 'I do not advise you to read it [right] through,' she told him, 'or you might go mad, and that would be a great pity. Even a skip through gives one an idea of his mentality, ignorance and obvious sincerity.'

The King attended his last summer camp for working class boys, in the grounds of Abergeldie Castle, and the Queen joined them for supper one evening. On these occasions she always seemed rather overdressed, as though prepared at a moment's notice either to open a bazaar or to receive a bouquet. Her uncreased day dress, hat and handbag were in marked contrast to the King's open-necked shirt and bare knees. One of the most revealing photographs ever taken of the Queen Mother, in a supposedly informal setting, shows her beside the swimming pool at Fort Belvedere, fully attired. Surrounding her are the Duke of York, Lord Louis Mountbatten and Prince Gustav Adolf of Sweden, and the Hon. Mrs Jock Gilmour, Princess Sybilla of Sweden, Princess Ingrid of Sweden and Lady Furness – all in swimming costumes. The Duchess looks shy and sly, in a hat and dress, like an intruder at a nudist colony.

'On the day war broke out' (as the comedian Rob Wilton would have said) the King noted in his diary, 'I broadcasted a message to the Empire at 6.0 pm.' On 11 November the Queen followed suit, and 'broadcasted' a message to 'the women of the Empire'. She expressed her deep and abiding sympathy with the women of Poland, and also with those who had bravely consented to separation for the sake of their 'little ones'. As always she put her trust in God, who was 'our refuge and strength in all times of trouble'. She declined, however, to be parted from *her* little ones. There was talk at the beginning of the war of the Princesses being shipped to Canada, but in order to allay public alarm, the Queen put her foot down. The family made Windsor Castle their wartime headquarters, taking with them the crown jewels, wrapped in newspaper. In the event of an invasion, however, it *was* planned to evacuate the heir presumptive, and suitcases remained packed throughout the war ready for a dash to Liverpool. Madresfield Court, a country house in Worcestershire with romantic associations with Elgar (it had been the home of Lady Mary Lygon, the subject of the 13th of the *Enigma Variations*), was kept in readiness for emergency use by the King and Queen. There was also talk in 1940 of Queen Mary moving into Windsor Castle, but after inspecting the air raid shelters and anti-aircraft guns she told Lady Bertha Dawkins, a lady-in-waiting, the place was 'like an armed camp!' and retired, with a staff of 63, to Badminton, the home in Gloucestershire of her niece, the Duchess of Beaufort. Queen Mary may also have had the sense to realise that Windsor Castle presented a conspicuous target from the air. Indeed, 300 high explosives landed in the park.

Although the King advised Leopold of the Belgians to continue his country's struggle from exile, one can only speculate about what action the King and Queen might have taken in the event of an invasion. But the concept of leading a nation at war excited them both and bestowed the sense of a final purpose behind their accession to the throne.

In July 1940 Harold Nicolson was invited to lunch by Mrs Arthur Jones to meet the King and Queen, and when Nicolson told the Queen that sometimes he got homesick (for Sissinghurst Castle in Kent, presumably, which he only visited at the weekends anyway) the Queen said, 'But that is right. That is personal patriotism. That is what keeps us going. I should die if I had to leave.'[1] Harold told his wife he noticed a change in the King. He was gay, 'like the Duke of Windsor', and the Queen so calm. She had at the time been taking revolver lessons in the garden at Buckingham Palace, so if the worst came to the worst, they planned to go down fighting. Asked many years later if she had been alarmed to hear that a gunman had attempted to hijack Princess Anne in the Mall, the Queen Mother remarked, 'Oh, people have been shooting at kings and queens for centuries – often with very good cause!' And then, perhaps recalling the dangers of possible assassination during her state visit to Paris, and the very real possibility that she might have been captured during the war, she added, 'Being a queen is doing a job. There isn't *anything* I wouldn't do for England.'[2]

If the war was to be the King's ultimate testing ground, no competition could be tolerated from the Duke of Windsor, and it soon became apparent that he did wish to do his part in rallying the troops. The Duke returned briefly in 1939, accompanied by the Duchess, but only managed to see the King on condition the Duchess did not go to Buckingham Palace. He never saw the Queen at all. On 31 August the Queen had sought advice. 'What are we going to do about Mrs S?' she asked Queen Mary. 'Personally I do not wish to receive her, tho' it must depend on circumstances; what do you feel about it, Mama?' There is no record of Queen Mary's response.[3]

The brothers met on 14 September, to discuss two possible appointments for the Duke – either as a member of the British Mission in Paris (where it was proposed he would serve with the rank of Major General) or as an assistant Regional Commissioner for Civil Defence in Wales. It was their first meeting since the Abdication, and lasted about an hour, 'with no recrimination on either side', according to the King's account in his diary. He told the Prime Minister, 'The whole tone of our meeting was a very friendly one. He seems very well, & not a bit worried as to the effects he left on people's minds as to his behaviour in 1936. He has forgotten all about it.'

But when writing to the Duke of Kent on 26 September the King seems to have revised his view, describing the encounter as 'very unbrotherly', the Duke being 'in a very good mood, his usual swaggering one, laying down the law about everything'. There had been evidence of serious Fascist support for the Duke only two years previously, and in September 1937 the King had told his mother he had impressed upon three of his ministers 'that David cannot come back here'. It was small wonder he now decided that Wales was out of the question, and gave instructions that his brother should be posted to Paris. At the same time, he appointed the Queen Commander-in-Chief of the three women's defence services.

Forbidden to visit the front, the Duke soon became bored. Full of resentment that the new British ambassador to Paris, Sir Ronald Campbell, had not received him, he flew back to London, on 21 January 1940, to make a complaint at the Foreign Office. He failed to inform Buckingham Palace that he was coming, and was soon looking up old cronies like Lord Beaverbrook, whom he met at the home of Walter Monckton. In a letter to Oliver Harvey, now Minister at the British Embassy in Paris, dated 26 January 1940, Charles Peake, head of the Press Section at the Foreign Office, penned a report of the meeting as recounted to him by Monckton himself. Both the Duke and Lord Beaverbrook, Peake said, 'found themselves in agreement that the war ought to be ended at once by a peace offer to Germany. The Beaver suggested that the Duke should get out of uniform, come home, & after enlisting powerful City support, stump the country in which case he predicted that the Duke would have a tremendous success. W. M. contented himself with reminding the Duke that if he did this he would be liable to income tax. This made the little man blench & he declared with great determination that the whole thing was off.' Peake later told Harold Nicolson that the Duke had spoken 'about the inevitable collapse of France and said that he would return to England and conduct a movement for peace with Germany.' After Beaverbrook left, Monckton told the Duke he had been speaking high treason.[4]

Some minion in the Foreign Office dropped a brick when in June, attempting to extricate the Windsors from Spain, whence they had fled from France, he telegraphed to the British Embassy in Madrid, 'Please invite Their Royal Highnesses to proceed to Lisbon.' This resulted in a reprimand from Alexander Hardinge. From Madrid the Duke put out further feelers, asking for the King and Queen, whose country he had been plotting to hand over to the enemy, to meet him and his wife 'just once, for 15 minutes'. According to Sir John Colville, Private Secretary to Churchill, he tried to 'impose conditions, financial and otherwise', about his return to England. 'It is,' Sir John wrote in his diary on 29 June, 'incredible to haggle in such a way at this time, and Winston proposes to send him a very stiff telegram pointing out that he is a soldier under orders and must obey. The King approves and says he will hear of no conditions, about the Duchess or otherwise.' We may safely assume the King was bolstered in his determination by the Queen. Even the faintest whiff of disloyalty, let alone treachery, was – and still is – high on her list of unforgivable sins. By now they knew about the Duke's conversation with Beaverbrook; Charles Peake informed the Prime Minister, and the Prime Minister would have been failing in his duty had he not informed the King. Only those who at the time knew nothing about all this were surprised when the Duke was fobbed off with the Governorship of the Bahamas.

Following the faux pas at Madrid, the Lord Chamberlain sent word ahead to the staff at Government House that the Duchess was not entitled to a curtsey and should be addressed as Your Grace. (Only by servants, in point of fact; her social equals would expect to call her Duchess.) A salient fact had been overlooked, however; as Governor, the Duke acted in a quasi-regal position, and instantly countermanded the instructions. So almost everyone in the Bahamas dutifully curtsied and called the Duchess Your Royal Highness. But the Duke still wanted the matter placed on a formal footing, and in November 1942, while submitting names for the New Year Honours List, he asked Churchill to request the King to restore the Duchess's 'royal rank', not only as 'an act of justice and courtesy to his sister-in-law, but also as a gesture in recognition of her two years' public service in the Bahamas.'

After consulting the Queen, the King sent a memorandum to Churchill, marked Private and Confidential, saying he was sure there were still large numbers of people 'in this country and in the Empire' to whom 'it would be most distasteful to have to do honour to the Duchess as a member of our family.'

Writing in his diary on 11 January 1941, John Colville said he had no doubt it was the 'astonishing success' of the King and Queen's visit to the US that made America give up its partisanship towards the Windsors. He noted also that a yachting trip the Duke had taken with a 'violently pro-Nazi Swede' had not created a good impression with the Americans either. Had the Duke seen the King's memorandum he might have spared himself the trouble of making one last effort to circumvent his relatives, when he wrote to Churchill on 3 October 1944 to say:

Were the King and Queen to behave normally to the Duchess and myself when we pass by England, and invite us merely to tea at one of their residences, a formality which as a matter of fact is prescribed by Court protocol in the case of Colonial Governors and their wives, it would avoid any division of feeling being manifested . . . It could never be a very happy meeting, but on the other hand it would be quite painless, and would have the merit of silencing, once and for all, those malicious circles who delight in keeping open an eight-year-old wound that ought to have been healed officially, if not privately, ages ago.

Churchill went through the motions of laying this latest plea before the King, but to no avail. By 1946 the King had come to the conclusion that the best place for the Duke and Duchess to make their permanent home was in the United States.

Winston Churchill's first official dealings with the King were as First Lord of the Admiralty, the post to which he was appointed when Chamberlain formed a war cabinet. It says much for the King's magnanimity that he welcomed Churchill warmly, although, when Chamberlain was finally forced to resign in May 1940 after the failure of the Norwegian campaign, the King wanted Lord Halifax as his wartime prime minister. The Queen might also have taken a few moments to get used to the idea. For Christmas 1940 Churchill gave her a copy of *Fowler's English Usage*. Fortunately the comic side of Churchill's nature greatly appealed to her.

The King's initial partiality for Halifax had more to do with wishing to work closely with someone he knew well and liked enormously than with any political appreciation of the situation. Although born without a left hand, Halifax was a fearless rider to hounds, a keen shot, the inheritor of great estates and the possessor of an Oxford First in Modern History. Greatly in his favour also, as far as the King was concerned, was his interest in ecclesiastical affairs. His wife was a lady-in-waiting to the Queen. Unfortunately, like so many bred to rule in a leisurely era of patrician politics, Halifax never took the Nazi bully boys seriously. He found Göring 'frankly attractive', and likened him to the 'head game-keeper at Chatsworth'. The King toyed with the idea of having Halifax's peerage (he had succeeded his father as Viscount Halifax in 1934; in 1944 he was created Earl Halifax) placed in abeyance, so that as prime minister he could answer to the House of Commons. But he quickly realised 'there was only one person whom I could send for to form a Government who had the confidence of the country, & that was Winston.' It is interesting that he referred to Churchill by his Christian name even then, and always in private the King and Queen called him Winston. Churchill was also the only commoner whom George VI met at the top of the stairs at the equerries' door although Churchill consistently arrived late for his weekly audience. Even in 1944 he thought nothing of leaving a cabinet meeting at 1.28 pm to lunch with the King at 1.30 pm. A monarchist par excellence, he amply repaid the King and Queen for their friendship, faith and hospitality.

But parting with Chamberlain had been a painful business. The King had relied on him precisely because he exuded self-confidence. He had endeared himself at Balmoral by fishing with the Queen. And, as a Nonconformist, he had been suitably shocked by the antics of Edward and Mrs Simpson. As early as 23 November 1935 he had told his sister, Hilda, that the Duchess of York was 'the only royalty I enjoy talking to, for although she may not be an intellectual she is always natural and moreover appears always to be thoroughly enjoying herself.' After he had been to the Palace to offer his resignation, the Queen took it upon herself to write to him to say, 'I must write you one line to say how deeply I regretted your ceasing to be our Prime Minister. I can never tell you in words how much we owe you. During these last desperate & unhappy years, you have been a great support & comfort to us both, and we felt so safe with the knowledge that your wisdom and high purpose were there at our hand. I do want you to know how grateful we are, and I know that these feelings are shared by a great part of our people.' Knowing that Chamberlain was dying, on 14 October 1940 the King and Queen drove from Windsor to spend half an hour with him – 'a characteristic bit of kindness and sympathy' Chamberlain noted, in his last diary entry.

By January 1941 Churchill was writing to the King to say, 'Your Majesties are more beloved by all classes and conditions than any of the princes of the past.' But by that time both the King and Queen had, quite literally, been through the fire. So far as the nation was concerned, they could never now do any wrong. The Luftwaffe saw to that. While they slept at Windsor, and spent the weekends there, the King (and often the Queen) drove to Buckingham Palace each day. It was thought a sound principle to keep the royal standard flying from Buckingham Palace, as a rallying point for Londoners. It was also important for the King to be in London to attend to state business. On 13 September 1940 they arrived at the Palace in the middle of an air raid. The windows of the King's sitting room had already been blown out, so they went upstairs to a small sitting room overlooking the Quadrangle. 'All of a sudden,' the King told Churchill later that day, 'we heard the zooming noise of a diving aircraft getting louder and louder, and then saw two bombs falling past the opposite side of Buckingham Palace into the Quadrangle. We saw the flashes and heard the detonations as they burst about eighty yards away. The blast blew in the windows opposite to us, and two great craters had appeared in the Quadrangle. From one of these craters from a burst main water was pouring out and flooding into the passage through the broken windows. The whole thing happened in a matter of seconds, and we were very quickly out into the passage. There were six bombs: two in the Forecourt, two in the Quadrangle, one wrecked the Chapel, and one in the garden.'[5]

'We all wondered that we weren't dead,' the King wrote in his diary. Three men working in the plumber's workshop were injured. 'E and I went all round the basement talking to the servants who were all safe, & quite calm through it all . . . There is no doubt that it was a direct attack on Buckingham Palace.' Wellington, on the field of Waterloo, with Napoleon in his sights, forbade anyone to take a pot shot at the Emperor. But the King was well aware the Nazis paid no heed to such gentlemanly rules of conduct in battle. Not only was he sure it had been a direct attack on the Palace, he was convinced the attack had been aimed at him personally. Calm as he may have appeared immediately afterwards, he was very badly shaken, and suffered delayed shock. 'Unable to read,' he wrote in his diary, 'always in a hurry, & glancing out of the window.' The Queen's long-term reaction took the form of inate hostility to Germany and Germans; in fact, although obliged to inspect British troops in the Federal Republic, she felt unable to go to Berlin until 1987, when she finally paid a visit. She told the British Minister she could not have gone sooner for she had never forgiven the Germans for the way they bombed London.[6] She approved of the retaliatory bombing of Dresden by Bomber Command, which reduced that ravishing city to a smoking heap of rubble. And in 1992 she sailed forth to unveil a statue of the man responsible, Marshal of the Royal Air Force Sir Arthur Harris, whose aggressive tactics had been so controversial at the time that he was passed over for a viscountcy in 1945 and had to wait eight years for the return to power and patronage of Churchill before being compensated with a baronetcy.

In the aftermath of the raid the Queen was quick to capitalise on the danger, saying she was pleased the Palace had been bombed, for now she could look the East End in the face. She and the King showed their support in countless informal chats to bemused knots of homeless Londoners, whose houses had come crashing round their ears the night before. On one occasion the Queen, in a brilliant piece of public relations (there was a photographer on hand to record the event), rolled up in an armoured car.

In October the Archbishop of Canterbury lunched with the King and Queen and noted afterwards, 'The war has fully secured the affection they had already won. The fact that they had been bombed at Buckingham Palace brought them close to humble folk who had gone through much more terribly the same experience. They both seemed well and full of eager spirit.' Lang himself was lucky not to have been a victim of the Blitz. A bomb exploded in the drawing room of Lambeth Palace only a week after Buckingham Palace was hit, but worse was to follow on the night of 10 May 1941. Four bombs fell in the courtyard, setting alight the library roof. Incendiaries ignited the roof of the chapel also, and the fifteenth-century Lollards' Tower was gutted. 'A dreadful night of screeching bombs and crackling flames,' as the old man recalled.

But the Queen, who found her visits to bomb sites something of a strain ('I feel quite exhausted after seeing & hearing so much sadness, sorrow, heroism and magnificent spirit' she told Queen Mary), did not confine her ministrations to victims of bombing in London. The King and Queen both went to Coventry when 400 people were killed in November 1940, and in January 1941 the Queen was at Sheffield. Afterwards Lord Harlech, North-Eastern Regional Commissioner for Civil Defence, told Harold Nicolson that when the car stopped the Queen 'nips out into the snow and goes straight into the middle of the crowd and starts talking to them. For a moment or two they just gaze and gape in astonishment. But then they all start talking at once.'[7] And small wonder. No queen consort had ever behaved with such dignified informality before. Queen Alexandra would have been inhibited not just by protocol but deafness, Queen Mary by shyness. Nicolson was correct when he told his wife, 'She has that quality of making everybody feel that they and they alone are being spoken to. It is, I think, because she has very large eyes which she opens very wide and turns straight upon one.'[8]

This was a gift Harold Nicolson again noted, in a letter to his younger son Nigel, after the King and Queen had visited Parliament on 17 May 1945: 'The Queen has a truly miraculous faculty of making each individual feel that it is him whom she has greeted and to him that was devoted that lovely smile. She has a true genius for her job.' It is a gift the Queen Mother can even utilise from the back of a car. Driving down a street she can look back at a crowd in such a way as to convince each individual that she has looked back expressly at them. Each wave is a personal acknowledgement. She never once relaxes eye-to-eye contact. Hence thousands of people who have never in reality met the Queen Mother firmly believe they have.

In April 1941 the Queen was at West Ham. She wrote to Lord Halifax afterwards to report: 'The whole place is flat, and everywhere we stopped the people were magnificent. Words fail me – you know this spirit – it is unbeatable.' Unbeatable too were the efforts the press were making to aid and abet the King and Queen in their propaganda war. A photograph of the royal couple appeared in the *Daily Mirror* on 24 April 1940 with the caption: 'Look at this photograph – the King and Queen, the cop, the kids, the crowd – and not a gloomy face among them. The picture was taken yesterday when the King and Queen were in the bombed areas of London's East End; everyone in it has known the horror of Nazi hate raids, but knows, too, that though the War news is grave, IT'S NOT ALL BLACK.'

Use of royal propaganda was nothing new; Clive Wigram, when Assistant Private Secretary to George V, had first formed the concept of 'using the royal family as a public relations organisation' during the First World War, and it was he who first suggested having a full-time press secretary at Buckingham Palace, 'to publicise the work of the King'.[9] But, thanks to the stimulus of war, there was now developing a rapport between the monarchy and the people that can only be described as an act of chemistry. All the ingredients had come together – a king who had stepped into the breach, a war, shared danger, a common foe and a queen consort who had broken down the traditional barriers of restraint while retaining a sense of theatre. Never shaking hands to say goodbye (unless to an official in attendance) the Queen had mastered the art of seeming to drift away rather than suddenly vanishing, leaving her audience wanting more. In Canada she had invented the royal walkabout. The most Queen Mary could manage by way of a wave was a kind of stunted flapping of her wrist, but the Queen had perfected the long, slow royal acknowledgement. Like all great performers she laid herself open to imitation but never to mockery. Someone who once imitated the famous royal wave, to the amusement of the crowd, was a council employee bringing up the rear of a procession on a dustcart. The Queen Mother was so upset when she learned that he had been sacked that she asked the council to reinstate him.[10]

During the First World War Windsor Castle went on the water wagon, and during the Second World War meals at Buckingham Palace became fairly spartan. In the autumn of 1943 the Queen invited Mrs Roosevelt to stay, promising to 'try to make your visit pleasant'. Mrs Roosevelt's abiding impression was of meagre rations eaten off gold plate, but the menu at dinner didn't sound too bad: fishcakes, cold ham and chicken, salad, pudding, a savoury and fruit.[11] Her visit had been very hush-hush. When Cecil Beaton was summoned to take photographs he was not at first told who to expect. The Queen came in and said, 'Mrs Roosevelt is just taking her hat off. After she's had a cup of tea we'll come in again right away.' Beaton had to work in a room with glass cupboards stripped of china. He noted too the fireplace was empty, and that the temperature in the corridors and many of the rooms 'was little above freezing'. There were not even any flowers. Mrs Roosevelt was photographed with the Royal Family. They 'smiled nervously' and Princess Margaret tittered. After Mrs Roosevelt had left the room Beaton took more pictures of the family alone. The Queen was 'as sympathetic and full of charm as ever,' and the King was 'amenable', but Beaton found himself uninspired.

> While waiting for a brainwave (Cecil Beaton wrote in his diary) I played for time by scrutinizing an enormous vase covered with dragons. 'This is a strange object but it casts nice shadows.' 'Isn't it hideous!' remarked the King. 'Where did it come from, I wonder?' After we had surveyed it for some seconds in silence the King ventured, 'It's Chinese, I suppose.'

Conscious of those far less well off, the King and Queen sent £3,000 to the Red Cross, £1,000 being specifically earmarked for Russia. And the Queen continued her broadcasts, all of which were filmed for the newsreels – sending words of sympathy to France, of thanks to America. 'The warmth and sympathy of American generosity has touched beyond measure the hearts of all of us living and fighting in these islands,' she said on 10 August 1941. 'We can, and shall, never forget that in the hour of our greatest need you came forward with clothes for the homeless, food for the hungry, comfort for those who were sorely afflicted . . . We like to picture,' she said, 'you knitting on your porches, serving in your committee rooms, and helping in a hundred ways to bring relief to our civilian garrison here.' Twice a week, in the Blue Drawing Room at Buckingham Palace, the Queen herself conducted knitting sessions for the troops and the Red Cross.

On 12 December that year the Queen had the Archbishop of Canterbury to stay a night at Windsor, when he told the King of his decision to resign. 'The King and Queen were full of understanding sympathy,' he wrote, 'especially the Queen, who spoke about my intention with her usual quiet wisdom. She recognises that this is no time for the leadership of elderly gentlemen!' Lang was succeeded by William Temple, Archbishop of York, whose tragically premature death after only two and a half years in office robbed the Church of England of a potentially great post-war leader. Lang seems to have had few savings – so few that a generous benefactor sent him a cheque for £15,000 – and the King, grateful for the paternal support he and the Queen had received, loaned him York Cottage, a grace and favour residence at Kew, assuring him it was not in fact a cottage 'but a roomy Georgian house'. This was an imaginative gesture on the part of the Supreme Governor of the Church of England that might have been expected to have set a precedent. But when, in 1988, another former Archbishop of Canterbury with few savings, Michael Ramsey, died, he was allowed to do so in a retirement home.

One of Lang's last services to the Royal Family was performed on 28 March 1942. In 'the ugly private Chapel at the Castle', as Lang described the seat of the devastating fire of 1992, he confirmed Princess Elizabeth. He had spent the previous night at the Castle, when he enjoyed 'a full talk with the little lady alone'.

In his official life of George VI, Sir John Wheeler-Bennett categorises Churchill as the one man, of courage, imagination and steadfastness, 'in whose leadership the British people could un-waveringly place their trust'. But just as succinctly he remarks that 'behind the Prime Minister, supporting him with all the weight of the strength and tradition of constitutional monarchy, stood the King, who, by the example of conduct set by himself and the Queen, afforded his people a standard of behaviour and a criterion of courage which none other than one in his high office could have proffered.' Certainly the King never wavered, in public or in private, in his belief in ultimate victory. He had a stubborn nature anyway, but he was bolstered in his belief, certainly in the summer of 1940, when he did expect an invasion, by an equally stubborn wife. With her unique gift for talking at a basic yet intelligent level to absolutely anybody, the Queen imbued others with her own calm self-confidence. The King, immaculate in naval uniform, presented the perfect image of youthful majesty, handsome, his chest suitably beribboned. The Queen combined regal deportment with self-evident humanity.

Somehow it never seemed incongruous that the Queen should turn up at a salvage workshop wearing four strings of pearls or at a preserving depot in a fur-trimmed costume, any more than she should arrive at St Paul's Cathedral in October 1939 for a Day of National Prayer carrying a gas mask. In hospitals she lingered by patients' beds, and visited severely wounded soldiers. If it is true, as has been alleged, that she has 'an instinctive distaste for disease, maiming, malformation of any kind', she hid her feelings with stoical fortitude. In the first five months of the war, 50,000 civilians were killed or injured, and

Plaistow Hospital was only one of many the Queen went out of her way to tour. Conscious of the need to encourage vital wartime industries, she also inspected aircraft factories, shipyards and coal-mines. She saw evacuated children in the country. And at Sandringham, while the King and the Princesses rode on bicycles, the Queen conducted tours of the ploughed-up golf course in a Governess cart, taking the reins herself.

'Let no one be mistaken,' the King said in a broadcast on Empire Day 1940, 'it is not mere territorial conquest that our enemies are seeking. It is the overthrow, complete and final, of this Empire and of everything for which it stands, and after that the conquest of the world.' The royal couple took it as axiomatic that everyone shared their religious certitude. It was, at that time, almost impossible to admit to atheism. All the great institutions of the Establishment – parliament, the BBC, even the press – were geared to propagating Christian beliefs and attitudes. 'At this fateful hour,' the King continued, 'we turn, as our fathers before us have turned in all times of trial, to God Most High . . . Let us with one heart and soul humbly but confidently commit our cause to God, and ask His aid that we may valiantly defend the right as it is given to us to see it.'

No doubt believing that God had always intended the Empire to triumph, after the war the Queen told a meeting of the World's Evangelical Alliance that she and the King longed to see the Bible 'back where it ought to be, as a guide and comfort in the homes and lives of our people'. She said she knew from personal experience 'what the Bible can mean for personal life'.

The King and Queen's belief in Providential protection was absolute, and material arrangements for their safety were almost non-existent. At first a housemaids' sitting room in the basement of Buckingham Palace was commandeered as a makeshift shelter, but it was not until 1941 that a properly equipped concrete air raid shelter was constructed. Buckingham Palace must have appeared a potential deathtrap to German bombers taking their bearings along the Mall. Incarcerated there were at one time Queen Wilhelmina of the Netherlands, King Haakon of Norway and his son, Crown Prince Olav, who, as King Olav, was to remain, until his death in 1991, a favourite private guest of the Queen Mother. King Haakon, a son-in-law of Edward VII, once asked the King what would happen if German parachutists attempted to snatch a few royal prizes. Guards would spring to everyone's defence, the King assured him, pressing an alarm bell to prove his point. The King, Queen and King of Norway repaired to the garden to witness events, but nothing happened. Eventually a contingent of guardsmen was rounded up, who proceeded to thrash their way through the undergrowth in the manner of beaters at Sandringham. King Haakon failed to see the funny side of this inspired British amateurism, but the Queen was convulsed.

Having been made aware of how vulnerable the nation's treasures had become (most of the paintings at Buckingham Palace belong to the Royal Collection, and as such are held in trust for the nation by the reigning sovereign), the Queen busied herself chivvying the appropriate authorities to get them safely out of London. One day in 1942 she telephoned the Duchess of Wellington at Straffield Saye, her country house in Hampshire, to enquire if it was true the treasures at her London home, Apsley House, had not been removed to a place of safety. When the Duchess, freezing to death in one room, admitted as much, the Queen said, 'Well, then, I am coming round at 11 with a van to take them to Frogmore.' Sure enough she turned up, along with the King, and decided what should be moved and what left behind. The Duchess's sister, Mrs Lotti Adams, told James Lees-Milne the Queen said, 'You mustn't be sentimental, Duchess. Only the valuable pictures can go.'[12]

In 1941 the King and Queen joined the ever increasing ranks of ordinary citizens who were suffering personal bereavement when the Queen's nephew, the Master of Glamis, was killed in action with the Scots Guards. At 1.30 pm on 25 August the following year, the Duke of Kent, flying in a Sunderland from Scotland to Iceland, was killed along with his secretary, his valet and all but one member of the crew, when their aircraft crashed into a mountain. His younger son, Prince Michael, had only been baptised, at Windsor Castle, three weeks before. The King and Queen were at Balmoral at the time. With the Duke of Gloucester, the King was out shooting in the mist and rain. Why it took until the early evening for the Secretary of State for Air, Sir Archibald Sinclair, to telephone Balmoral with the news remains only a part of the mystery surrounding the Duke's death. The King consoled himself with the thought that his brother had died on active service, but few officers, embarking on active duties, do so accompanied by a secretary and a valet. Rumours later circulated that much of the cargo consisted of alcohol, a good deal of which had been consumed by the crew.

Sinclair telephoned in the middle of dinner. When the King left the dining room to take the call everyone remained at the table in silence, 'each one of us,' Princess Alice, Duchess of Gloucester, recalled, 'and particularly Queen Elizabeth, suspecting something awful had happened. The King came back and sat in silence. I could feel he was in deep distress.'[13] The Queen caught her sister-in-law's eye and led the ladies from the room. 'In the drawing room we all assumed the news must be of Queen Mary's death,' but in that supposition they were 11 years premature. The Queen returned to the dining room, to be told the news by the King, and they both went to the drawing room to explain to the others.

There was a funeral service at St George's Chapel, Windsor, on 29 August. 'I have attended very many family funerals in the Chapel,' the King wrote in his diary, with fairly typical disregard for grammar, 'but none of which have moved me in the same way . . . Everybody there I knew well but I did not dare to look at any of them for fear of breaking down.' According to Noël Coward, who had had an affair with the Duke of Kent and was himself at the funeral, in floods of tears, both Mountbatten and the King *were* seen to weep. The Duke of Windsor, too, 'wept like a child' throughout a memorial service for the Duke of Kent in the cathedral at Nassau.[14] A fortnight later the King paid what he called a pilgrimage to the site of the crash, partly to see the scene, partly to thank members of the search party who had found his brother's body.

In June 1943 the King flew to North Africa. Thick fog prevented his 'plane from landing at Gibraltar to refuel, and since she lacked any precise information, the thought crossed the Queen's mind that the King's 'plane, too, had crashed. 'I have had an anxious few hours,' the Queen told her mother-in-law, 'because at 8.15 I heard that the plane had been heard near Gibraltar, and that it would soon be landing. Then after an hour & a half I heard that there was a thick fog at Gib. & that they were going on to Africa. Then complete silence till a few minutes ago, when a message came that they had landed in Africa, & taken off again. Of course I imagined every sort of horror, & walked up and down my room staring at the telephone.'[15]

On this two-week tour of his troops, the King journeyed 6,700 miles, and in Libya decorated a member of the 4th Indian Division with the Victoria Cross.

When the worst of the bombing was over, the Queen turned her attention to patronage of the arts. On 14 April 1943, accompanied by the Princesses, she attended a bizarre poetry reading at the Aeolian Hall, organised by Edith and Osbert Sitwell. T. S. Eliot recited from *The Waste Land*, Osbert Sitwell, a minor poet at the best of times, read several eclogues from *England Reclaimed*, and Edith, determined to shine as the star of the afternoon, recited in grand style her new poem, 'Anne Boleyn's Song'. Walter de la Mare, however, was unable to reach the gigantic lectern provided by Osbert, who was considerably taller than de la Mare, and W. J. Turner of the *Spectator* went on so long he had to be silenced by the chairman. Unfortunately, the royal party missed the best performance, staged by Dorothy Wellesley, whose husband, Lord Gerald Wellesley, later that year succeeded to the dukedom of Wellington when his nephew was killed in action. Lady Gerald was much addicted to the bottle, and just after the Queen had left she struck Harold Nicolson with her umbrella and had to be restrained by the actress, Beatrice Lillie. Dining at Brook's six days later with James Lees-Milne, Harold Nicolson told him Lady Gerald was now determined to sue somebody – anybody, apparently, and Nicolson was afraid it might be him – for saying she was drunk. Harold's wife Vita Sackville-West had been convinced she was too drunk to recite before the Queen and, according to Harold, had never let her out of her sight except when she went to the lavatory, which she did five times, emerging each time less sober than the last. Recording Harold's account of events, Lees-Milne wrote in his diary on 20 April, 'At last Vita said, "But Dotty, you can't possibly want to go again!" She sat down on the Bond Street pavement screaming, and banging with her stick, because she had been prevented from being presented to the Queen.'[16]

When Denton Welch, still an aspiring young writer and painter, lunched with Edith Sitwell at the Sesame Club five days after the poetry reading he asked her if the Princesses had listened well. 'They sat very still in the front row and stared straight at one,' she told him.[17] No doubt it had been an effort for them not to laugh. 'The Queen,' Edith Sitwell added, 'has a real interest in books,' which indeed is true. The Queen and the Princesses attended a second Sitwellian poetry reading, this time at the Wigmore Hall, on 14 May 1946, organised by the Society of Authors. In Hollywood, in 1951, Osbert Sitwell was asked if it was true that he advised the Queen on what to read, and replied that it was the other way round – that the Queen advised him.[18]

The Queen was not the only member of her family with a serious interest in literature. Her cousin Lilian Bowes-Lyon was a poet of some repute, who also took a practical part in caring for the bombed and poor in the East End. She ferried children to places of safety in the country and helped to evacuate the dead and wounded. Although in considerable pain from arthritis, made worse by an injury received when a bomb landed near a bus she was travelling in, she remained throughout the war tireless in her efforts to distribute food and hot drinks. But Lilian's life was one of tragedy and suffering. By the time she died in 1949 she had lost both legs through the onset of gangrene.

By 1944 Allied forces had begun the liberation of Europe, and Germany unleashed a new device on British civilian targets, the V-1 bomb. It was a pilotless aircraft which everyone could see and hear, but no one knew, until the engine cut out, on whose head it was going to land. Within two weeks, 600 flying bombs fell in London, killing 1,600 people and injuring 10,000. Two-hundred thousand houses were damaged. 'There is something very inhuman about death-dealing missiles being launched in such an indiscriminate manner,' the Queen wrote to Queen Mary. Almost every day windows at Buckingham Palace were shattered, and the King and Churchill were obliged to retreat to the air raid shelter for their weekly luncheon. On 8 September 1944 the first V-2 rocket, which arrived completely out of the blue, fell in Chiswick. Some 1,250 of these lethal missiles landed in London and the south-east. Between September and December 1944, 1,425 people were killed by them and 3,134 injured.

However, on 8 May 1945 the King was able to record in his diary, 'The Prime Minister came to lunch. We congratulated each other on the end of the European War . . . No more fear of being bombed at home & no more living in air raid shelters.' That afternoon and evening he and the Queen, sometimes with the Princesses and Churchill, appeared eight times on the balcony of Buckingham Palace. 'We were given a great reception,' he noted. But the Princesses did not appear as often as their parents. Because the King allowed them to mingle with the crowd. 'Poor darlings,' he wrote in his diary, his grammar as awry as ever, 'they have never had any fun yet.'

A fortnight later, after an exhausting round of thanksgiving services, carriage drives through east and south London, and an address to parliament by the King delivered almost faultlessly until, at mention of his brother's death, his voice broke, the King and Queen retired to Windsor, where the King recorded, 'We have been overwhelmed by the kind things people have said about our part in the war. We have only tried to do our duty during these 5½ years.' To Lang, in his retirement, the King wrote, 'The Queen and I have been overcome in the last fortnight with everybody's great kindness, which has been overwhelming. We have tried to do our duty in these 5 long exacting years.' Ominously, the King added in his diary entry on this occasion, 'I have found it difficult to rejoice or relax as there is still so much hard work ahead to deal with.'

Even under the benign influence of the Queen, the King found it hard to relax. He was a natural worrier, constantly prone to nervous irritation over quite trivial matters, a sartorial error, for example, or some remark that rubbed against his own ingrained prejudices. It would not be true to say he looked ill at the end of the war, but he was desperately tired. To the Duke of Gloucester he wrote from Sandringham at Christmas, 'I have been suffering from an awful reaction from the strain of the war I suppose & have felt very tired especially down here . . . Medican, not even Weir's [Sir John Weir was the King's personal physician], is of no use as I really want a rest, away from people & papers but that of course is impossible.'

Hanoverian duty called, and after the profound disappointment at losing Churchill as prime minister after the 1945 General Election the King braced himself to deal with a Labour administration, which presided over strikes, nationalisation, the creation of the welfare state, Independence for India and the physical and economic rebuilding of a country bankrupted in the cause of defending freedom. In one of the earliest audiences the King gave to the new Prime Minister, Clement Attlee, the King and Attlee discussed the shortage of clothing. 'The P.M. told me,' the King recorded afterwards, 'all available suits etc. go to the Demobilised Men, & the Women's clothes stocks are much exaggerated. I said we must all have new clothes & my family are down to the lowest ebb.'[19]

This was a slight exaggeration. The Queen was shortly to purchase a vast wardrobe for a visit to South Africa, a visit which captured the imagination of a public sick of austerity. The tour took place between February and April 1947, and was chronicled in detail by the press and newsreels. It coincided, unfortunately, with an acute fuel shortage at home, where rationing was still in operation, and some people were beginning to wonder whether Britain had won the war or lost it. But the idea of a tour had been germinating since the King had enjoyed numerous wartime meetings in London with the Prime Minister of the Union, Field Marshal Jan Smuts, whom he greatly liked and admired. On 1 February the Royal Family left Portsmouth for Cape Town in the battleship *Vanguard*, launched by Princess Elizabeth only two years before. The Queen took with her two ladies-in-waiting and her private secretary; the Princesses shared a lady-in-waiting. Also on board, as equerry, was Wing-Commander Peter Townsend.

Townsend, greatly to his surprise, had been seconded to the Palace as an equerry to the King in 1944 on a three-month assignment. Warned to take no notice if the King shouted at him, Townsend immediately warmed to the King's essential humanity and simplicity. The attraction was mutual, and he was to remain in royal service for nine years – until he became embroiled in a constitutional crisis. By this time the King was dead and the Queen Mother was left to cope.

It took *Vanguard* three weeks to steam through the Atlantic, while the Royal Family, the Queen swathed in a white turban hat, played games and took ciné films on deck and the British people at home nearly froze to death. 'This tour is being very strenuous,' the Queen wrote to Queen Mary after they had landed, 'as I feared it would be & doubly hard for Bertie who feels we should be at home. But there is very little he could do now, and even if he interrupted the tour & flew home, it would be very exhausting, & possibly make it difficult to return here.' But, she assured Queen Mary, 'We think of home all the time, & Bertie has offered to return but Mr Attlee thought that it would only make people feel that things were getting worse, & was not anxious for him to come back.'

'The fatigue factor was terrible,' a member of the Household has recalled.[20] 'The King lost pounds in weight. [17lbs to be precise.] At the end of that tour he was absolutely flaked out.' Thirty-six nights were spent in what was called the White Train. It stretched for a third of a mile, and one of its ten ivory and gold carriages had an observation platform on which the Royal Family appeared repeatedly. The King opened parliaments in Cape Town and in Salisbury.

It was noticed that Townsend, who was 32 and married with two sons, was often quite sharp with the 16-year-old Princess Margaret, whom he evidently regarded, at this stage, as little more than an over-privileged schoolgirl. But everyone's nerves were frayed. On one drive the King began a barrage of backseat driving. Townsend turned round and snapped, 'For heaven's sake shut up or there's going to be an accident.' And for once in her life, the Queen overreacted. When an excited black man started running alongside the car, clutching something in his hand (which turned out to be an intended birthday present for Princess Elizabeth), the Queen dealt him 'several deft blows' with her parasol.

The birthday in question, the Princess's 21st, occurred on 21 April. It was celebrated in Cape Town, where she broadcast from Government House, declaring that her whole life, 'whether it be long or short', would be devoted to 'the service of our great Imperial Commonwealth'. Little did she imagine that in five years' time she would be Head of that Commonwealth.

Staying on a farm at Maseru at the time of the South Africa tour was the novelist and playwright Enid Bagnold. An assiduous correspondent, she sent an amusing letter to Diana Cooper.[21] 'You can't believe the wild excitement there is about the King and Queen,' she told Lady Diana three weeks before their arrival in Basutoland. 'The K and Q's every breath and movement is blown through Africa at all hours on the wireless so that I myself am worked up and wait with excitement to know what they are wearing. There was a woman commentator in Cape Town who completely lost her head and kept shouting on the first day, "But she's LOVELY! OH, SHE'S LOVELY, LOVELY . . ." just like someone yelling at a football match.'

When eventually, on 19 March, she saw the Royal Family herself, Enid Bagnold reported, 'I must tell you I'm swept into the upward rush about the Queen. She is now surrounded by an actress-aura. She is like Irving after a First Night and oneself at the stage door. I watched her closely . . . when she was inspecting ex-servicemen right under my nose . . . She has an extraordinary control of every facial muscle, a very delicate control, so that she makes valuable every look and half smile in a very expressive way. We others, and the princesses, just smile or don't smile, but the queen has a much bigger range and a delicacy of holding or tilting her head or casting a small look for an instant that gives a rain of pleasure here and there and on whoever gets one of the fragments.' She also told Lady Diana that at one point 'The King had to stop pinning the decorations on because he couldn't get through the leopard skins.'

Later Enid Bagnold saw the White Train passing, 'and suddenly there was the queen in her garden party dress sitting in the window. I waved, and she gave one more sickly wave like a dying duck, a sketch of her other waves. She looked as though she would die if she saw just one more woman to wave to.'

The Royal Family had only been home two months when Princess Elizabeth's engagement to Lieutenant Philip Mountbatten was announced. As Prince Philip of Greece he had stayed at Sandringham for Christmas in 1943, by which time, although the King regarded them both as 'much too young' (Philip was 22, Elizabeth only 17), there was serious speculation about a possible marriage. The King was keen to test his daughter's love rather than the Prince's suitability. 'I like Philip,' he wrote to Queen Mary on 17 March 1944. 'He is intelligent, has a good sense of humour & thinks about things in the right way.' Prince Philip, like Princess Elizabeth, was a great-great-grandchild of Queen Victoria. He was a naval officer, and although of Greek origin he had been brought up in England since the age of eight.

In March 1947 (while the Royal Family were in South Africa) Prince Philip, having declined the King's offer of British royal status, renounced his Greek and Danish royal pretensions, took British nationality, and assumed the surname Mountbatten.

All that remained was for the future husband of the future Supreme Governor of the Church of England to be received into the Anglican Church. So off to the chapel at Lambeth Palace the naval lieutenant went to receive the ministrations of the Archbishop of Canterbury, Geoffrey Fisher.

Writing to Princess Elizabeth on her honeymoon, the King apologised for perhaps seeming 'hard hearted' over making the Princess wait a long time before becoming engaged. But it is inconceivable the decision was not one taken jointly by the King and Queen. As it happens, the Princess had written to her mother to say she thought the long wait had been for the best, and the King paid tribute in the letter he sent her on her honeymoon to the Queen's contribution to her upbringing – and by implication, to her training for the throne. 'I have watched you grow up all these years with pride under the skilful direction of Mummy,' the King wrote, 'who as you know is the most marvellous person in the World in my eyes.'

By 26 April 1948 the King had shared 25 years of marriage with 'the most marvellous person in the World', and he decided they should cheer up austerity Britain by driving in a state landau to St Paul's Cathedral for a Service of Thanksgiving. The Home Secretary, Chuter Ede, wanted the service, for security reasons, to be held at Westminster Abbey. But George V and Queen Mary had gone to St Paul's on their silver wedding and the Queen remained adamant. Afterwards they appeared on the balcony at the Palace and both the King and Queen made a broadcast. The poet laureate, John Masefield, celebrated the occasion with the following words:

> To These, to-day (to them a sacred day)
> Our hopes become a praying that the stress
> Of these, their cruel years, may pass away
> And happy years succeed, and Wisdom bless.

But these were dark days for Great Britain. The King felt personally responsible for both affairs of state and the conduct of international affairs. Constant worry about the economy at home and the threat from overseas of nuclear annihilation began visibly to wear away at his health. By January 1948 the King was suffering from cramp in both legs. By August he was in discomfort most of the time. By October his left foot was perpetually numb and pain kept him awake at night. Then his right foot became affected. When the King had it examined on 20 October by a manipulative surgeon, Morton Smart, Sir Morton was so alarmed he called in a heart specialist.

On 30 October four eminent doctors gathered round the King. They called in a fifth, and advised Sir Alan Lascelles that a proposed visit to Australia and New Zealand should be cancelled. But the King continued to fulfil official engagements at home, and forbade Princess Elizabeth, now pregnant, to be told about his condition, which had been diagnosed as arteriosclerosis. There was talk of amputation. On 23 November the public were informed that the King was suffering 'from obstruction of the circulation through the arteries of the legs'. Complete rest had been advised, and 'treatment to improve the circulation in the legs' had been initiated. The doctors further announced: 'There is no doubt that the strain of the last twelve years has appreciably affected [the King's] resistance to physical fatigue.'

He tried to follow doctors' orders, but became 'tired & bored with bed'. On 14 November Princess Elizabeth gave birth to a son and heir. At least the King had lived to see the succession secured. At Sandringham, after Christmas, he went shooting, but back in London, on 3 March 1949, half a dozen specialists gathered at Buckingham Palace, and advised a 'right lumbar sympathectomy' – 'excision of part of a sympathetic nerve'. An operating theatre was constructed in the Palace overlooking the Mall, and the operation was carried out on 12 March. By 29 March the King was holding a Privy Council, and on 9 June he drove to Horse Guards Parade in a carriage for Trooping the Colour. By 18 June he was dancing at a ball at Windsor (as was the Queen, who 'danced every dance vigorously', according to Chips Channon[22]). 'I feel ever so well in this good fresh air,' the King reassured Queen Mary from Balmoral on 24 August, '& am trying to worry less about matters political.' By the end of the year, satisfied they had prevented the King from suffering a heart attack, his doctors were prepared to reconsider plans for a tour of Australia and New Zealand in 1952.

But by the time the King went to Westminster Abbey on 24 May 1951, to install the Duke of Gloucester as Great Master of the Order of the Bath, he was looking extremely ill. That evening he retired to bed with influenza. A shadow was discovered on his left lung. 'The doctors are happier about me tonight than they have been for a week,' he told Queen Mary on 31 May, although why they should have been, heaven only knows. By 11 September it was decided a portion of tissue should be removed for examination. The King had a malignant growth. While the strain of being king may have 'affected his resistance to physical fatigue' it had not been the cause of his cancer; smoking had. He was told his left lung must be removed, but not the reason why. The public, who flocked in their hundreds to the Palace to read the medical bulletins, likewise were fobbed off. Structural changes had developed in the lung, they were told. Whatever the King's understanding of his condition, he suddenly decided to make a fraternal gesture of good will to the Duke of Windsor, who was staying in London. Just before undergoing a life-threatening operation he asked the Master of the Household to send the Duke three brace of grouse!

But he made a good enough recovery to welcome back Winston Churchill as his prime minister on 26 October. The second of December was designated a Day of Thanksgiving for the King's recovery. However, when Princess Elizabeth and the Duke of Edinburgh left for a 35-day tour of Canada the Princess had taken with her a sealed envelope containing a draft Accession Declaration, in case the King died while she was away. On their return the King made them both Privy Councillors. He told the Princess to come at noon on 4 December 'so that I can show you what you will have to do'.

On 30 January 1952 the Royal Family went to see *South Pacific* at Drury Lane. The next morning the King and Queen, the King hatless in the wind and looking drawn and haggard, went to London Airport to wave goodbye to Princess Elizabeth and the Duke of Edinburgh. They were off to East Africa, and then – hopefully – to Australia and New Zealand. On 5 February, back at Sandringham, the King went shooting. At half-past ten he retired, and around midnight a watchman in the garden saw him fixing a latch on his bedroom window. He was the last person to see the King alive.

8
'Nannie Of Us All'

IN SNOW AND SLEET, for three days more than 300,000 people joined a queue sometimes four miles long to pay their last respects to George VI in Westminster Hall. For 17 years his body remained in a vault at St George's Chapel, Windsor, until in 1969 he was finally laid to rest in a small side chapel on the north aisle, beneath a plain black slab. Here, eventually, Queen Elizabeth the Queen Mother will one day join him. The King's chapel has glass by John Piper, who was commissioned to execute a series of watercolours of Windsor Castle. 'You seem to have very bad luck with the weather, Mr Piper,' was the King's considered verdict.[1] Today they hang at Clarence House.

The day before the King died the Queen and Princess Margaret had driven to Ludham, to cruise on the Norfolk Broads as the guest of another painter, Edward Seago. They returned to Sandringham with some of Seago's paintings. As so often, the Queen got back 'rather late'. She wrote to Seago: 'as I always did, I rushed straight to the King's room to say that I was back and to see how he was. I found him so well, so gay.' The pictures had been deposited in the hall, where the King duly inspected them. Then, wrote the Queen, 'We had such a truly gay dinner . . . One cannot yet believe that it has happened.'

The King seems to have had a premonition of his early demise. One evening Lady Hambleden was sitting beside him at dinner at Windsor and asked when the new stands at Ascot would be ready.

'Oh,' said the King, 'I don't think I shall see them finished.'

'However long are they going to take, Sir?' asked Lady Hambleden in surprise.

'Oh, two or three years.'

'I think,' says Lady Hambleden, 'the King was aware how ill he was but the Queen wouldn't accept the fact. She can put her head in the sand like an ostrich.' And with a gentle sweep of her hand across her own face, Lady Hambleden indicates how, for the Queen Mother, problems can simply float away.[2]

Princess Margaret, too, seems to have been taken by surprise. In view of the prematurely aged aspect of her father (he was only 56 when he died, and looked ten years older) it seems extraordinary that she could have written to Lady Diana Cooper six days after his death, 'We miss him dreadfully but we are comforted by the fact that he was so *well* and in good spirits when he died, in peace at his beloved Sandringham.' The Princess's letter paints a touching vignette of the tiny nuclear Royal Family as it was constituted in 1952. 'We were such a very happy and close family,' she wrote, 'and we are so lucky to have countless lovely memories of my darling Papa. He was such a lovable person and he was greatly loved by people who had never met him, simply because they knew he was a sincere person and that they could trust him completely.

'We are so thankful that he was such a delicious person and so *alive* always that we never took him for granted, & he was always doing nice little things for one so that one was continually being touched by his kindness and generosity to us all.'[3]

The position of the monarchy, in 1952, seemed eminently secure, and a 'second Elizabethan era' was confidently predicted. Its advent was confirmed by the brilliantly timed conquest of Everest on the eve of the new Queen's coronation. By a strange coincidence, Elizabeth II succeeded at the age of 25, the same age as her great predecessor, in 1558. She had been married only four years, without much experience of the chores of royal life and with practically no experience of the lives of ordinary people. Hers had been a sheltered childhood and adolescence, and tinkering around with a spanner in the ATS for a few months had been no substitute for a boarding school or a spell at university. She knew absolutely nobody outside the enclosed world of upper-crust courtiers. Princess Margaret's social circle of wealthy landowners and lounge lizards had not appealed to her. With the exception of Lord and Lady Rupert Neville, her closest friends (people like Sir Henry and Lady Zia Wernher, with whom she frequently stayed at Luton Hoo) were old enough to be her parents. Without exception, all were rich (the Duke of Edinburgh, by contrast, scarcely owned a decent suit when he was courting her), and the Wernhers were very rich indeed.

Two other important people had been bereaved very young; Prince Charles, who was only three and could never carry into adult life any personal recollections of his grandfather, and the Queen Mother, who had been widowed at the age of only 51. Quite apart from the prospect of a long and lonely widowhood ('One cannot imagine life without him,' she told the new American President, General Eisenhower) this opened up a very real chasm, for what role was she now supposed to play, ousted by fate overnight from her position as queen consort, too young to play Widow Twanky, and overshadowed by the presence of a queen mother already firmly in command of that position, Queen Mary? The first problem to be solved was a practical one: a choice of title by which she would be known in future. After assuring the nation that their concern had sustained her in her sorrow, she said her only wish was to be allowed to continue the work that she and the King had 'sought to do together', but even as she penned these words she must have wondered what work that was, what particular tasks would be allocated to her now that she was a widowed queen consort, a spare cog in the Constitution like Queen Alexandra and Queen Mary before her. She made it known that she would henceforth be styled Queen Elizabeth the Queen Mother, 'Queen Mother' neatly differentiating her from Queen Mary. To her family and Household she became generally known as Queen Elizabeth, Elizabeth II being referred to simply as the Queen.

By the time of the coronation, on 2 June 1953, Cecil Beaton was already describing the Queen Mother in his diary as 'The great mother figure and nannie of us all,' using the term nannie not in the sense of a children's nanny but as a grandmother. But it was not until a Canadian journalist first coined the phrase that the Queen Mother became known universally as the Queen Mum. No monarch or consort in history has ever been accorded a more appropriate or affectionate soubriquet.

But before the Queen Mother could settle into the cosy role of the nation's favourite granny she had a good deal of anger to deal with. For the past 29 years she had supported and been supported by someone largely fashioned by herself, who as King in the aftermath of an abdication and then in war had amply rewarded her efforts. Suddenly she was alone, stripped of her only equal and total confidant, the person with whom she had planned to spend her old age in shared contentment. She had created the position of a modern queen consort, and by undertaking a wide range of public engagements quite unconnected with state ceremonies she had set a precedent for other female members of the Royal Family – which in years to come was to prove a disastrous legacy. What she needed in the initial years of bereavement was a scapegoat for her husband's far from robust constitution and heavy smoking, the two constituent factors that had led to his premature death and to her isolation. The obvious focus for her grief and disappointment was the Windsors.

Bertie had loved his eldest brother, and just how fond of David the Queen Mother had been can be judged from a letter she wrote to him on 13 January 1925: 'I hope your affairs are going well, and that neither your heart nor your staff are giving you cause for worry. These two seem to give you most trouble in life, and also of course you are *very*, very naughty, but delicious.' It seemed to Elizabeth now that Edward's infidelity to the Crown had been rewarded with personal happiness while her reward for keeping the ship of state afloat was deep despair.

The grievance the Queen Mother entertained for her husband's death became focused primarily on the cause of the Duke of Windsor's continuing domestic bliss, Wallis. Even though in 1942 Queen Mary had managed to write to the Duke, 'I send a kind message to your wife,' George VI's widow made sure no invitation was extended to the Duchess of Windsor when the Duke was invited to Bertie's funeral. Yet even as the Duke was sailing the Atlantic in the *Queen Mary* to attend his brother's funeral he was nursing hopes of a family reconciliation. 'I hope,' the Duchess wrote to him on 12 February, 'you can make some headway with Cookie and Mrs Temple Jr.' The Duke was at first planning to report to the Duchess (addressing her as 'My own darling Peaches') that 'officially and on the surface my treatment within the family has been entirely correct and dignified.' But these words were part of a draft letter he never sent, probably because he related its contents in a telephone call. 'I suggest that you see the widow and tell her a little of your feelings,' the Duchess advised as a result of that telephone conversation. 'So anxious to see you walking in the funeral,' she continued. 'Try to see the Queen and Philip casually just so they will know what you are like etc.'

When, on television, Wallis did see the Duke 'walking in the funeral' he was swaying behind the gun carriage like a seasick duck. On discovering he was to lose the £10,000 a year allowance paid personally by the late King, the Duchess wrote, on 17 February, 'They are beasts to continue to treat you the way they do. Anyway do the best you can my darling but I am afraid Mrs Temple Sr will never give in.'

The Duke cabled back, 'Have asked to see Cookie but general atmosphere frustrating.' On 22 February he reported, 'Cookie was sugar as I've told you and M [Mountbatten, who had been created an earl in 1947] and other relatives and the Court officials correct and

friendly on the surface. But gee the crust is hard & only granite below.'
He mentioned the £10,000 allowance in connection with the Queen
(who had invited him to lunch at Clarence House, her home since her
marriage) and the Queen Mother. 'It's hell to be even this much
dependent on these ice-veined bitches.' He was hoping to see Cry
Baby again. 'Cry Baby' was Churchill.

Before she had even buried Bertie, the Queen Mother was aware that
the mother-in-law upon whose advice and support she had so
depended was ailing. The Duke of Windsor noticed this too. 'Mama as
hard as nails but failing,' he jotted down. 'When Queens fail they make
less sense than others in the same state . . . Cookie listened without
comment & closed on the note that it was nice to be able to talk about
Bertie with somebody who had known him so well . . . Clarence
House was informal & friendly. Brave New World. Full of self-
confidence & seem to take job in their stride.' Mountbatten, he noted,
was 'very bossy & never stops talking. All are suspicious & watching
his influence on Philip.'

Anxious though the Queen Mother may have been to talk to David
because he had known Bertie well, she remained averse to discussing
anything with his wife. When Queen Mary died shortly before the
coronation, the Duke of Windsor was again invited to come on his
own to the funeral, but family chat seems to have petered out in St
George's Chapel; a dinner for 28 was held afterwards, to which the
Duke was not invited. He and Wallis had previously failed to get
tickets for Princess Elizabeth's wedding – as had the Duke of
Edinburgh's sisters. The close-knit family invented by George VI and
Queen Elizabeth seemed determined to remain very close-knit indeed.

In the immediate aftermath of the King's death the Queen Mother
contemplated retiring into private life. She had no wish for the
popularity she had earned as Duchess of York and then as Queen to
deflect the spotlight from the new young monarch. But within three
months she had flown to Fife to wish the 1st Battalion the Black Watch
Godspeed before they left for Korea. In the late spring she decided that
a visit to Sissinghurst Castle in Kent, the home of Harold Nicolson and
Vita Sackville-West, might cheer her up. Normally Vita slopped
around in jodhpurs, but realised on this occasion that she would have
to put on a skirt. Harold, who had met the Queen Mother on a number
of occasions, nevertheless sought advice about protocol from Diana
Cooper. She told him to tell Vita to place the Queen Mother at the end
of the table. He was to sit on her left. In the event, Harold sat on her
right and his younger son Nigel on her left. Vita sat opposite the

Queen Mother, at the other end of the table. After lunch Queen Elizabeth walked round one of the loveliest gardens in England. Then she stayed to tea. 'Everything goes *comme sur des roulettes*,' Vita recorded in her diary.

But inevitably, one outing for lunch could only serve as a temporary painkiller. In September Edith Sitwell sent the Queen Mother an anthology of poetry, *A Book of Flowers*, which she sat down by a river to read on a day, she told Edith in a letter of thanks, 'when one felt engulfed by great black clouds of unhappiness and misery'. She admitted that sorrow was 'small and selfish', but 'it bangs one about until one is senseless.'[4] On 3 May the Queen Mother had written to Edith's elder brother, Osbert, echoing Princess Margaret's sentiments about her father's apparently improved health.

> It is very difficult to realise that the King has left us, he was so much better, & so full of plans & ideas for the future, and I really thought that he was going to have some years perhaps less anguished than the last fifteen. I think that those years after the war were terribly anxious & frustrating and that it was all very hard & grinding work, and I longed for him to have some peace of mind. He was so young to die, and was becoming so wise in kingship. He was so kind too, and had a sort of natural nobility of thought & life, which sometimes made me ashamed of my narrower & more feminine point of view. Such sorrow is a very strange experience – it really changes one's whole life, whether for better or for worse I don't know yet.

In due course the Queen Mother was to decide to follow Queen Mary's example by attending the coronation (it had not normally been the practice for a widowed queen consort to do so), and she appeared wearing a train that had belonged to her mother-in-law. By 1954 she would be up and off again on overseas tours. What she did in the meantime helped speed her recovery, but may also have fuelled rumours about her impending retirement.

While staying privately with friends in Caithness she heard that a small castle – a fortified house, really, which she rather quaintly referred to as a villa – on the Pentland Firth was for sale. It was called Barrogill and was about as far north, windswept and isolated as any hermit could desire (it stands in fact in the same parish as John O'Groats). After a little hesitation, for the place was damp and leaking, the Queen Mother bought it, and restored to it its original name, the Castle of Mey. It took three years to renovate the sixteenth-century building, a task which the Queen Mother closely supervised. Starting from scratch, for the castle contained none of the Empire chairs and tables so beloved of European royalty, she toured antique shops and furnished the place to her own taste. When eventually electricity arrived she exclaimed that this was 'Such a joy!' There were originally 25 acres of land, including trout ponds and a deer park, and – much needed in that part of the world – a walled garden. The Queen Mother later added to the estate a 120-acre farm, where she breeds Aberdeen Angus cattle.

The Castle of Mey, where the Queen Mother goes into residence in August and again in October, was the first home of her own, the first place she had ever purchased. It proved to be a refuge where she was not continually distracted, as she was for many years at the Royal Lodge, at Balmoral and at Sandringham, with reminders of the King. The King once said of her that she could make a home anywhere. But no matter how adept one may be at flower arranging, to make a mausoleum like Buckingham Palace into a home would require skills verging on the miraculous. At Mey however the Queen Mother had a house with proportions both inside and out that enabled her to create a real home, which favoured friends and relatives vie to visit. She shops in Thurso, chats to farm workers and fishes for salmon – or she did until very recently. As a lady-in-waiting put it, 'Everything at the Castle of Mey is bent double because of the wind. But Queen Elizabeth doesn't feel the cold at all. In fact, she prefers the cold to the great heat she has sometimes had to endure overseas.'[5] In August, the Queen Mother has all her former equerries to stay, and entertains a lot of young people. In October she enjoys the castle almost entirely alone.

The new Queen inherited from her father the private properties of Sandringham and Balmoral, so the Queen Mother again took possession of Birkhall. She retained the use of the Royal Lodge for life, but in London there was an inevitable change of address. Since their marriage in 1947 the Queen and the Duke of Edinburgh had been living at Clarence House, halfway along the north side of the Mall. But, on her accession, the Queen was due to take up residence at Buckingham Palace. A simple swap was arranged, and on 18 May 1953 the Queen Mother and Princess Margaret, accompanied by Peter Townsend as Comptroller to the Queen Mother's Household, moved in. Named after the third son of George III, the Duke of Clarence who eventually succeeded as William IV, the house was substantially improved in the nineteenth century by Nash, and became the London home of Victoria's mother, the Duchess of Kent, and later of Victoria's second son, the Duke of Edinburgh. During his occupancy the Tuscan portico, entrance gate and lodges were added to the south front. From 1900 until his death in 1942 Clarence House was the home of Victoria's third son, the popular Duke of Connaught, and, before Princess Elizabeth moved in, it had served as headquarters for the Red Cross. It was not long before the Queen Mother was lavishing taste and expenditure on what was to be her London home for 40 years. Here she has hung most of her considerable collection of modern art, which includes work by Duncan Grant, a 1938 portrait of Bernard Shaw by Augustus John and an unfinished one of herself by John. She also owns a very remarkable portrait of George V with his racing manager by Sickert, and paintings by Paul Nash, John Bratby, Graham Sutherland and Lowry.

No doubt the Queen Mother was glad to be away from Buckingham Palace. In his diary Cecil Beaton has left a sad account of her days alone there immediately after the King's death, 'picnicking', according to a lady-in-waiting, and being taken care of by a 'skeleton staff'. His assistants were told by some of the senior Palace servants they 'couldn't think why the Queen Mother stayed on here so long – not that she will relish the move to Clarence House for there won't be the number of servants there that she's accustomed to.' When Beaton passed the Queen Mother's old rooms there was a strong whiff of decorator's paint; electricians whistled as they walked down the Picture Gallery. As in wartime, he found the rooms to be freezing cold, and when he asked for a vase of flowers to use in his photographs the lady-in-waiting returned to say there was not one in the Palace. Yet when the Queen Mother arrived, 'her smile and warmth of sympathy made it seem as if the sun had come out.' Everything had gone wrong for this photo session; even Beaton's camera shutter had jammed. 'Of course,' he wrote, 'there is something of the great actress about her, and in public she has to put on a show that never fails, but it is her heart and imagination which guide her. She will always say just the one thing that puts people at ease and makes them feel a glow of happiness, because she understands and appreciates the reality of any situation – whether it be tragic or gay.'

On the way home Beaton stopped at a florist and ordered a bouquet of spring flowers to be delivered 'to that adorable human being living in that cold, bleak palace'. He was amply rewarded. Thanks to the Queen Mother, he was commissioned to take the official photographs at the coronation.

As the date grew nearer, it was clear Queen Mary was failing. She made it plain that if she were to die, arrangements for the coronation

were to go ahead. After a somewhat distressing few weeks she died on
24 March. Queen Mary's death set the Queen Mother free to pursue a
new phase of her career. Queen Mary had vetted and approved the young
Lady Elizabeth Bowes-Lyon, had taken her under her wing, trained her
in her royal duties, advised her how to appoint her own Household in
1937, and shared with Elizabeth her anguish at the prospect of Bertie
mounting the throne. For 15 years Queen Mary had acted almost as a
surrogate mother. As queen, the Queen Mother had been assiduous in
keeping Queen Mary informed about what was going on, in asking her
advice, in constantly drawing her into the centre of affairs. She was
solicitous for her welfare and punctilious in the respect she paid towards
her position as the widow of a sovereign. When the Queen Mother
herself became queen, there was no one in the world to whom she would
ever curtsey again, but she thought up a subtle and rather charming
method of conveying respect. When greeting Queen Mary in public she
would invariably kiss her hand.

Queen Mary's death meant the Duke of Windsor, the spectre at the
feast, was to return to England for another funeral, again on his own.
A 'ridiculous and costly trip' was how the Duke described his journey
by sea to attend his mother's sickbed when he wrote to the Duchess on
9 March 1953. After hearing that 'the old lady's condition' had
improved slightly, he observed that 'ice in place of blood in the veins
must be a fine preservative.' He was accompanied by the Princess
Royal and her equerry, 'the incredible old Colonel Balfour', whom the
Duke found an insufferable and seldom sober bore. At Marlborough
House he discovered a letter from the Duchess urging him to work on
'Cookie' and 'Shirley' for the restoration of his allowance. When he
wasn't fretting about money the Duke spent plenty of it shopping, and
on 21 March, with Queen Mary still lingering, he told the Duchess that
'hanging around someone who has been so mean and vile to you my
sweetheart is getting me down.'

But he only had three more days to wait for his mother's death. On
27 March he wrote to the Duchess from Paris to say, 'Well, thank God
the nightmare of watching Mama die is over. I couldn't have taken it
for much longer, for her sake or for mine.' It was in this letter that he
described how, while he was at Marlborough House towards the end,
'the Archbishop of Canterbury showed up to "give Mama a blessing"
as he called it and Mary and I had to kneel in the next room while he
said some prayers. An unctuous hypocrite like all the rest I should
judge.'

Hospitality during the funeral was offered by the Unknown Soldier

– the Duke of Gloucester. The Duke of Windsor thought 'maybe age has softened him a little like it seems to have done to Mary.' Afterwards, he returned to Marlborough House to make sure Princess Mary knew which of his mother's possessions he wanted. As he told the Duchess in a letter from the Duke of Gloucester's residence, York House, on 31 March, 'I wanted some nice things but of course I'll be at a disadvantage being away when the division is made and the "vultures" will have had first pick . . . What a smug stinking lot my relations are and you've never seen such a seedy worn out bunch of old hags most of them have become.' But, he told her, 'let us skip this rude interlude and enjoy our lovely full life together far removed from the bordom, the restrictions and the intrigues of the Royal Family and the Court.'

There was one intrigue brewing up that, when it surfaced, must have given inordinate pleasure to the Windsors. It was the first test of the new Queen's reign, and the first occasion for the Queen Mother to use her subtle influence behind the scenes since finding herself bereft of total regal status. Princess Margaret and Group Captain Peter Townsend had fallen in love. He declared his feelings in the Crimson Drawing Room at Windsor Castle, and the Princess broke the news to the Queen and the Queen Mother. It was revealed to the rest of the world by the *People*, just 12 days after the Princess had been seen in Westminster Abbey flicking a speck of dust from Townsend's uniform. The news raised two important questions. The first related to rank: Townsend was a commoner; Margaret was only third in line of succession. The concept of a woman so close to the throne marrying a commoner was not yet firmly established. That was why Lieutenant Philip Mountbatten (who at least had been royal) had been loaded with honours on the eve of his marriage to Princess Elizabeth. The other question related to the Abdication; Townsend had been divorced. Had Princess Margaret wanted to cock a snook at the Establishment she could not have mismanaged her affairs more neatly. That said, the pair were genuinely in love – which did not of course mean they were under any obligation to announce the fact, or to get married.

Townsend had a distinguished war record. Initially flying in a Hurricane, later in a Spitfire, he brought down the first German bomber to crash in England since the First World War, and eventually won the DSO and two DFC's. He was brave, amusing, charming and good at his job. While he may not have been treated as a member of the family, he was regarded as a friend, and his promotion within the Household had been rapid. After only three years as an equerry he had been appointed a Commander of the Royal Victorian Order by the

King, and eventually he was made Deputy Master of the Household. But if Princess Margaret had been relying on her mother's support or on Townsend's proven abilities she was in for a disappointment. The official line was made abundantly clear to Townsend himself when he confided to Alan Lascelles that he and the Princess had fallen in love. 'Either you're mad or bad,' was the response. It is said, by a former member of the King's Household, that Princess Margaret felt badly let down by Lascelles, on the grounds that he ought to have told her there and then she could not possibly marry Townsend and retain her rights of succession to the throne. There would have been no need for the Princess to forego her royal status. She could have remained a Royal Highness, as Prince Michael of Kent, having renounced his rights of succession, remains a Royal Highness. She would have ceased to be eligible for funds from the Civil List, but the Royal Family are not hard up, and private financial arrangements could have been sorted out. Having renounced her rights of succession, there would have been no impediment, even though she was married to a former divorcé, to her carrying out royal engagements. None of this seems to have been discussed, but as the same former courtier has observed, with the King dead there was no one to cut the Gordian knot. 'The temptation was to wait and see, and hope the cloud would pass by.'[6]

Margaret was only 13 when she first met Townsend, and any suggestion that on the South Africa tour three years later Princess Margaret had lured Townsend away from his wife is absurd. Townsend's marriage, to Rosemary Pawle, had been a hasty wartime one. It came under considerable strain from the unsocial hours an equerry inevitably works, even if the ostensible cause of the divorce was Rosemary Townsend's adultery with John de Laszlo, whose father had painted a portrait of the Queen Mother.

Under the 1772 Royal Marriages Act, until she was 25 Princess Margaret required the consent of the Queen to marry, and even after 25 she would need the permission of both Houses of Parliament. The Queen Mother kept her feelings to herself, however, hoping either that the romance would blow over or that the Establishment – the politicians and churchmen – would sort out the affair for her. In the words of someone closely involved in the drama, she was to exercise 'benign authority', exerting behind the scenes 'the terrific power of her personality'.[7] Whenever Townsend and Margaret were discussing their problems and the Queen Mother came into the room 'she was absolutely sweet', and Princess Margaret never told Townsend that her mother was completely against their getting married.[8]

In the event, the Establishment made all the running, as the Queen Mother had hoped they would. Lascelles alerted Churchill, who forgot his earlier championship of King Edward and suggested exporting Townsend without delay. Lascelles concurred, and proposed exiling Townsend to Singapore or Johannesburg, where he would have been separated from his eleven and eight-year-old sons. Eventually, without troubling to inform the ambassador, Lascelles settled for Brussels, where Townsend found himself posted as air attaché.

The Queen Mother, her morale much improved by having the Castle of Mey to tinker with and Clarence House to organise to her taste, had already banished thoughts of a graceful retirement clad in widow's weeds by accepting an invitation to tour Rhodesia. Princess Margaret was to accompany her. Margaret had only had a minor role to play on the South Africa tour in 1949, and it would be useful training for her future life. Chanting choirs and triumphal arches (one read, Greeting Great White Queen and Great White Princess) augured well. But two days before they were due to return to England, it fell to the Queen Mother to break the news to Princess Margaret that there was to be no reunion with Peter Townsend. He had already been posted to Brussels.

Lady Hambleden, who was in waiting, recalls, 'That was all very awkward!' It was indeed. Margaret threw a fit and retired to bed. The Queen Mother explained she had a cold. Shortly after their return to England, the Queen Mother was due to tour gardens in Stoke Newington, something she greatly enjoys, enabling her as it does to 'look the East End in the face' without the distraction of German bombers. But now it was Princess Margaret who had to step into the breach and deputise for her mother, who had in turn taken to her bed, exhausted with bereavement and now her daughter's unhappy love affair.

'I think,' Lady Hambleden recalls, 'the Queen Mother was basically against the marriage because she thought Princess Margaret was too young, but the fact that Peter Townsend was divorced was an additional distraction. It was too soon after the Abdication, and people just didn't get divorced then. As far as the Queen's attitude was concerned, I can only say she depended a great deal on her mother's help and advice when she first came to the throne, and the fact that the Queen Mother did not positively endorse the affair meant, as far as the Queen was concerned, it was not on.'[9]

Townsend's exile to Belgium was supposed to be a cooling off operation. But for three years he continued to live in the hope of marrying Princess Margaret. They telephoned one another constantly. Margaret also sought the advice of a close friend, a young university chaplain, with whom she was in almost daily contact at one time in her struggle to reconcile her personal desires with her sense of public duty and genuine religious convictions.

With the approach of Princess Margaret's 25th birthday, she and Peter Townsend took refuge in the Berkshire home of one of the Queen Mother's nieces, and a lady-in-waiting to Princess Margaret, the Hon. Mrs Wills. By now Anthony Eden, himself a divorcé, was prime minister, and on 18 October 1955 he took time off to discuss the marriage problem with the Queen. Two days later the Attorney General, Sir Reginald Manningham-Buller, was dragged out of court to attend a cabinet meeting. The Marquess of Salisbury, a High Anglican descendant of Elizabeth I's Lord Burghley, Leader of the House of Lords and a blue-blooded blimp of the old school (he was once playing racing demon with the Queen Mother and complained he was 'suwwounded by howwible, howwible Queens'), was threatening to resign from the Government. As he was an old and valued friend of the Queen Mother, serious notice was taken. And the Archbishop of Canterbury, no doubt irked because he had only been kept informed of events by Princess Margaret's private counsellor, intervened to announce it had all along been nothing more than 'a stunt'. 'If they want to marry, why shouldn't they?' the *Sunday Express* demanded to know. Delighted at Cookie's discomfiture, the Windsors purchased a pug and called it Peter Townsend. When the joke had worn off they gave it away.

With the Queen Mother only offering what one might term negative support – she didn't say No but she didn't say Yes – it was left to Princess Margaret to resolve the first constitutional crisis of the new reign herself. This she did after the Queen, too, made sure her sister did not feel under pressure from her family. On the day in 1955 when Princess Margaret left Balmoral for London to thrash out the issues finally with Townsend, she naturally expected the Queen to be in the hall to say goodbye. Afraid she might find herself saying, 'Do be careful,' the Queen deliberately absented herself.[10] It was the Princess's affection and admiration for the Queen and her fear of doing damage to the Church which resulted in the statement she issued on 31 October: 'mindful of the Church's teaching that marriage is indissoluble' she had decided not to marry Group Captain Townsend.

In 1959 Townsend married Marie-Luce Jamagne, with whom he made his home in France and by whom he had a son and two daughters. Princess Margaret's clerical confidant recalls feeling 'terribly sad at the outcome but immensely relieved'.[11] No one was more relieved than the Queen Mother. But as one of her ladies-in-waiting says, 'She has had to get used to divorce up to a point. But she still doesn't approve.'[12] Ironically, one of the divorces that she had to get used to a quarter of a century later was Princess Margaret's, from the Earl of Snowdon.

Once Princess Margaret was divorced, the rule banning divorcés from the Royal Enclosure at Ascot was lifted. It would hardly have done for Princess Margaret to be banned. But even as early as 1955 it can be seen how trapped in history the Queen Mother had become by the stand she had taken in keeping the Duchess of Windsor, and effectively the Duke as well, out of England. Commenting on the Margaret–Townsend affair in his diary, a great admirer of the Queen Mother, Noël Coward, wrote: 'It has all been a silly, mismanaged lash-up and I cannot imagine how the Queen and the Queen Mother and Prince Philip allowed it to get into such a tangle.'

The answer to Noël Coward's musings is simple. The Queen and the Duke of Edinburgh were both very young and inexperienced. The Duke was not yet in control of his own home, and the Queen was surrounded by old-fashioned and, in some crucial instances, incompetent courtiers. Alan Lascelles had lived through the Abdication and could scarcely credit that a daughter of the man hurtled on to the throne in 1936 could contemplate marriage to a divorcé only 17 years later. The Queen's press officer, Commander Richard Colville, was a sailor by profession. He had received no training for the job and had no aptitude anyway. He was one of that breed of press officer who resorts to saying 'No comment'. He left Townsend to face the press alone, and when Townsend departed for Brussels, Colville tried to turn him into a non-person, denying the Queen Mother even had a Comptroller. He also called upon the press for restraint, which prompted the *Manchester Guardian* to comment: 'If we in this country behaved with the same good manners towards Royalty as they do in Scandinavian countries there would be no need for the appeal. People would treat the members of the Royal Family with the same tolerance and decency that they would think due to themselves. But,' the paper concluded, 'the public attitude towards Royalty has come rather too near idolatry to be easily influenced by such counsels.'

The reason the Queen Mother allowed things to drift was because she could do nothing else. If she had allowed Princess Margaret to marry a divorcé, how could she possibly justify the morganatic marriage handed out to the Duke of Windsor? She had engineered the Letters Patent, and consistently resisted attempts by the Duke to reinstate himself in England. To have countenanced Margaret's marriage to Townsend would have meant a betrayal of much of her life's work.

9

A Very Private Person

AT A COCKTAIL PARTY on 5 November 1947 King George VI had 'naively' remarked to one of the other guests, the Countess of Moray (so she relayed to James Lees-Milne later than evening), 'We keep wondering whether Philip realises what he is in for.'[1] The child of a disastrous marriage, now a mere prince consort and expected to produce an heir to the throne but always to walk two paces behind his wife, Philip, and the Queen, were in for a rougher ride than they could ever have imagined on the day that Elizabeth II inherited the throne. Since the Abdication crisis, the Royal Family had enjoyed 21 years of unalloyed, indeed cloying, admiration.

But in 1957 such a storm of criticism broke that the Queen Mother was hard pressed to imagine how, in the five years since her husband had died, everything could have turned so sour. What really shocked her was that a peer, Lord Altringham, had led the assault. At least he made some amends, in the Queen Mother's eyes, by disclaiming his peerage for life in 1963. Altringham owned an obscure monthly magazine, the *National and English Review*, in which he wrote an article suggesting that the personality of the Queen 'conveyed by the utterances which are put into her mouth' was 'that of a priggish schoolgirl, captain of the hockey team, a prefect and a recent candidate for confirmation!' As a result, he was challenged to a duel. His words, picked up by the national newspapers, emboldened others to join in the fray. Altringham, who is now known as Mr John Grigg, was only 33, and he had struck a chord with many other young people, who believed the Queen, although only 30 herself, was not in touch with the modern world.

The reason she was not was because she remained in thrall to an outmoded generation of courtiers. Sir Edward Ford, Assistant Private Secretary to George VI from 1946 to 1952, and from 1952 until 1967 Assistant Private Secretary to the Queen, was recruited not by the

King but by Sir Alan Lascelles. Sir Edward recalls that when asked how Sir Martin Charteris was appointed Private Secretary to Princess Elizabeth in 1950, Charteris replied, 'By the best of all possible ways, nepotism!' Sir Edward makes a spirited defence of the system. 'It is perfectly true to say that on the whole we came from the same stable; public schools, Brigade of Guards. But it is frightfully important that members of the Court should get on with each other. And there's always at least one private secretary in attendance. Princess Anne resented the fact that when she came home for the holidays from Benenden there was a private secretary always hovering around. You are treated by the Royal Family like a guest, and they have therefore got to employ people who fit into the same sort of slot. And I agree that much of the criticism in 1957 was directed at the people around the Queen – at the likes of me!'[2]

John Osborne, flagwaver once upon a time for all angry young men – and women – announced in *Encounter* that the whole panoply of royalty was symptomatic of a deeply sick society. 'It distresses me,' he wrote 'it bores me that there should be so many empty minds, so many empty lives in Britain to sustain this fatuous industry; that no one should have the wit to laugh it into extinction or the honesty to resist it.' When Malcolm Muggeridge stuck his oar in, in articles in the *New Statesman* and the New York *Saturday Evening Post*, he was suspended from the BBC.

The Duke of Edinburgh, who had come to loathe the press, operates at the best of times on a fairly short fuse. Behind the scenes, the Queen Mother found herself pouring oil on troubled waters, to calm her son-in-law and reassure her daughter. She had by now been a member of the Royal Family for 34 years. Without her string of public appearances and her whimsical comments on the passing scene at home it might have been more difficult for the Queen and her husband to weather the early criticisms of the Queen's presentation (her voice was embarrassingly high pitched and upper-crust) and of the Duke's prolonged forays abroad without her, of the expenditure on cars and trains, aeroplanes and yachts, banquets and holidays, criticisms which amounted to a questioning of Britain's post-war role. The Suez debacle of 1957 was another blow to the morale of a nation whose entire raison d'être had been transformed by economic decline and loss of Empire. If the monarchy was to remain a stabilising agency at the service of a nation deeply ambiguous about itself, it clearly needed to do more than act as part of the constitution. It needed to become more popular without becoming vulgar. But few monarchs are ever truly popular until they are old.

The Queen Mother realised the Queen had yet to establish herself, and that what she needed was a bulwark between herself and her critics, a mother-figure who could float serenely above the boredom of royal chores, leaving the Queen to her boxes and audiences. She decided to go on tour.

She had made her first solo visit overseas in October 1954 when she flew to the United States, accepting a cheque at the Waldorf-Astoria representing funds donated in memory of the King. At Columbia University, where she received an honorary doctorate, she was told she was 'a noble queen, whose quiet and constant courage in time of great stress sustained a nation and inspired a world.' By the time she had toured the Metropolitan Museum of Art, been received by Congress, requested the band to play 'Hernando's Hideaway' at a ball and gone shopping for a magnetic bottle opener she had New York at her feet.

Intoxicated by her success, by the knowledge that she was no longer dependent on a king by her side and, conversely, that she conveyed even greater sexual allure now that she was a single woman again, she decided to dazzle millions of her daughter's Commonwealth subjects face to face, adorned in Hartnell creations and priceless jewellery. The total itinerary is fairly breathtaking. She has been to Rhodesia and Nyasaland twice, to Southern Rhodesia four times. Canada has received no fewer than nine visits. In 1958 she undertook a strenuous tour of Australia. The next year she was received at the Vatican by Pope John XXIII. New Zealand, Fiji and Honolulu have twice played host to Queen Elizabeth. Despite her aversion to Germany, the Army of the Rhine was eventually inspected, for the Queen Mother is particularly fond of visiting the 18 regiments of which she is Colonel in Chief. Where else? Tunisia and Sardinia, Jamaica and the Caribbean, Kenya and Uganda, Cyprus and Iran, Venice and Paris. Helicopters hold no terrors for the Queen Mother, so that visits to Northern Ireland became almost routine. Denmark and Holland received her. Between 1958 and 1985 the Queen Mother made at least half a dozen private visits overseas and some 30 official ones.

A large part of the Queen Mother's successful renaissance was due to the distance she placed between herself and the reigning court at Buckingham Palace. Relations between the Queen Mother and her daughters have always been symbiotic, and Clarence House developed not as a rival court but as a magnet for clever and amusing people, actors, writers, dancers and painters. A large part of her success was also due to an illusion she was able to foster that in every tiresome aspect of life she was non-partisan. Politics, racial discrimination, rearmament, world poverty, these were all somehow subjects on which not only was she not expected to express an opinion, she was not expected to hold one.

Another contributing factor to the image she was building up, of the innocent abroad, the spreader of goodwill to all men, was the feeling of reassurance which old age, and hence presumed wisdom, can convey – the feeling that she constituted a fixed focal point in an otherwise insecure and uncertain world. Hence there were shock waves of horror when a rumour was floated that she contemplated marrying her Treasurer, Sir Arthur Penn. She could, in theory, have remarried, but as Lady Penn the perimeters of her life would have narrowed somewhat. Her revenues from the Civil List would have stopped. Her tenure of Clarence House, Birkhall and the Royal Lodge would in all probability have been withdrawn. And invitations to patronise over 300 organisations of one sort or another, ranging from the Injured Jockies Fund to the Church Army, would have dried up. At all events, it was rather an uninspired rumour; Sir Arthur, like so many gentlemen of the Queen Mother's Household, was not of an inclination to marry.

Until she donned the mantle of Queen Mother, Queen Elizabeth was perceived by the public as the charming companion of the King, but not as an icon in her own right. As she grew older she carefully cultivated habits and activities that peculiarly appeal to the English, who are, on the whole, much more fond of flowers and animals than they are of children. Hence the annual traipse round the Chelsea Flower Show and the visits to Holloway and Finsbury to congratulate the proud owners of neat front gardens on their awards. Before the Second World War, the Royal Lodge was a canine refuge. Golden retrievers and labradors shared the royal retreat with a cocker spaniel, a couple of corgies and a Tibetan lion dog. One of the original corgies, Dookie, bit Lord Lothian. At Windsor, in more recent years, another of the Queen Mother's corgies committed the unforgivable indiscretion of killing one of the Queen's dogs.

'Why Queen Elizabeth ever had corgies I can't imagine,' says one of her ladies-in-waiting. 'I don't like them myself, although the two she's got now are rather nice.'[3] But by and large it is the Queen who is perceived as a dog-lover, aeroplane-loads of corgies following the itinerant royal calendar. The Queen Mother decided to become identified far more with the turf, the one sport participated in and approved of by every class. Starting in a very modest way as an owner, by the mid-sixties the Queen Mother had 15 horses in training, and by 1993 she had chalked up 400 winners. She has achieved three racing hat tricks, one at Sandown Park on January 1967, which she watched on television in hospital having undergone what in the *1978 Country Life Book of Queen Elizabeth the Queen Mother* Godfrey Talbot coyly refers to as 'a major abdominal operation'. It was in fact a colostomy.

The Queen Mother had already received the ultimate sporting loser accolade from the public, when disaster overtook Devon Loch in the 1956 Grand National. Running in the Queen Mother's colours of Strathmore pale blue, buff stripes, pale blue sleeves and black cap with gold tassel, Devon Loch looked a certain and overwhelmingly popular winner. Racing for home he suddenly stopped still, and virtually did the splits. A silence of disbelief descended on Aintree. The first person to pull herself together was the Queen Mother, who hid her bitter disappointment and went straight to the enclosure to congratulate the winner and commiserate with her own jockey, Dick Francis, to whom she afterwards sent a generous cheque and a beautiful silver cigarette case engraved with her signature. It was, thought one of those thousands of bemused spectators, Harold Nicolson, 'the most perfect display of dignity' he had ever seen.

Only days after undergoing a general anaesthetic in 1993, the Queen Mother insisted on attending the Derby. Indeed, very little will keep her away from a race meeting. However much she may be enjoying her after-luncheon glass of port, the Off will find her at the window of the Stewards' dining room, transfixed with her binoculars. Not all her Household share this enthusiasm, however. After lunch one day, bored with the topic of horse racing, a lady-in-waiting actually dropped off to sleep.

In 1954 the Queen Mother entered academia, accepting the post of Chancellor of London University. (From 1967 to 1977 she was the first Chancellor of the University of Dundee.) As London's first woman Chancellor, the Queen Mother served the University for a quarter of a century. She spent an inordinate amount of time, at both official and informal occasions, with the students. At a party for students given at Clarence House she was asked for her opinion on Watergate. 'If I were the President,' she mused, as though about to come out with some astounding words of wisdom, 'I think I should look in the bag.' What the remark meant no one has ever fathomed.

When she arrived at the University Church of Christ the King in Gordon Square, Bloomsbury, in 1974 she passed through glass doors which were held open by two American students in unaccustomed morning dress. (One of the young men had fitted himself out for the occasion for £5 at a jumble sale.) Looking spectacular herself in black, for she was in mourning for the Duke of Gloucester, she delayed the procession a moment by going back to say, 'You've added such an air of distinction to the occasion.' Because of the Duke's death there had been some doubt whether the Queen Mother would fulfil the engagement, which was a service for the Royal Free Hospital Medical School. Rejoining the procession, and chatting to the chaplain, the Reverend Victor Stock, she mentioned how she and Princess Alice had been the first two commoners to marry into the Royal Family, and how the Duke's death had brought back to her memories of the Abdication. 'Then,' Father Stock recalls, 'she shed a tear, so I gave her a little hug. "Which way do we go?" she asked. "Left, Ma'am," I said. "No we don't, we go right," the Queen Mother corrected me, very fiercely and firmly. She had never been in the building before but she knew perfectly well what she had to do! By this time *I'd* gone completely to pieces!'[4]

The Queen Mother generally presided each year over two degree presentations, which could take up to two and a half hours, and in 1974 and 1977 they developed into family affairs, when she conferred honorary doctorates on Prince Charles and her Private Secretary, Sir Martin Gilliat. In 1979, opening the University's new library, she quoted Ruskin – not entirely to her own advantage. 'Ruskin,' she recalled, 'in a lecture once made the somewhat stern observation: "What do we, as a nation, care about books? How much do you think we spend altogether on our libraries, public or private, as compared with what we spend on our *horses*?"'

Apart from her one big operation, most of the Queen Mother's physical afflictions have been minor and self-inflicted, caused in the main by an unfortunate habit of stumbling. In the same year that Devon Loch came to grief his owner fell at Clarence House. In 1960 she sustained an injury to her leg at the Royal Lodge, and the next year fell at the Castle during an Ascot Week house party. This time she broke a bone in her foot, and managed to break it again by stumbling at Birkhall the following year. In 1981 she ran the risk of missing Prince Charles's wedding when she again stumbled, at Ascot Race Course, and ran a temperature as a result. The most dangerous misadventure occurred during dinner at the Royal Lodge when she was 82. A bone had found its way into the fish mayonnaise, and accompanied by Princess Margaret the Queen Mother motored to London to have the bone removed from her throat under anaesthetic. There was a recurrence of a throat blockage ten years later, at Birkhall. This was the occasion when the Queen Mother spent a few nights at the Aberdeen Infirmary which she and the Duke of York had opened in 1936.

One reason the Queen Mother dislikes ill health or injury is because she is fiercely independent and resents the need to be offered a helping hand. 'She is,' Lady Elizabeth Basset has remarked, 'a very private person.'[5] This aspect of her character extends not just to unnecessary physical contact but to a seeming need to keep little secrets to herself. It also, very conveniently, enables the Queen Mother to avoid involving herself in unpleasant family entanglements which, were it not for the fact that she had married into the Royal Family, would never have come to light.

A Strathmore niece, Anne Anson, daughter of John Bowes-Lyon, was divorced in 1948, and although it was to Prince Georg of Denmark that she was remarried two years later, the Queen Mother refused to go to the wedding. 'She didn't disapprove,' the Archbishop of Canterbury, Geoffrey Fisher, told James Pope-Hennessy, 'but she wouldn't go. Didn't want to get muddled up in it, if you see what I mean.'[6] Her attitude to life, according to Dr Fisher, was 'to make everything as easy as possible'. He added: 'She's a profoundly religious woman, mind you, profoundly religious.' At a kindly, personal level the Queen Mother was not prepared to be uncharitable, but publicly she would not be seen reneging on the stand she had taken over remarriage in 1936. It was a stand she was going to have to alter very considerably when her granddaughter the Princess Royal remarried in 1992.

In 1950 Lady Nancy Bowes-Lyon, sister of the 16th Earl, was divorced, getting remarried in 1954 even while Princess Margaret and Peter Townsend were enduring their enforced separation. In 1967 a nephew by marriage, the Earl of Harewood, 18th in line to the throne, was divorced, and shortly afterwards married Patricia Tuckwell, by whom he already had a son. Harewood's brother Gerald Lascelles divorced too. By the time a royal nephew, Prince Michael of Kent, married a divorcée in 1978 the past was looking distinctly foggy. No one suggested that Princess Michael was unfit to take the automatic appellation Royal Highness. On this as on so many other matters, the Queen Mother remains inscrutable.

Apart from failed marriages there were renewed family tragedies for the Queen Mother to ignore. Her brother Patrick, the 15th Earl, became a recluse. His heir, Timothy, became an alcoholic. When he married a nurse at the home where he was undergoing treatment, the Queen Mother ignored his wedding. The bride was a Roman Catholic.

In 1959 the new Lady Strathmore gave birth to a baby girl, who died at the age of three weeks. Eight years later, the Countess committed suicide. Queen Elizabeth at least sent a wreath, but there was no further contact until she attended Timothy's funeral in 1972. Whether, had she not married into the Royal Family, the Queen Mother would have kept in closer contact with her own family we shall never know. It does seem that commitment to the House of Windsor became a full-time consideration, to the almost total exclusion of her Strathmore relations. Yet the problems they caused her were to prove a mere bagatelle compared to the later antics of her grandchildren.

The first grandchild born to the Queen Mother, Prince Charles, created Prince of Wales and a Knight of the Garter at the ludicrously early age of nine, became so close to her that she has been blinded to his faults. As with her brother-in-law King Edward VIII, she has found a scapegoat for them. That scapegoat is his wife, the Princess of Wales. It would have been natural for the Queen Mother to have hoped to produce an heir to her husband's dukedom; even more natural for her to have regretted not producing a male heir to the throne. But Princess Elizabeth's birth had been by Caesarian section, and Princess Margaret kept the Home Secretary waiting two weeks and was presumably born late. The Queen Mother is not a particularly maternal person, and children as such have never been of much interest to her. It is often the case with women who have found it difficult to cuddle their own children that they compensate by extending physical and emotional affection to their grandchildren. This the Queen Mother has done most conspicuously in the case of Prince Charles, a boy who was himself denied physically affectionate parents. He was four before he even spent a birthday with his father.

Had Bertie lived, there is no doubt he would have exercised enormous influence over the education and training of Prince Charles. But with Lord Mountbatten, whose ambitions and judgements the Queen Mother deeply suspected, trying to exercise a strong influence over Prince Philip, and with Philip so often away from home and the Queen tied up with official duties and overseas tours, the Queen Mother stepped into the breach. Here in any case was a ready-made little boy to spoil, the perfect substitute for a son of her own. There were also a great many reasons why Charles could ease the early pain of bereavement, for in so many ways he reminded the Queen Mother of Bertie. Like Bertie, he had few friends. Indeed, before he married, his two closest friends, for he saw more of them than anyone else, were his personal detectives. Like Bertie, he liked dancing. He even had the courage to hunt – as Bertie had done. In the case of Charles, this required a strangely inverted moral courage, for it was a provocative act in defiance of a large chunk of public opinion. But the Queen Mother approved, for she cares very little for public opinion, and is scarcely in touch with it.

When Charles was five his parents were abroad at Christmas, and in fact left their already emotionally deprived son with his grandmother for six months. No wonder he began, like his great-uncle David, to develop an attachment to older women. A more satisfactory result of his grandmother's influence was his attachment to the Christian religion, in view of the fact that, again like Bertie, his destiny was to become Supreme Governor of the Church of England.

The Queen Mother quite simply saw Charles as the heir to the throne she had done so much to stabilise. What she imbued him with above all else was her own conservative instincts. Charles may have spent much time and energy proving his masculinity by leaping out of aeroplanes and playing polo, but, unlike his great-uncle, he is no radical. Like his grandmother, he likes to surround himself with a conservative Household, looking no further for a private secretary on one occasion than the son of his mother's private secretary – who was none other than the grandson of George V's private secretary.

As a boy, Prince Charles would always dash to sit beside his grandmother on picnics, and even now, according to one of the Queen Mother's ladies-in-waiting, 'he comes to see her on every possible occasion.'[7] There was not much to gladden the eye at home except inherited gilt Empire furniture, and the Prince, the nearest to an intellectual the Royal Family has produced by birth or marriage since Prince Albert, has always needed a bolt hole. The Royal Lodge provided just that. The Queen Mother realised that, far from needing to be toughened up by being sent to his father's old school, Gordonstoun, which he loathed, Prince Charles required a great deal of affection, sympathy and support. All of this she has supplied. Under her tuition he learned to paint, to play the 'cello and to love, in particular, the music of Elgar. He succeeded the Queen Mother as president of the Royal College of Music. Above all else, the Queen Mother's most positive contribution to the development of the Prince of Wales was to instil in him a sense of duty. When the Prince implored his grandmother to intercede with his parents and have him released from Gordonstoun she refused, saying that instead she would help him to endure something he found unpleasant.

In 1978 Prince Charles wrote, in a Foreword to *The Country Life*

Book of the Queen Mother, 'Ever since I can remember, my grandmother has been the most wonderful example of fun, laughter, warmth, infinite security . . . For me she has always been one of those extraordinarily rare people whose touch can turn everything to gold.' It may seem odd that a 29-year-old man with an immense fortune, plenty of servants and as much food and drink as any reasonable human being could wish to consume should need a Midas in his midst, but the word 'security' is the key to the Prince's sentiments.

If one was drawing a graph to demonstrate the rise and fall of the modern monarchy's popularity, mid-Victorian England would have seen a very low dip, with open talk of Republicanism. As Queen Victoria grew older, more mellow and more respected, the needle began to rise, and remained at a steady level throughout the reigns of Edward VII and George V. With the shock of the Abdication there was a sudden dip, but recovery was soon under way, and by the time the King and Queen had emerged from war to victory in 1945 the Royal Family had never been more popular or adulated. This was the situation that pertained until in 1957 there was a major reaction against the Court, when the graph took a sudden nose dive. Between 1957 and 1977, the year of the Queen's Silver Jubilee, popularity was gradually and steadily restored, and remained high on the graph until in 1992 a kind of collective mad cow disease gripped the younger members of the family, and the monarchy itself became derided. The watershed in the family's fortunes was 1981, the year of the marriage of the heir to the throne.

This is not to say that life has been lived on an even keel between the highs and lows of popularity. An obvious blip to appear on the graph was the Queen's unfortunate decision in 1966 to postpone a visit to Abafan. Had the Queen Mother still been queen she would have gone in a flash, seeing the disaster as akin to wartime bombing. But for better or worse she has always hesitated to telephone advice to her daughter, whose private secretary is paid to make sure she reacts to outside events as she should.

It may be assumed that by 1965 the Queen Mother believed the vigilance she had exercised over the return to England of the Duke and Duchess of Windsor as permanent residents could safely be relaxed. That year the Duke entered the London Clinic. After he had undergone a second operation on his eyes, the Queen called to see him, meeting at the same time the aunt she had not clapped eyes on since she was a little girl. It is inconceivable that the Queen would have made this gesture of goodwill without informing her mother of her intentions, and presumably the Queen Mother did no more than shrug her shoulders. The Queen, after all, was not going to receive the Duchess formally. The two women were merely to meet on neutral territory, and chat about the Duke's health. The Queen Mother herself was still quite prepared to discuss the Abdication – she had done so in 1962, with Noël Coward – but by now the subject had slipped into historical perspective.

The year before, when the Duke underwent open-heart surgery in New York, the Queen had sent him a telegram to commemorate his 70th birthday. The heavens had not fallen in. This was not to say the Queen was feeling her way towards rescinding the Letters Patent of 1937. To have done so would have been tantamount to admitting that her father (and in effect her mother and grandmother) had made a mistake.

By this time, in any case, the Duke had virtually given up all hope of his wife being officially accorded the title Royal Highness. His mind, as ever, was concentrated on money. In 1968 he procured the Queen's agreement to a pension of £5,000 a year for the Duchess after his death – not that she needed it. By now the Duke was a very rich man, living in luxury in Paris. If ever the Duchess had found herself short of funds she would only have needed to sell a few of the fabulous pieces of jewellery he had given her over the years. 'Mrs Simpson was literally smothered in rubies,' Chips Channon had noted in his diary as early as 27 July 1936.

An opportunity for the Queen to ease the situation of the Duke and Duchess socially, however, did occur in 1967, when she invited them both to attend the unveiling of a plaque outside Marlborough House to mark the centenary of the birth of Queen Mary. This invitation to the Duchess to accompany the Duke at a public ceremony was as good as acknowledging that the Duchess was a member of the family, if only a morganatic member.[8] Even more significantly, the Queen Mother was to be present, and was scheduled to meet the Duchess as well. It was a strategic moment in the long drawn-out war of attrition, and one which the Queen Mother seems to have fluffed. The Duchess curtsied to the Queen but not to the Queen Mother. But she was given no encouragement to do so, and under the circumstances she needed some encouragement, a quid pro quo at least. The Duke bowed to the Queen Mother, kissed her hand and was embraced by his sister-in-law. Had the Queen Mother, on extending her hand to the Duchess, done her the courtesy of kissing her too (she had just kissed her husband, and the Duchess was, whether she liked it or not, her sister-in-law) there can be little doubt the Duchess would automatically have completed the greeting by curtseying. The truth is, she was snubbed, although in fairness to the Queen Mother it could be argued that she doubted whether the Duchess would curtsey, and was not prepared to be snubbed herself – especially in full view of the world's press. Having agreed to this brief meeting in public the Queen Mother had done her duty whatever transpired. Afterwards she and the Queen and Prince Philip went to the Derby, leaving the Duchess of Kent to give the Windsors lunch at Kensington Palace.

In 1969 the Queen invited the Duke of Windsor to attend the investiture of Prince Charles as Prince of Wales (the first investiture since the Duke's in 1911), an imaginative and appropriate thought on her part; but she did not extend the invitation to the Duchess. 'I have hesitated to enquire whether you would like an invitation considering the circumstances,' the Queen wrote to her uncle on 26 February 1969, 'but if you would reply to this indirect form of invitation in whatever way you feel, I shall quite understand.' He declined, by saying he did not think his presence would add much to the 'colourful' proceedings. The Queen invited him to a public ceremony again a few weeks later, when new Garter windows were due to be dedicated in St George's Chapel, Windsor. The Duchess was not specifically included in the invitation, and once again the Duke declined. 'You see,' he patiently explained to his niece, 'after more than thirty years of happy married life, I do not like to attend these occasions alone.' All such a mild rebuke required was a letter from the Queen saying of course your wife will be welcome. The only conclusion that can be drawn is that the Queen had persuaded her mother to make one, and only one, symbolic gesture of reconciliation with the Duchess; a resolve that remained absolute until the year of the Duke's death.

At one time, the Duke of Windsor considered being buried in Baltimore. Later, he suggested he and his wife should emulate Victoria and Albert by having a special mausoleum erected for themselves at Frogmore. In 1968 the Duchess of Kent pulled out of a garden party the Queen and Prince Philip gave for the Lambeth Conference, for she was beginning to suffer the fatal consequences of a brain tumour. When the Duke came to England for her funeral he decided it would be nicer if he and his wife ended up with the rest of those members of the family not interred in St George's Chapel, and asked the Queen if he might change his mind. In August 1970 she agreed to both the Duke and Duchess being buried behind Queen Victoria's hideous mausoleum, and not a moment too soon. Inoperable cancer of the throat was diagnosed in 1971. The Duke faced the end with dignity and courage. In May 1972, while the Queen was in Paris, she called on her uncle to bid him farewell. By manipulating the drip that was keeping him alive he managed, with heroic determination, to receive the Queen standing, for he intended to bow. The Duchess curtsied to the Queen as she said goodbye at the door. Nine days later, the Duke of Windsor died.

The RAF having collected the Duke's body, which lay for a night in the Albert Memorial Chapel at Windsor and for two days in St George's Chapel, the Queen then sent an aircraft of the Queen's Flight to Paris to fetch the Duchess, who was met at Heathrow by Lord Mountbatten, and escorted to Buckingham Palace where she stayed. Peeping from behind a partly drawn curtain, the Duchess watched the Queen ride out to attend the Trooping the Colour on Horse Guards Parade. Meanwhile, 57,000 people (the population of a large market town) were filing past the Duke's coffin to pay their last respects. By the day of the funeral the grass in front of St George's was knee-deep in wreaths. On the 35th anniversary of her wedding day the Duchess drove from Buckingham Palace to Windsor Castle where, escorted by her 23-year-old great-nephew, the Prince of Wales, she quietly slipped into the Chapel. The service, held on 5 June, was a unique historical occasion, with the Queen present at the funeral of her penultimate predecessor. Also there was the Queen Mother, veiled and bejewelled, solicitous towards her newly widowed sister-in-law, thankful that she still had all her wits about her. The Duchess, by contrast, was clearly tranquillised. 'There was no love lost between Queen Elizabeth and the Duchess' a member of the Queen Mother's Household has remarked. 'Although the reason there was no friction at the Duke's funeral was because by that time the poor Duchess was rather losing her marbles.'[9]

After a sombre lunch the funeral cortege drove off to Frogmore, where the Duke was laid to rest in his great-grandmother's favourite garden. Fourteen years later, having suffered from paranoia, senile dementia and eventually a prolonged and gruesome death, the Duchess was laid beside him, insulted in death as she had been in life, her rightful title Royal Highness even now withheld from the inscription on her grave.[10]

There was drama of a theatrical nature in store for the Queen Mother. Barely five months after the Duke of Windsor's funeral the Queen Mother found herself depicted, as Duchess of York, in a play at the Theatre Royal, Haymarket, called *Crown Matrimonial*. Although much of the dialogue put into her mouth was pretty smug, the actress who played the Duchess of York, Amanda Reiss, who was not exactly a star at the start of the run, received thunderous applause when she appeared. She looked amazingly like the Queen Mother when young, and audiences refused to suspend their disbelief, preferring to pass a judgement on the real Queen Mother's public performance, which reached its zenith, so far as the Duchess of Windsor was concerned, in October 1976. While staying at the British Embassy in Paris the Queen Mother sent two dozen red roses to the ailing Duchess, with a note that read 'In Friendship'.[11] She had no idea, of course, that after staying with the Windsors in 1958 James Pope-Hennessy had noted that the Duchess reserved a particular facial contortion for speaking about her. It seemed to him, he wrote, 'akin to frenzy'.[12]

10

Frustrated and Furious

WITH THE BIRTH IN 1977 of Peter Philips, Princess Anne's first child, Queen Elizabeth the Queen Mother became a great-grandmother. She already had six grandchildren and was to become a great-grandmother half a dozen times also. But her eldest grandchild, the Prince of Wales, seemed to show no inclination for marriage. 'The first duty of an heir to the throne is to ensure the succession,' Philip Ziegler writes in his life of Edward VIII.[1] That may be right in principle, but Prince Charles was well aware there was by now no shortage of heirs to the throne in direct succession to his grandfather, King George VI. There were his two brothers and his sister, his sister's son, and his aunt Princess Margaret and her two children. It scarcely mattered if he did not marry at all. And after all, had not his guru, Earl Mountbatten, told Charles, when he was 25, to 'sow his wild oats' and have as many affairs as he could before settling down with a 'suitable, attractive and sweet-charactered girl *before* she met anyone else she might fall for'.[2] This must have seemed like sound male chauvinistic advice, because it perfectly suited the character of the heir to the throne. Brought up since birth to snap his fingers and expect anything he desired to be delivered on the spot, Prince Charles correctly read into his great-uncle's advice the message that no matter how many women he slept with, the one chosen for his ultimate bride must be a virgin.

By the time he had sown his wild oats, or thought he had, he was in his thirties, and contemporary virgins were becoming somewhat thin on the ground; hence he had increasingly to look over his shoulder for a wife, for someone a good deal younger than himself. This, after all, was the fourth quarter of the twentieth-century, not the first, the era his grandmother the Queen Mother had grown up in. There could be no guarantee that even a young woman of 22 or 23, eligible in every other way to be queen consort one day, would still be a virgin on her wedding night.

The year 1979, however, which saw the Queen Mother become the first woman to be appointed Warden of the Cinque Ports, witnessed also the gruesome removal of Lord Mountbatten from any influence over the Prince of Wales. Together with his 83-year-old mother-in-law, the Dowager Lady Brabourne, one of his grandsons, Nicholas Knatchbull, and a young Irish friend, Paul Maxwell, Mountbatten was blown up by the IRA. Mountbatten had been nursing perfectly reasonable hopes that his granddaughter Amanda Knatchbull would marry Charles. The Queen Mother approved, but she and Mountbatten had not always seen eye to eye, and his death now left her in sole receipt of her grandson's confidences, in particular in relation to his girlfriends. The Queen Mother told one of Prince Philip's biographers, Tim Heald, 'We always took Dickie with a pinch of salt.'³ And one of the Queen Mother's Household has remarked, 'I don't think the family miss Mountbatten. They admired him, but only Prince Charles was fond of him. I wouldn't say that he was tremendously popular with the Royal Family. Like Edward VIII, he too had rather a dual personality. The Queen Mother's influence on the training of Prince Charles was far greater than that of Mountbatten.'⁴ The fact remains however that Charles had never known his paternal grandfather and could scarcely recall his mother's father, and he regarded Lord Mountbatten not so much as a great-uncle as an honorary grandfather. 'I have no idea what we shall do without you when you finally decide to depart. It doesn't bear thinking about,' Charles had told Mountbatten less than a year before the Earl's assassination.⁵

In 1978 Princess Margaret's marriage came to an end, and she took up very publicly with a much younger man, Roddy Llewellyn. But neither that unfortunate occurrence, nor even the murder of Lord Mountbatten, was permitted to mar the celebrations in August 1980. It was the Queen Mother's 80th birthday, and the *Daily Mail* announced, 'She is much more than everyone's lovable old granny. She is a woman of greatness whose wholly beneficial influence upon our history ought to be acknowledged.' For a Service of Thanksgiving at St Paul's Cathedral on 15 July the Queen accorded her mother a singular honour, providing her with a Sovereign's escort of the Household Cavalry. She rode not from Clarence House but from Buckingham Palace, in a state landau accompanied by Prince Charles, to be received at the Cathedral by the Queen and Prince Philip. After the service she again took precedence, leaving first. It was a unique occasion and one the London crowds enjoyed to the full. There was a spontaneous realisation that the Queen Mother was not just the Queen Mum, a figure of some fun to those who believe she is permanently tipsy or hires a double to smile and wave into her ninth decade, but a remarkable link with great historical events, someone who rises above the squabbles of party politics and the squalid murders committed by heartless terrorists. Forty-five years before, it had occurred to Lady Furness, as it has to many since, that if ever she had to live 'in a bungalow in a small town' the Duchess of York was the woman she would most like as a next-door neighbour.[6] The reception the Queen Mother received wherever she went during the year of her 80th birthday confirmed a bond she seemed to have forged in an effortless way between herself and 'ordinary' people. She remains the only member of the Royal Family who has been placed by taxi drivers and judges alike beyond normal criticism. That bond, forged by an amalgam of dignity and fun, which are perhaps the hallmarks of the Queen Mother's public appearances, has now become epitomised by the ritual of her birthday, when no one attempts to upstage the children who gather outside Clarence House to hand her flowers and cards, and the band marches past playing 'She Must Have Been a Beautiful Baby'.

On the 80th birthday itself the Speaker of the House of Commons acknowledged the debt the nation owed the Queen Mother for the loving care with which she had nurtured the Royal Family. In her reply to both Houses of Parliament, the Queen Mother recalled how, during the war, 'The King and I, on our visits round the country, were sustained and inspired by the steadfastness, courage and compassion shown by our people.' She said it was encouraging 'to find today that, in our schools and universities and among the younger generation these same qualities live on'. She added that she felt deeply grateful to have been given the opportunity 'to serve our beloved country in some small way', and characteristically she added, twisting her grammar as royalty often do, 'I have been always helped and uplifted by the love of my family, the loyalty and understanding of our people, and by my faith in Almighty God.'

Writing an obituary for the *Independent* in 1993 of the Queen Mother's Private Secretary, Sir Martin Gilliat, Sir Edward Ford described the Queen Mother as 'perhaps the most loved person in the Western world'. Maybe the Queen Mother's patent adherence to orthodox Christianity is one of the explanations for her massive popularity. The majority of people do not go to church on Sunday or believe in God, but they like someone else to do so for them. Then there is her indomitability. Physical infirmity can overtake a million-aire in middle age, and no amount of luxurious cushioning can account for the Queen Mother's stamina. Years after the age at which Queen Mary had taken to a wheelchair the Queen Mother was striding around, only beginning to walk somewhat unsteadily in her 92nd year due to a painful knee. Years after the age at which the Queen had succumbed to wearing glasses (she once had to abandon a speech because she could not find her spectacles) the Queen Mother still refuses to be seen wearing reading glasses, using them at home but in public having her speeches written out in very large capital letters. At the age of 93 she was acting as a Counsellor of State in the absence of the Queen overseas.

'Performing public engagements, continuing her duties, has become such a habit with her that she can't stop,' remarked a former member of King George VI's Household, still active in royal affairs. 'She has a great sense of what people expect of her and she's not going to let them down.'[7] On one occasion, having cracked a bone in her foot, she launched the 22,000-ton *Northern Star* at Newcastle-upon-Tyne in a wheelchair. There was another occasion, in 1983, when she was due to tour an old soldiers' home; she had influenza and had not eaten for some time, and although her Household tried to persuade her to cancel the engagement she insisted on going ahead. As usual, she stayed longer than expected, and on her return home, as she got out of the car, she said to Lady Elizabeth Basset, 'There, you see, you *can* do it!'

'Queen Elizabeth doesn't believe in being ill at all,' according to another member of her Household. 'She is interested in homoeopathy but is very anti-pills. She only takes painkillers or antibiotics when it is absolutely necessary.' While her eyesight is no longer brilliant, her bearing remains formidable, allied as it is with an ability to concentrate on someone she is speaking to while listening at dinner to everything being said around her.

Some extremely rude comments were made about the Queen Mother's clothes when she was younger. 'Her Majesty's clothes . . . are still something of a problem,' *Time* magazine informed its readers in 1941. 'Compared to her fashion-plate sister-in-law, Marina, Duchess of Kent, Elizabeth looks like a middle-aged matron.' The magazine put this down to the lack of a French maid. The truth is, the Queen Mother has never been fashion conscious and resolutely has presented herself to the public as she is, very small and, in middle-age, prone to tubbiness because she adores food and drink. Apart from an occasional game of tennis when first married, she is not best known for taking exercise. Walking her dogs after a picnic hardly counts. 'She's not really interested in clothes,' a friend of many years reports. 'They bore her to bits. I think she has been very sensible just to dress in a style that suits her, and the public have come to identify her with the chiffon and tulle. That's the Queen Mother! As for her stamina, she is very, very tiny and I think if you're small it's easier to stand for a long time, because you haven't got such a long back.'

That stamina is truly astonishing. In 1991 the Queen Mother undertook 100 engagements. In 1992, at the age of 92, she undertook 91. Like Queen Alexandra, the Queen Mother is renowned for unpunctuality, but unpunctuality of a different kind. 'If you don't come now you won't get crowned!' Edward VII bellowed up the stairs as he paced up and down waiting for Queen Alexandra to emerge on the day of their coronation. The Queen Mother's unpunctuality takes the form not of arriving late but of leaving engagements, both private and public, long behind schedule, simply because she refuses to be rushed and wants to make sure she has spoken to as many people as possible. This unhurried approach to her duties has become a firm part of the legend that guarantees her popularity. 'The great thing about the Queen Mother,' in the opinion of Lady Hambleden, still in attendance after 57 years, 'is that she's so interested in people. She likes people. If she goes to the theatre she'll always take a peep in at the box office. She's never bored, because she always finds something interesting or amusing, and this enjoyment of life is very infectious. She enjoys her outings, and she communicates that enjoyment. She finds her job very rewarding, and people instinctively realise and appreciate this. You are never bored when you are with her, because she always has something amusing or interesting to say. And in 50 years I've only once seen her cross. And then she wasn't really cross. Someone hadn't opened a door or something! Normally she never loses her bait. Never. She's very serene.'[8] Asked if the Queen Mother was easy to chivvy along, another lady-in-waiting said, 'No! Even if we're running late she pays no attention whatsoever!'

Sometimes the Queen Mother does set out for an engagement late, perhaps because she has given a large lunch party and the guests have been reluctant to depart, but she usually catches up with the schedule. It is not always her fault when she doesn't. One day she attended the reconsecration of a church. In attendance was Lady Elizabeth Basset. The vicar was supposed to preach for ten minutes but went on at inordinate length, which meant they left late for the next engagement. They only managed to catch up by staying for one course of a delicious lunch. Passing through numerous villages the car slowed down so that the Queen Mother could wave. But between villages, the chauffeur put his foot down hard and Lady Elizabeth found herself sitting on the floor of the car beside the Queen Mother. Both were convulsed with laughter.

Laughing together is something the Queen Mother and Lady Elizabeth Basset do a good deal of. 'What sets her off? It could be anything. That's what's so delightful. There was a very funny book by a circuit judge she had in Scotland, called *A Case of Bananas*, and we read it alternately to each other with the tears pouring down our cheeks. And of course, Prince Charles and the Queen Mother set each other off.'[9]

The Queen Mother's taste in literature is extremely catholic – she greatly enjoys P. G. Wodehouse – and forms one of her shared interests with Lady Elizabeth. In 1973 the Queen Mother contributed a Foreword to an anthology compiled by Lady Elizabeth, *Love is my Meaning: An Anthology of Assurance*.[10] 'We live in a world of unusually rapid change,' the Queen Mother wrote. 'It is no wonder, therefore, that thinking and sensitive people want to know what is fundamentally changeless. It is my hope and belief that this book can help to assure us that we can, at one and the same time, be truly contemporary men and women *and* have our thoughts and lives rooted in truths that do not change. Moreover, for many of us it is difficult to convey at all clearly the faith and hope that is in us. I am sure, therefore, that those who read this anthology will find expressed in the pages what in our hearts we believe but find so hard to say.'

Lady Elizabeth believes the Queen Mother draws her own strength from 'a very strong faith, but a very private one'. This, she says, is how the Queen Mother rises above 'awful worries and illness, and family problems, and is always so cheerful on the surface'. Lady Elizabeth was in waiting soon after the Queen Mother's brother, David, died at Birkhall. 'When I left, Queen Elizabeth said she was sorry things had not been as cheerful as usual, but you would not have known. I suppose she's a very good actress. But how she does it I don't know. It's not that she doesn't feel.'

There are people – Lady Elizabeth Basset is one – who believe the Queen Mother possesses some kind of healing power. 'When you are with her,' Lady Elizabeth says, 'not only do you feel better, you are better. It's the most extraordinary thing. It's not just the aura of royalty rubbing off, it's something much deeper than that. However much you have made up your mind not to grumble about your own worries you find yourself telling her everything! She is such a marvellous confidante, and so wise.'

The Queen Mother has four regular women of the bedchamber, who go into waiting for a fortnight approximately every six weeks. Over a period of perhaps 40 or 50 years this has proved a massive commitment, only made possible in the early days by the ladies-in-waiting having nannies or compliant husbands, and in more recent years by their being widowed. The two ladies of the bedchamber attend the Queen Mother on special occasions, and there are extra women who may be called upon from time to time. There is no training to be a lady-in-waiting. At the time of her appointment in 1959 Lady Elizabeth Basset scarcely knew the Queen Mother, and the invitation came as a great surprise. 'You aren't told anything, really,' she says. 'You play it by ear.'

Although all the ladies hesitate to presume a friendship with the Queen Mother, they undoubtedly rank as personal friends in the Queen Mother's eyes. She is daily dependent on them for companionship, for help with correspondence and entertaining, and for sympathy when things go wrong. Asked if she would describe herself as a friend of the Queen Mother, Lady Elizabeth Basset said, 'She treats you as a friend. And we have enormous laughs. But at the same time you are very aware that she's the Queen Mother. The tradition is very important. You wouldn't take liberties at all. But at the same time she's tremendously approachable and a really wonderful person to serve. I really love her. Speaking of Lady Radnor in her old age, E. F. Benson said, "To be with her was like sitting in the sun." That always makes me think of Queen Elizabeth.'

The Queen Mother becomes more dependent on her Household the older she gets, for as they die or drop out she dreads having to replace them. When Lady Jean Rankin suggested some years ago it was about time she retired, the Queen Mother said, 'If you retire, I retire.' Appointed a woman of the bedchamber in 1946, Lady Jean has now been compelled to retire, for she is confined to a nursing home. Most of the remaining ladies find standing for lengthy ceremonies very tiring, but they feel that as long as the Queen Mother carries on, they must. 'Queen Elizabeth's idea of duty is what she calls *devoir*,' Lady Elizabeth Basset explains. 'I wouldn't think she'd ever let the side down in the smallest possible way.' Lady Elizabeth admits to being one of those who find the standing a strain, and Lady Hambleden is now much dependent on a stick, but still attends the Queen Mother whenever she feels up to it. In 1993 the Queen Mother lost two of her most faithful retainers, her Private Secretary for 37 years, Sir Martin Gilliat, who had been longing to retire but died in harness at the age of 80, and Ruth, Lady Fermoy, grandmother of the Princess of Wales, who was 85 and, like Sir Martin, had served the Queen Mother, as a lady-in-waiting, for 37 years. The most extraordinary achievement must be that of the Queen Mother's second cousin, Lady Victoria Wemyss, appointed in the first year of George VI's reign. She remains an extra woman of the bedchamber at the age of 103.

For secretaries, comptrollers and treasurers it has been almost a sine qua non that they be the non-marrying sort, for hours are long and unsociable, and duty may call them to Windsor or Scotland as well as Clarence House, and, in the past, they had to be available to accompany the Queen Mother on her world-wide peregrinations. But another explanation for the Queen Mother's preference for employing homosexuals, and her partiality for their company generally, may be discerned in the perceptive diaries of James Lees-Milne. After staying at Bury Farm, in June 1948, adjacent to the Queen Mother's childhood home in Hertfordshire, he drove the brother of whom she was so fond, David Bowes-Lyon, to London the following day, and noted, 'His conversation very strange. Did I think women's thighs ugly? Men's figures more aesthetic? Did I like wearing shorts? He did not disapprove of any sexual practices – and so on. Trying not to be too distant, I did not commit myself to any opinions. He must have found me either a dolt or a prude.'

Lees-Milne met David Bowes-Lyon again at a dinner party early in 1949, and recorded that he had been 'insinuating all sorts of forbidden things in veiled terms and proposing a trip with me in the spring. He is an extraordinary, complicated, buttoned, perhaps not so buttoned-up man who cannot call a spade a spade and is a walking riddle.' At the Chelsea Flower Show that year, Bowes-Lyon 'seemed keen that we should go on a motor tour in August. A curious man he is.'[11] The clear implication from these diary entries is that while David Bowes-Lyon may indeed have been curious, he was almost certainly bisexual, a fact which could well have become a commonplace to his sister, colouring for life her own laissez-faire attitude to personal sexual morals, which very much reflects the dictum of her near contemporary, Mrs Patrick Campbell: don't do it in the street and frighten the horses.

Behind the scenes the Queen Mother has always displayed her aristocratic upbringing. She never fails to thank the cook when she goes out to dinner, or the entire staff when she leaves a country house. On returning to Buckingham Palace from her 80th birthday Thanksgiving Service the first thing she did was to tell the groom the horses had gone beautifully – and then stood around trying to remember the name of one of the horses. 'Of course!' she exclaimed when the groom reminded her. She always thanks her chauffeur when she returns to Clarence House from an engagement. 'William and Reginald, her pages, would go out into the street and get run over if it suited her,' one of the ladies-in-waiting believes.

'She is not a rich woman,' says a seasoned royal biographer, David Duff.[12] Then he adds, 'judging by the standards of some Royalties.' Apart from the Dutch Royal Family it is hard to imagine which Royalties are better off than the British. And, even with assistance from the Civil List, it is difficult to comprehend how anyone who is not seriously rich can manage to run four homes. The Queen Mother draws £640,000 a year from the Civil List to meet her official expenses (cars, wages, clothes required for the job, donations to charities) and to enable her to live in a style thought appropriate for a queen dowager. Her private fortune is considerable. Yet it worries the public not one jot that she is materially well off. In matters of finance the Queen Mother has somehow escaped all public censure. Instead of pressing charges, the press and public prefer to fantasise, accusing her of those two socially acceptable foibles, drinking and gambling. But the Queen Mother never places a bet. So far as drink is concerned, she enjoys gin and loves champagne. She regards champagne as some people regard mineral water. She has been known to enjoy two glasses of white wine at a midday reception before driving off to a luncheon, where, whilst moving through a suite of rooms, she has sipped at least three separately prepared gin and Dubonnets before enjoying a glass of vintage champagne. At the same luncheon two glasses of white burgundy would seem normal, followed by a glass of claret. When offered a fine Château Yquem with the pudding, she exclaimed, 'Oh, no, I mustn't drink any more. I'll just have another glass of champagne, if that's agreeable.'

'Drink doesn't affect her one bit,' according to a member of the Queen Mother's Household. 'I mean, she can drink quite a lot, and it doesn't affect her in any way. Which is odd, as she eats very little now.'[13] This is not to say her guests are stinted. Her chef, Michael, is renowned for producing the best food at any royal table. Not for nothing does the Queen invariably remain at the Royal Lodge for lunch on Sunday after attending service with the Queen Mother at All Saints, next door. After the service Queen Elizabeth will sometimes invite the canon who has conducted the service for a pre-lunch drink.

He often finds it necessary to ring the doorbell twice, for the sound of the bell tends to be drowned by barking corgies. Then the door may well be opened by the Queen. In the drawing room the Queen Mother will ask what the canon would like to drink, and then ask the Queen to pour the drinks, from a trolley behind the door. 'The trouble is,' as one of the canons has remarked, 'the Queen Mother can be so relaxed and friendly there is a danger you will forget who she is, especially on a Sunday morning when there is not a footman in sight. But you learn to take nothing for granted. There are very few people with whom she can relax, and it is the privilege of the clergy at Windsor to help to fill that gap.'

David Herbert was invited to lunch one day, and the Queen Mother said, 'Now David, I'm going to make you one of my special martinis.' When they had both enjoyed a second drink, the Queen Mother said, 'You see, I can't possibly get through all my engagements without a little something, so before I go out I might just have a third martini – and why not? And then at dinner perhaps some whisky, and after dinner a glass of champagne. And do you know, it has no effect on me whatsoever!'[14]

Allied to the Queen Mother's reputation as a bonne vivante is her alleged partiality to mildly louche forms of entertainment. She was quite capable of sharing her husband's enjoyment of music hall jokes, musical comedy and stand-up comedians like Flanagan and Allen. But her own tastes are broad, embracing drama and ballet as well as *Dad's Army*. Although not as accomplished at the piano (or as a mimic) as Princess Margaret, she would think nothing of singing 'My Old Man Said Follow the Van' as a duet with Noël Coward after dinner at Sandringham. Her musical weekends at the Royal Lodge, to which some 30 people may be invited, including Eton schoolboys, will still find the Queen Mother, accompanied by Lord Hailsham, singing popular French songs like *Sur le pont, d'Avignon*.[15]

The British music hall, the old girl who likes a nip in the local . . . these are the images, if slightly blurred at the edges, that have helped 'ordinary' people to identify with the Queen Mother. A member of a London congregation, whose life is normally far from glamorous, was suddenly one day pulled out of the crowd to be presented to the Queen Mother. 'When things get a bit difficult, Ivy and I have a glass of martini, Ma'am,' said the rector. 'How lovely!' the Queen Mother exclaimed, 'my favourite drink!' 'As far as the Queen Mother's concerned,' said the rector involved, 'it's all *fun*. She doesn't start pawing the ground as the Queen does. That's why she's a star.'[16]

Charm must be the most ambiguous of all virtues, the hardest to define and the most difficult to manufacture. Yet it remains the most acceptable and appealing quality, infinitely preferable to good looks or even a brilliant mind, both of which can make those who possess neither feel inferior. Charm puts everyone at their ease. The Queen of Rumania thought the young Duchess of York 'one of the dearest, sweetest, most gentle . . . and most agreeable women I have ever met.'[17] Perhaps it is charm that has proved to be the Queen Mother's most effectual secret weapon. Writing to her 19-year-old daughter Mary on 2 November 1941, after she and Churchill had lunched alone with the King and Queen, Clementine Churchill said the occasion had been 'all most enjoyable, becos' The Queen is so gay & witty & very very pretty close up.' On 20 February 1945 the Churchills dined at the Palace. Next day Mrs Churchill wrote to Mary to say, 'It really was great fun,' because after dinner she had an hour alone with the Queen, 'but it passed like a flash because she is gay and amusing and has pith and point.' A month later (on 17 March) Mrs Churchill was back at the Palace for tea, and found the Queen looking 'very sweet & soignée like a plump turtle-dove'. On 20 November 1947 Mrs Churchill was describing to her lifelong friend Horatia Seymour the Queen's 'dazzling & magnetic charm'. The year before, *Time*'s London correspondent, Alfred Wright, was at the opening of an exhibition of American art at the Tate, and caught most perceptively and concisely a contemporary impression of the Queen Mother which in fact captures the permanent essence of her:

> Instinctively my attention was first attracted by the Queen. She was not beautiful and she was not wearing a spectacular get-up. It is just that she is the real star of the team.
> She has a superb complexion; everyone notices it right away. She moves with the unselfconscious ease of a person who knows she is alone in a room and won't be disturbed. When someone is talking to her, she concentrates completely on what he is saying, despite any & all distractions. During all the time I watched her the Queen maintained a remarkable expression on her face – as if this was an experience she had been awaiting months, and it had turned out better than she hoped.[18]

David Herbert recounts that one night the Queen stayed up until four in the morning (perhaps a slight exaggeration) 'doing her boxes', and said to Lady Hambleden, his sister, 'Patricia, do be an angel and help me,' and at the end of the session she said, 'You know, I do work awfully hard, but Mummy has all the charm.'[19] Paradoxically for someone to whom not a shred of scandal has ever become attached, another strong card in the Queen Mother's hand is her ability to be safely flirtatious. The way she has of looking a man straight in the eye goes perfectly with ballroom dancing and a weakness for chocolates. Nothing wicked; just a bit naughty. Fun, in other words.

In 1959 the Queen Mother attended a Women's Toc H evening at the Royal Albert Hall. (Toc H is a society formed in England after the First World War to encourage Christian fellowship.) A young journalist – he was only 25 – had been commissioned to write a masque for the occasion. Determined not to come out with a cliché at the end of the performance, and equally determined to say what she really thought, the Queen Mother searched for some time for an appropriate phrase. Eventually she said, 'I thought it was – *just* right.' A quarter of a century later, on the 50th anniversary of Elgar's death, the Queen Mother attended a concert of Elgar's music at Westminster Abbey. The author of the masque had on this occasion been invited to present to the Queen Mother a copy of his biography of Elgar.[20] Whilst talking to Queen Elizabeth about her meeting, in 1933, with the composer, the hapless man was stricken by a form of mental paralysis not infrequently experienced in the presence of royalty even by the most hardened politicians and accomplished entertainers. 'Of course, Ma'am,' he heard himself saying, 'it is difficult now to think of you all those years ago as . . .' and out came 'the Duchess of Gloucester.' The Queen Mother roared with laughter, and then performed a spectacular feat of spontaneity. She happened to be holding a bouquet of white roses. 'Now,' she said, plucking a rose from her bouquet, 'remember, white roses for York.'

The Queen Mother has always been in demand as a guest. One of her favourite hostesses, despite the fact that she used to curtsey to the Duchess of Windsor, was Lady Diana Cooper. Who would not want to entertain the Queen Mother when you could be assured of a bread-and-butter letter like the one the Queen Mother wrote from the Royal Lodge on 4 June 1978?

Dearest Lady Diana,

I always love coming to lunch with you, and I think that last Thursday was one of the best and most enjoyable of many memorable feasts. The moment that I enter your heavenly house I feel engulfed by the gay and glamorous atmosphere that you create, and I come away greatly cheered & uplifted. With my love, and a thousand thanks from Your ever affec: Elizabeth R.

It is interesting that even with a friend as frequently visited and written to personally, on her blue notepaper folded into small blue envelopes and sent in the registered post, the Queen Mother never got around to addressing Lady Diana Cooper by her Christian name, a favour seemingly only ever bestowed by senior members of the Royal Family on members of their Household, not all of whom are as efficient as is generally made out. On one occasion an invitation for the Queen Mother to attend a private lunch party went astray, because all her letters had been placed in one large envelope and sent on from Clarence House to Sandringham, where it would appear they lay unopened. (During the war a letter from George VI to President Roosevelt actually got lost in the diplomatic bag.) A disastrous contretemps occurred in November 1977 when Queen Elizabeth had to cancel acceptance of an invitation to lunch with Diana Cooper. The Queen Mother explained as follows:

> I have had a terrible shock!
>
> I have been told that on Wednesday Dec: 7th I have a long standing engagement to attend the Smithfield Show, and this means I simply cannot get away to come & lunch with you – I am really miserable, and the reason for this idiotic muddle is that it was never put into my horrid engagement list, so when I saw Dec: 7th hooray free, I was so pleased & thrilled that you had asked me on that day, as I *love* coming to your heavenly lunch parties . . .
>
> When I am tramping unhappily round horrible carcases of beef (I hate raw meat), I shall be thinking of you, & of all the gaiety & fun I am missing.
>
> I am, ever you affec: & frustrated & FURIOUS Elizabeth R.

In spite of her understandable annoyance, it is all too easy to imagine the Queen Mother's tramp round Smithfield, smiling and chatting, without giving any hint of her frustration or fury, or indeed her aversion to raw meat. Nothing daunted, she was back at the Royal Smithfield Show at Earls Court on 1 December 1993. Just as easy to imagine is the letter the lady-in-waiting in attendance would have written to the organisers of the 'long standing engagement', thanking them on behalf of the Queen Mother for the wonderful arrangements, and assuring them how much Her Majesty had enjoyed the occasion. What is perhaps less easy to grasp is how on earth an official engagement, to which the Queen Mother must have given her consent, could not have been entered in her diary. Having said that, the punctiliousness and courtesy of members of the Queen's and the Queen Mother's Households, who telephone if time is short and who normally reply to letters by return of post, compares more than favourably with the incompetence that in recent years has seized the Households of the estranged Prince and Princess of Wales, whose members not infrequently fail to reply to letters altogether. But it is perhaps a comfort to know that royal engagements, like everyone else's, are subject to the vagaries of human conduct. In 1965 Princess Margaret set off for lunch with Diana Cooper, who lived at 10 Warwick Avenue, London W2. The chauffeur cheerfully headed for Warwick Avenue, SW5, where they found themselves outside 'a not very nice school in Earls Court'. The chauffeur, the Princess told Lady Diana when writing to thank her, had been 'amazed!'.[21]

The Queen Mother has a penchant for clergymen, preferably High Church and slightly camp. Lady Diana Cooper was a great procurer of such. On 23 June 1979 the Queen Mother told Lady Diana, 'I loved those two dear little clergyman. What luck to have them, & how it must help them to be encouraged by you.' On 28 March 1981 she was writing to say, 'Once again I am writing to thank you for a perfect lunch party, and a *most* enjoyable noon cocktail party – your neighbours are so delightful and amusing and varied, and it is great fun to watch the famous HOUSE POISON doing it's [sic] work, voices rising, conversation becoming more & more sparkling, & even the dear faces of the clergy becoming a tiny bit roseate – Oh, it is such fun, and I adore coming to see you, & I enjoy myself madly in the lovely & relaxed atmosphere that you create round you, & I am deeply grateful to you for giving me such a heavenly treat.'

On 4 April 1982 the Queen Mother told Lady Diana that her own dear clergy, by which presumably she meant the canons at Windsor, 'seem quite boorish & tweedy' in comparison to the 'exquisite clergy in Little Venice'. It was following a visit to Diana Cooper, when three clergymen had come in for drinks before lunch, that as she was leaving the Queen Mother said to Lady Diana, 'I did enjoy meeting your bouquet of clergy.'[22] Among those invited in 1980 for a drink was a guest whose name, Sir Martin Gilliat assured Lady Diana Cooper, met with the Queen Mother's approval – Edward Fox. He had recently played the role of Edward VIII in a television series called *Edward and Mrs Simpson*.

Envoi

WHEN, ON THE OCCASION of the Queen Mother's 80th birthday, the Speaker of the House of Commons commended 'the loving care with which she had nurtured the Royal Family' his remark was nothing less than perceived wisdom. When the future Lord Alanbrooke stayed at Sandringham in 1944 he had described his hosts as a 'thoroughly close-knit and happy family all wrapped up in each other'. He thought the King and Queen and their two daughters provided 'one of the very best examples of English family life'.

But their family life was in no way typical of other English families. They were royal, after all, and constantly protected from the outside world by a ring fence of protocol manipulated by time-serving courtiers. Hence they were very much driven in on themselves for companionship, and what went on within the family circle became, for them, the absolute norm. The range of their conversation and criticisms, their sense of humour, all tended to produce a pattern of family behaviour to which outsiders, either friends or those marrying into the family, were expected to conform. There was little scope for improvisation or for rivalry.

It was the Queen Mother, in her bid to rescue the domestic respectability of the monarchy, who had created the concept of the modern happy royal family. By the time she was 80 that family had expanded somewhat from the cosy foursome so beloved of her husband. Indeed, by 1988, the year that extensive rewiring of Windsor Castle had given the Queen an excuse to abandon the ritual of a Christmas family gathering, the number of immediate relatives deemed worthy of an invitation had grown to 38.

With three divorces, the image of the happy royal family so carefully nurtured by the Queen Mother was already beginning to splinter. Since the marriage in 1978 of Prince Michael of Kent to an independent-minded, strong-willed and vibrant Austrian, rejoicing in the name of Baroness Marie-Christian Agnes Hedwig Ida von Reibnitz, a lady who was determined to demonstrate to the British Royal Family how a princess ought to behave, the road show dominated for so long by the Queen, the Queen Mother and Princess Margaret had begun to career downhill, out of control. One reason for this was because with the best of intentions the Queen, in concert with her mother, desired to give to the younger members of the family a large measure of freedom and independence. Hence the numbers of Royal Households began to swell. In addition to the Queen's, the Queen Mother's and the Duke of Edinburgh's, independent establishments were eventually set up for the Prince and Princess of Wales, the Duke and Duchess of York, Prince Edward, the Princess Royal, the Duke and Duchess of Gloucester, Princess Alice, Duchess of Gloucester, the Duke and Duchess of Kent, Prince and Princess Michael of Kent and Princess Alexandra.

All these Households were manned by private secretaries, Comptrollers, equerries and ladies-in-waiting. They operated from four or five different addresses, and failed to share information or plans. Instead of a family conference being held every six months or so, to allocate roles and tasks, to plan in fact an overall strategy for public appearances, various members of the Royal Family took to the streets and skies of Britain like Hollywood film stars, dashing from one engagement to the next bedecked in the latest off-the-shoulder (sometimes off-the-bosom) fashions, largely for the benefit of photographers. While the Queen Mother was soaking up heart-warming plaudits for her sterling efforts in the year of her 80th birthday, she could hardly have dreamed what disasters lay ahead. The ultimate watershed in her family's fortunes was a fateful day in July 1981, the day her eldest grandson, the Prince of Wales, drove to St Paul's Cathedral to marry Lady Diana Spencer.

The new Princess of Wales was 19, shy, ill-educated (she had been brought up on a diet of Barbara Cartland novels) and in love with a man who had been informed by *Woman's Realm* when he was 30 that he was perhaps the most accomplished young man in Britain. Such hyperbole was palpable rubbish. The Prince of Wales was reasonably artistic, extremely well-travelled and in many ways intelligent. He was also 31, a martyr to unsatisfactory affairs of the heart and dangerously set in the selfish mould of a bachelor gay. Like so many English men of his breeding, what he actually knew about women would probably not have gone on the back of a postage stamp. The Princess, coming from a traumatised family background, needed a mentor. Impatient, like his grandmother, with illness in others, Prince Charles was to prove an unsympathetic husband lacking in tact and gentleness towards the person who had sacrificed her freedom to marry him. Because he was so obviously eligible, Prince Charles had become a sex symbol. When the same thing happened to his wife, he resented it. Soon it dawned on the Princess that her sole role was to keep her mouth shut and produce an heir to the throne.

This she dutifully did, producing in fact two potential heirs, in quick succession. Prince William of Wales was born within 11 months of the marriage, Prince Henry a little over two years later. Both, by all accounts, are delightful children. It would be amazing if they were not. Their mother, to the surprise and eventually dismay of the Royal Family, especially the Queen Mother, developed into a mature and beautiful woman, becoming, like the Queen Mother herself, very much her own person. She discovered gifts she had no idea when she married that she possessed, and in a journey of self-discovery she determined to exploit those gifts for the benefit of herself and others. While at first her relationship with the press and public seemed like the result of self-gratification, it was soon transformed into a dazzling virtuoso performance such as the Queen Mother herself might have envied. Which, unfortunately, she did. One thing the Queen Mother does not care for is competition, and this is a trait strongly inherited by her family. Princess Anne cannot stand competition, which is why after divorcing one nonentity she promptly married a second. Prince Charles cannot stand competition. Before his marriage he held the crowds in his hands, and, like the previous Prince of Wales, his great-uncle Edward VIII, he absorbed adulation like a sponge. Girls would race across the beach to kiss him. European princesses were sized up and discarded. Ever since his days as an undergraduate at Cambridge he had escorted and entertained the crème de la crème. Daughters of dukes, marquesses, earls, barons, knights and Governor Generals all received the royal invitation to dine and wine but never the final accolade, to wed. Foolishly, Prince Charles once let slip that he thought 30 was the right age for him to take the plunge, and by the time his 30th birthday was approaching he found himself, from his family in particular, under increasing pressure to make up his mind.

One of many friends of Prince Charles who gave up waiting to be asked and married someone else was Camilla Parker-Bowles – whose great-grandmother was Alice Keppel, mistress to Edward VII. Another extraordinary fact is that her husband is a member of the Queen's Household, the improbable Silver Stick in Waiting, in which capacity, in 1990, he had the honour to organise the celebration parade along the Mall for the Queen Mother's 90th birthday. Alas for the future of the British Royal Family, Mrs Parker-Bowles has remained close to Prince Charles, so close that his marriage, like his sister's and that of his brother, the Duke of York, is heading for a divorce.

As recently as 1990 a *Daily Mirror* columnist wrote that the Queen Mother had now perfected her role to the point where no other actress need apply.[1] Unfortunately for the Queen Mother, one did. As the former Lady Diana Spencer grew up it became increasingly obvious that one day she would be more than capable of fulfilling the role at present held by the Queen Mother. Her spontaneity, charm and understanding of ordinary people fitted her precisely to become a Queen Mother to King William V. But a very different sort of Queen Mother. Because Queen Elizabeth cannot cope with illness or disease she could not comprehend how the Princess of Wales could shake hands with lepers and embrace men with Aids. And in turn, the Princess saw the Queen Mother as nothing more than a smiling icon, holding out her hand when she waved but never touching people. The Princess is immensely tactile, and has an instant rapport with small children – unlike her husband, her mother-in-law and the Queen Mother herself. Instead of welcoming Diana into a family which once again, as in 1923, was in need of fresh blood, the Royal Family simply found her conduct inexplicable. It almost beggars belief that at one time, in his exasperation at his wife's unhappiness and ill-health, Prince Charles compared her unfavourably to the Queen Mother, and even to his wayward sister-in-law, the Duchess of York.

It was no coincidence that the Princess's grandmother, Ruth, Lady Fermoy, was a lady-in-waiting to the Queen Mother and an intimate friend. While the two old ladies may not exactly have plotted the match, and even allowing for the belief among some that Lady Fermoy warned Diana Spencer against marrying into the almost hermetically sealed Royal Family, they both believed that from Prince Charles's point of view she would make an ideal bride. Her family had been in royal service for many years, Diana had had no former boyfriends, she seemed the dutiful type. Little did they know that deep down she was as tough as her father, whose partial recovery from a massive stroke was little short of miraculous, and that from a marriage that was to shatter her hopes of personal happiness she would emerge an international star. It is a mystery to the rest of the world why the British Royal Family cannot absorb her talents, but they never made the faintest attempt in the early days to comprehend the sort of woman she would turn out to be. Clarence House has been described as a sort of charm school, to which young girls are invited prior to marriage to princes to receive a few tips on royal etiquette, but this is a myth. Instead of trying to cement the marriage of the Prince and Princess of Wales, the Queen Mother fell victim to her uncritical devotion to Prince Charles. Foolish she may sometimes think him, but his foibles, like keeping on a mistress, are always forgiven.

It is a strange contradiction in the Queen Mother's attitude towards personal morality that while she finds divorce distasteful she has never been puritanical about mistresses. She liked Lady Furness, and strongly disapproved of Edward VIII's cowardly dismissal of Freda Dudley Ward, when he merely instructed the switchboard operator at York House to cease putting through her calls. But the Queen Mother was reared in an era when many men in public life (Lloyd George for one) kept a mistress, and sensible wives (Queen Alexandra could not have been a more notable example) turned a blind eye to their husband's infidelities. She has never grasped that Diana Spencer was a modern girl who wanted a monogamous marriage. As Princess of Wales, Diana came increasingly to resent the Royal Family's lack of support, and their connivance at her husband's selfish and uncaring conduct. Too late alas, Princess Margaret, who refers affectionately to her former husband as a Rat, told a dinner guest on New Year's Eve 1993 that Prince Charles had tried to undermine everything Diana did.[2] Her sympathies are now entirely with the Princess of Wales.

As for the Queen Mother, her attitude has always been that dirty family linen should not be washed in public, and any lurking sympathy she had for Diana's plight evaporated on publication in 1992 of *Diana: Her True Story* by Andrew Morton.[3] This painted a lurid picture of Diana's marriage, and left the Prince of Wales looking a far less attractive character than before. Diana's crime, so far as the Queen Mother was concerned, was to have aided and abetted Morton in his research. Certainly a number of Diana's friends assisted, and she has never withdrawn her friendship from them, but Prince Charles's biographer, Anthony Holden, is convinced the Princess did not assist Mr Morton, indeed, that she regards his book as one more betrayal. On the other hand, there are those who assert that she actually paid a visit to the publisher's office to check the proofs.[4] Whatever the truth, the Princess found herself an outcast. At the Trooping the Colour in 1992 the Princess was in the room from which the Queen Mother and other members of the Royal Family watch at Horse Guards Parade, and was virtually ostracised. 'You could have cut the atmosphere with my sword,' a senior army officer on duty commented afterwards.[5]

If the unravelling of the marriage of the Prince and Princess of Wales, who with their good-looking and well-mannered sons could have safely steered the monarchy into the foreseeable future, can be seen as nothing less than a Greek tragedy, the disastrous five-year marriage of the Duke of York to Sarah Ferguson had all the hallmarks of a farce. Like the Princess of Wales, the Duchess of York had been brought up in an era that had seen the almost total collapse of authoritarianism, and she found it impossible to inhabit happily the royal world of make-believe. Not for nothing had Dr Robert Runcie, the Archbishop of Canterbury, told the Prince and Princess of Wales that their wedding was the stuff of which fairy tales are made. But although with hindsight one can see that Prince Andrew's choice of bride had been madness, the Queen Mother thoroughly approved the match. 'The Queen, too, was fond of Fergie,' Lady Hambleden recalls. 'They all were. But she went somewhat over the top, don't you think!'[6] In fact, no princess since Caroline of Brunswick, wife of George IV, has behaved so scandalously in public. But her conduct was at least in character. Born a Sloane Ranger, she had been taken on board by the Royal Family to compensate Prince Andrew for the loss of the unfortunately named but beautiful, talented and discreet Koo Stark, with whom the teetotal Prince Andrew deserved to be happy. The idea of Princess Koo, however, was too much for the Duke of Edinburgh, who considered the daughter of Prince Charles's polo manager more suitable as a daughter-in-law. Brash and vulgar by temperament, the Duchess of York knew quite well she was second choice.

Whether she intended to make the Royal Family pay for their folly or not, she succeeded, rushing around like a pop star without a manager, spending money on a scale Mrs Simpson might have envied, and finally getting herself splashed across the world's press half naked with an American friend. The Duchess's most foolhardy mistake, however, may have been to snub the Queen Mother, who on more than one occasion invited her to stay, in order to lend moral support and try to offer advice on how to settle into royal duties. Queen Elizabeth's invitations were always rejected. The Duchess, headstrong at the best of times, belonged to a generation that thought they knew best but had studied no history. Eventually even the Queen's Private Secretary and her press officer turned on her. She had built up no line of defence, and when the formal separation of the Duke and Duchess was announced on 18 March 1992 the Duchess became that saddest and strangest of all anomalies, a royal non-person – still a Royal Highness but stripped of her ladies-in-waiting and denied any royal duties.

By contrast, the Princess of Wales had built for herself a very strong power base. When, after 11 years, she and her husband decided they could no longer stand living together, she was in a position to retain her own Household, together with their apartments at Kensington Palace for her own exclusive use. The Prince moved into St James's Palace. The true victims of the Royal Family's failure to love and support the Princess of Wales are her children, after their father the heirs apparent and presumptive to the throne. They have taken on a great deal of their mother's unhappiness, but they are young enough to absorb also her concept of how the British Royal Family should, in some respects, adapt to the ways of Scandinavian monarchies, all of whom have proved it is perfectly possible to carry out a constitutional function while conducting their private lives in private. What continental royal families have never done is sell their souls to the press. The price being paid by the British monarchy for behaving like film stars, with the Princess of Wales carrying out 250 engagements a year before partially retreating from public life, is intrusion into their privacy which no ordinary family would be able to withstand.

Although the many charities the Princess of Wales supports may find that her decision to curtail her public engagements means a falling away of funds, in the long run her decision can only reap benefits for the monarchy and all who thrive on it. The less publicity the Royal Family receive in future the better for everyone, particularly Prince William and Prince Harry. By being so honest and true to herself, by admitting the failure of her marriage and by seeking a period in semi-retirement to think how best to bring up her sons, the Princess of Wales may eventually place the family who have so undervalued her greatly in their debt. The tragedy has been that while Lady Diana Spencer was not, through any fault of her own, the perfect choice of wife for Prince Charles, she became the perfect Princess of Wales. A victim of her own success, it now seems most unlikely that she will ever wear the mantle of the Queen Mother, who has failed to understand how Diana, never having been loved by her mother or her husband, could crave the love of the public in order to learn to love herself. If the Princess imbues her sons with her own hard-learned wisdom about the human condition they could emerge from the Windsors' present sorry mess as princes fit to inhabit the twenty-first century. Having matured through suffering, the Princess of Wales has more to offer the monarchy than any outsider since her husband's grandmother married Bertie in 1923.

Meanwhile, there was no denying, as the Queen well realised, that for her personally 1992, instead of being a glorious celebration of 40 years on the throne, had been a horrible year, with Windsor Castle bursting into flames in November, an event she dealt with with amazing sang-froid. Having just been informed the Castle was on fire she received the Latvian ambassador, who had called at Buckingham Palace to present his credentials. Not by a flicker of an eyelid did she disclose her anxiety, receiving his wife also and laughing and joking. It was only later that the ambassador realised that throughout the audience the Queen already knew of the conflagration.[7]

In March the Yorks had separated; in the summer Morton's book had been serialised and published. In December the Prince and Princess of Wales went their separate ways. It was also the year in which the Princess Royal was divorced. The Queen Mother stealed herself to attend the Princess's second marriage eight months later (neither the Princess of Wales nor the Duchess of York attended), but it required a good deal of Dutch courage. 'She's very upset about the divorces and separations,' one of her ladies-in-waiting says. 'She's very upset. But she definitely thinks the monarchy under Charles will continue. I don't think she would ever contemplate it not. She's a great royalist.'[8]

The monarchy itself will survive so long as parliament declines to find the time to abolish it – which could take years. Unfortunately, however, and greatly to the Queen Mother's chagrin, the reputation of Prince Charles for sagacity has taken a considerable knock. The monarchy does not, of course, in theory depend upon the morals of its inhabitants, but people in authority have to earn respect these days. An enormous fund of public sympathy, hope and goodwill was invested in the marriage of the Prince and Princess of Wales, and there is no question that the country feels let down by their rancorous behaviour. It looks increasingly likely that at whatever age Prince Charles eventually succeeds (and he could very well be 65 or older) he will do so without a queen by his side, for if his marriage ends in divorce, as it most probably will, the Princess of Wales will retain her present title until such time (if ever) as she remarries, but will never be queen. Whether the country would tolerate, even in the twenty-first century, a sovereign not only divorced but remarried, who was also Supreme Governor of the Church of England, must be wide open to question.

What the new reign will require, whenever it commences, will be far fewer members of the Royal Family rushing around undertaking far too many engagements. By the time the children of the Prince of Wales and the Duke of York are old enough to perform royal functions there will be no need for cousins of the sovereign to appear in public at all. What it will also require is the removal of courtiers who have served the monarchy badly. There are at present five members of the Queen's press office; judging by a television film in which she starred to celebrate the 40th anniversary of her coronation, the Queen knows more about public relations than the lot of them put together. Her Private Secretary grew up at Sandringham and is the brother-in-law of the Princess of Wales. Her Lord Chamberlain is a grandson of a lady-in-waiting to Queen Mary; Princess Alexandra is his sister-in-law, his wife is a lady of the bedchamber. It is this kind of self-perpetuating Court which has failed to follow through the vision and initiatives of the most successful 'outsider' ever to penetrate royal circles, Lady Elizabeth Bowes-Lyon.

But there remains much to be thankful for. The more one studies the life and character of King Edward VIII the more relieved one feels that he abdicated, and was prevented from staging any sort of comeback. When not fraternising with Nazis before the war he was castigating British Labour politicians as Communists after it. No one had his essentially fickle and dangerous personality in sharper focus than Queen Elizabeth the Queen Mother. No one had greater confidence in the potential ability, amply proven in the event, of King George VI to inspire his people while they were fighting for their lives. No member of the Royal Family has ever given so much innocent and charming pleasure to so many people over such an unbelievable length of time. At the Service of Thanksgiving for her 80th birthday, the Archbishop of Canterbury could not have recalled a more appropriate remark than the one made by a previous Queen Elizabeth, when addressing her last parliament in 1601: 'Though God hath raised me high, yet this I count the glory of my crown; that I have reigned with your loves.'

'Did Mummy survive?' Princess Margaret asked the Queen when she telephoned Sandringham House in the early hours of New Year's Day 1994. The enquiry was not too serious, just a jocular reference to the Queen Mother having sat up until midnight to see in yet another year, her 94th, fortified, as usual, by a comforting glass of champagne. When eventually Queen Elizabeth does decide to shuffle off this mortal coil she will leave not only a great sense of loss in the House of Windsor but a gap in the psyche of the nation impossible to fill.

Notes to Text

Chapter One: A Most Terrible Omen

1 Lockhart, J. G., *Cosmo Gordon Lang*, Hodder & Stoughton, 1949.
2 27 May 1953.
3 Lockhart, J. G., op. cit.
4 Ponsonby, Sir Frederick, *Recollections of Three Reigns*, Eyre & Spottis-woode, 1951.
5 Ziegler, Philip, *King Edward VIII*, Collins, 1990.
6 Donaldson, Frances, Edward VIII, Weidenfeld & Nicolson, 1974.
7 Ibid.
8 James, Robert Rhodes (ed.), *Chips: The Diaries of Sir Henry Channon*, Weidenfeld & Nicolson, 1967.
9 Donaldson, Frances, op. cit.
10 Minney, R. J. (ed.), *The Private Papers of Hore-Belisha*, 1960.
11 Letter from Michael Bloch to the author, 3 May 1993.
12 Letter from Viscount Norwich to the author, 31 July 1993.
13 Vincent, John (ed.), *The Crawford Papers*, 1984.
14 Lowndes, Susan (ed.), *Diaries and Letters of Marie Belloc Lowndes 1911–1947.*
15 Letter from HRH the Duchess of York to Edward VIII, 23 November 1936.
16 Private Secretary to Edward VIII as Prince of Wales from 1919–36. From 1937–58 Private Secretary to HRH the Duke of Gloucester.
17 Vincent, John (ed.) op. cit.
18 Letter from Viscount Norwich, op. cit.
19 Channon Diaries, op. cit.
20 Templewood, Viscount, *Nine Troubled Years*, 1954.
21 Letter from the Hon. Harold Nicolson to the Hon. Vita Sackville-West, 26 February 1936.
22 *The Country Life Book of Royal Palaces, Castles and Homes* by Patrick Montague-Smith and Hugh Montgomery-Massingberd (1981) states incorrectly that Birkhall was given to the Duke of York on his marriage by George V. Along with the rest of the Balmoral estate Birkhall has always

belonged to the Crown. Between 1923 and 1936 the Duke and Duchess of York sometimes stayed at Birkhall as the guests of King George V. Letter from Sir Alistair Aird, Private Secretary to Queen Elizabeth the Queen Mother, to the author, 28 April 1993.

23 Crawford, Marion, *The Little Princesses*, Odhams, 1950.
24 Bloch, Michael, *The Reign and Abdication of Edward VIII*, Bantam, 1990.
25 Helen, Lady Dashwood in conversation with the author, 1986.
26 According to Rickatson-Hall and recorded in *Walter Monckton* by Lord Birkenhead, 1969.
27 Windsor, Duchess of, *The Heart Has Its Reasons*, Michael Joseph, 1956.
28 Lady Diana Cooper quoted in: Ziegler, Philip, *Diana Cooper*, Hamish Hamilton, 1981.
29 Cooper, Diana, *The Light of Common Day*, Rupert Hart-Davis, 1959.
30 Windsor, HRH the Duke of, *A King's Story*, Cassell, 1951.
31 Eton College archives.

Chapter Two: A Pretty Kettle of Fish!

1 Young, Kenneth (ed.), *The Diaries of Sir Robert Bruce-Lockhart: 1915–1918*.
2 Bloch, Michael, op. cit.
3 Nicolson, Nigel (ed.), *Harold Nicolson: Diaries and Letters, 1930–1960*, Collins, 1980.
4 Letter from HRH the Duke of Windsor to the Duchess of Windsor, 27 March 1953.
5 Windsor, HRH the Duke of, op. cit.
6 Channon Diaries, op. cit.
7 Nicolson Diaries, op. cit.
8 Ibid.
9 Bloch, Michael, op. cit.
10 Monica Baldwin renounced her religious vows and in 1949 published a book entitled *I Leap Over the Wall*.
11 Memorandum written by HRH the Duke of York.
12 Brownlow Papers, quoted in: Ziegler, Philip, op. cit.
13 Eton College archives.
14 Bloch, Michael, op. cit.
15 Channon Diaries, op. cit., 7 December 1936.
16 Nicolson Diaries, op. cit., 10 December 1936. Baldwin told his niece there had been 'no moral struggle'.
17 Bradford, Sarah, *George VI*, Weidenfeld & Nicolson, 1989.
18 Nicolson Diaries, op. cit., 4 November 1936.
19 Sitwell, Osbert, *Rat Week*, Michael Joseph, 1986.
20 Channon Diaries, op. cit.

Chapter Three: Jacobite Blood

1 The children of the 14th Earl of Strathmore were: Violet, born 1882, who died at the age of 11; Mary, born 1883; Patrick, born 1884, who succeeded as the 15th Earl; John, born 1886; Alexander, born 1887, who died at the age of 24; Fergus, born 1889 and killed in action 1915; Rose, born 1890; Michael, born 1893, Elizabeth (the Queen Mother), born 1900; David, born 1902.
2 Lady Hambleden in conversation with the author, 6 May 1993. Speaking with the author on 10 September 1993, Lady Elizabeth Basset, who has known the Queen Mother 34 years, also denied all knowledge of Her Majesty's birth in an ambulance.
3 Ibid.
4 Ibid.
5 In conversation with the author.
6 Ibid.
7 Ibid.
8 Quoted in: Rose, Kenneth, *George V*, Weidenfeld & Nicolson, 1983.
9 Howarth, Patrick, *George VI*, Hutchinson, 1987.
10 Quennell, Peter (ed.), *A Lonely Business: A Self-Portrait of James Pope-Hennessy*, Weidenfeld & Nicolson, 1981.
11 Macmillan, 1963.

Chapter Four: Married to a Hanoverian

1 *See* Brooke, John, *King George III*, Constable, 1972, page 339.
2 Ibid.
3 *King George VI: His Life and Reign*, Macmillan, 1959.
4 Ibid.
5 *Time and Chance*, Collins, 1978.
6 In conversation with the author.
7 Ibid.
8 Op. cit.
9 Letter from the Hon. Harold Nicolson to Nigel Nicolson, 17 May 1945.
10 Lees-Milne, James, *Prophesying Peace*, Chatto & Windus, 1977.
11 Sitwell, Osbert, op. cit.
12 Hutchinson, 1927.
13 Viking, 1986.

Chapter Five: The Letters Patent

1 Letter from Edward Metcalfe to Lady Alexandra Metcalfe, 21 January 1937.
2 Duchy of Cornwall revenues for 1936 were £70,941 – Bloch, Michael, *The*

Secret File of the Duke of Windsor, Bantam, 1988. He had investments worth 'not less than £800,000'.

3 Memorandum, HRH the Duke of York, op. cit.
4 James, Robert Rhodes, *Victor Cazalet*, 1976.
5 Ibid.
6 Sitwell, Osbert, op. cit.
7 Letter from Queen Elizabeth to Queen Mary, 31 August 1939.
8 Bradford, Sarah, op. cit., page 287.
9 Letter from Edward Metcalfe to Lady Alexandra Metcalfe, 29 January 1937.
10 Letter from Sir Kenneth Scott to the author, 21 May 1993. In *Royal Feud* (Michael Joseph, 1985) Michael Thornton states that Windsor had never previously been used as a royal or non-royal title. This is not true. During the reign of Henry VIII Andrew Wyndesore, High Steward of the Borough, was created Lord Wyndesore, and the heir to the Earl of Plymouth is Viscount Windsor.
11 Memorandum made by Sir Clive Wigram, 10 December 1936.
12 *See* Ziegler, Philip, *King Edward VIII*, op. cit. According to Ziegler, King George V left all his children save the Prince of Wales 'some ¾ million'. He does not quote a source for this information, however, and royal wills are never published. The King, not unnaturally, assumed that his eldest son was already adequately catered for. When the Prince of Wales was 24 he came into £246,000, 'a very splendid sum of money' as his father told him, 'which will go on increasing until you marry and set up home.'
13 Bloch, Michael, *The Secret File of the Duke of Windsor*, op. cit.
14 Birkenhead, Lord, *Walter Monckton*, 1969.
15 Eton College archives.
16 Donaldson, Frances, *Edward VIII*, op. cit. In *The Queen Mother: With Unique Recollections by the Earl Mountbatten* by Donald Zec (Sidgwick & Jackson, 1990) the erroneous assertion is made that with the King's permission Lord Louis Mountbatten was best man to the Duke of Windsor.
17 Nicolson Diaries, op. cit., 5 August 1938.
18 Bloch, Michael, *The Secret File of the Duke of Windsor*, op. cit.
19 Payn, Graham, and Morley, Sheridan, (eds.), *The Noël Coward Diaries*, Weidenfeld & Nicolson, 1982.
20 Noël Coward to Lord Louis Mountbatten, quoted in: Ziegler, Philip, *Mountbatten: The Official Biography*, Collins, 1985.

Chapter Six: Cookie Doesn't Crumble

1 *A King's Story*, op. cit.
2 Bradford, Sarah, *George VI*, op. cit.
3 Sitwell, Osbert, op. cit.
4 Private conversation.
5 In conversation with the author.

6 Ibid.
7 Private conversation.
8 *Clean Young Englishman*, 1965.
9 Lord Birkenhead, op. cit.
10 *The Wanton Chase*, Collins, 1980.
11 Nicolson Diaries, op. cit.
12 Ibid, 27 May 1937.
13 A reference to *The Pilgrim's Progress*.
14 Nicolson Diaries, op. cit., 27 May 1937.
15 Ibid.
16 Letter from Sir George Allen to Sir Walter Monckton, 15 February 1938.
17 Quoted in *The Secret File of the Duke of Windsor*, op. cit.
18 Letter from Neville Chamberlain to George VI, 17 January 1939.
19 Letter from President Roosevelt to George VI, 17 September 1938.

Chapter Seven: 'The Most Marvellous Person in the World'

1 Letter from the Hon. Harold Nicolson to the Hon. Vita Sackville-West, 10 July 1940.
2 Queen Elizabeth the Queen Mother in conversation with the Reverend Victor Stock.
3 *King Edward VIII*, op. cit.
4 Quoted in: Bradford, Sarah, *George VI*, op. cit.
5 Letter from George VI to Winston Churchill, 13 September 1940.
6 Sir Michael Burton in conversation with the author.
7 Letter from the Hon. Harold Nicolson to the Hon. Vita Sackville-West, 7 January 1941.
8 Ibid.
9 Sinclair, David, *Two Georges: The Making of the Modern Monarchy*, Hodder & Stoughton, 1988.
10 Private information.
11 As itemised by Sarah Bradford in *George VI*, op. cit.
12 Lees-Milne, James, *Ancestral Voices*, Chatto & Windus, 1975.
13 *Memoirs*, Collins, 1983.
14 *The Secret File of the Duke of Windsor*, op. cit.
15 Letter from Queen Elizabeth to Queen Mary, 12 June 1943.
16 *Ancestral Voices*, op. cit.
17 De-la-Noy, Michael (ed.), *The Journals of Denton Welch*, Allison & Busby, 1984.
18 *Rat Week*, op. cit.
19 Diary of George VI, 26 February 1946.
20 In private conversation.
21 Eton College archives.
22 Channon Diaries, op. cit., 18 June 1949.

Notes

Chapter Eight: 'Nannie Of Us All'

1 James Lees-Milne's diary, 10 July 1945, published as *Prophesying Peace*, op. cit.
2 The Dowager Viscountess Hambleden in conversation with the author.
3 Eton College archives.
4 Letter from Queen Elizabeth the Queen Mother to Edith Sitwell, 15 September 1952.
5 In private conversation.
6 Ibid.
7 Ibid.
8 Private information.
9 In conversation with the author.
10 Private information.
11 Ibid.
12 In conversation with the author.

Chapter Nine: A Very Private Person

1 *Caves of Ice*, Chatto & Windus, 1983.
2 In conversation with the author.
3 Ibid.
4 Victor Stock, in conversation with the author.
5 In conversation with the author.
6 *A Lonely Business*, op. cit.
7 In conversation with the author.
8 There is a distinction between being a member of the Royal Family and being related to the Royal Family. Only those with royal status are members of the Royal Family, and Michael Bloch is in error in his book *The Secret File of the Duke of Windsor*, op. cit., when he suggests that Elizabeth II's consent, given in 1970, for the Duchess of Windsor eventually to be buried at Frogmore 'effectively granted the Duchess a posthumous status as a member of the Royal Family'. There are plenty of relatives buried at Frogmore – the Marchioness of Cambridge, for example, widow of Queen Mary's nephew – who were no more members of the Royal Family than are the children of Princess Margaret, the Duke of Gloucester, the Duke of Kent, Prince Michael of Kent or Princess Alexandra.
9 In conversation with the author.
10 In *Royal Feud*, op. cit., Michael Thornton states, 'The British people would never see their former King's last resting place, or [the Duchess's] which would be beside it. Although Frogmore Gardens are open for two days a year under the National Gardens Scheme, the public is never admitted to the royal burial ground, which is screened from view by a hedge.' This is incorrect. The two

days the gardens are open are usually the first Wednesday and Thursday in May, when it is perfectly possible to view both the Royal Mausoleum and the burial ground, and the graves of the Duke and Duchess of Windsor are clearly visible.

11 *Royal Feud*, ibid.
12 *A Lonely Business*, op. cit.

Chapter Ten: Frustrated and Furious

1 Op. cit.
2 Letter from Earl Mountbatten to the Prince of Wales, 14 February 1974
3 *The Duke: A Portrait of Prince Philip*, Hodder & Stoughton, 1991.
4 In private conversation.
5 Letter from the Prince of Wales to Earl Mountbatten, 27 November 1978.
6 *Double Exposure*, London, 1959.
7 In conversation with the author.
8 Ibid.
9 Lady Elizabeth Basset in conversation with the author.
10 Darton, Longman & Todd.
11 *Midway on the Waves*, Faber & Faber, 1985.
12 *Mother of the Queen*, Frederick Muller, 1965.
13 Private conversation.
14 The Hon. David Herbert in conversation with the author.
15 Private information.
16 Victor Stock in conversation with the author.
17 Quoted in: Howarth, Patrick, *George VI*, op. cit.
18 Quoted in: Bradford, Sarah, *George VI*, op. cit.
19 The Hon. David Herbert in conversation with the author.
20 De-la-Noy, Michael, *Elgar: The Man*, Allan Lane, 1983.
21 Eton College archives.
22 Retailed to the author by the Hon. David Herbert.

Envoi

1 Donald Zec, op. cit.
2 Private information.
3 Michael O'Mara Books.
4 Private information.
5 Ibid.
6 In conversation with the author.
7 Information: HE the Latvian Ambassador, in conversation with the author.
8 Private information.

Appendix A

Dear Lady Stair,

I must write & thank you both so very much for asking me to come to Lochinch. I did so enjoy my visit & you gave me such an Agapetum (delightful) time.

It was a great disappointment to me that my wife was unable to come too, & she is miserable at having missed the two Formosum (beautiful) days we had there. I am glad to tell you that she is much better, though I found her looking Microleucrum (small & white).

It was nice of you to say that I deputised well for her on Saturday but I feel that she could have done everything much better, as she has the Agastum (charming) way of Charidotes (giving joy). As we had arranged our visit for her, she Pothinum (much desired) to be there, & it was very sad for her to have missed it. However it is Sperabile (to be hoped for) Timeteum (to be honoured) with a future invitation.

As to my visit, I am overjoyed Eclecteum (to be chosen out) and Aberrans (wandering) Cyclium (round) so many Erastum (lovely) and Arizelum (notable) gardens in so short a time, has left me Charitostreptum (gracefully bent) with a Recurvum (bent back), & somewhat Lasiopodum (woolly footed). I must say I am filled Coeloneirum (with impressed nerves) at all the Agetum (wondrous) & Aperantum (limitless) beauties of the gardens cyclium (round) Lochinch.

But despite being Asperulum (slightly roughened) & having had time to examine my feet, Denudatum (naked) and Detersile (clean) I am glad to find they are neither Hypoglaucum (blue beneath) Hypolepidotum (scaly) nor Hypophaeum (grey) but merely Russatum (reddened). This Rufuscens (becoming reddish) will have Comisteum (to be taken care of) otherwise they will not be Eudoxom (of good report) for Clivicola (living on hillsides) in August. As a diversion I much enjoyed our chase after those Tephropeplum (ashy grey colour) Dumicola (dwellers in thickets) which we were lucky enough to find Telopeum (conspicuous) Lochmium (from a coppice). Knowing you to be an Ombrochares (lover of rain) I hope you will soon get some to revive the Species of Rhododendron; which as we are told by one Wallace: 'Of course it is over', and to make the snipe bogs Paludosum (marshy). It is too kind of you to have given me so many Axium (worthy) & Eucallum (beautiful) plants which will be Eritimum (highly prized) by me & are most Apodectum (acceptable).

After this I feel I cannot write English any more. It was really too kind of you to have had me to stay & I did so enjoy every moment of it. Thanking you both again so very much.

Yours very sincerely
Albert

Appendix B

The broadcast made by HRH Prince Edward from Windsor Castle, 11 December 1936

At long last I am able to say a few words of my own.

I have never wanted to withhold anything, but until now it has not been constitutionally possible for me to speak.

A few hours ago I discharged my last duty as King and Emperor, and now that I have been succeeded by my brother, the Duke of York, my first words must be to declare my allegiance to him. This I do with all my heart.

You all know the reasons which have impelled me to renounce the throne. But I want you to understand that in making up my mind I did not forget the country or the Empire which as Prince of Wales, and lately as King, I have for twenty-five years tried to serve. But you must believe me when I tell you that I have found it impossible to carry the heavy burden of responsibility and to discharge my duties as King as I would wish to do without the help and support of the woman I love.

And I want you to know that the decision I have made has been mine and mine alone. This was a thing I had to judge entirely for myself. The other person most concerned has tried up to the last to persuade me to take a different course. I have made this, the most serious decision of my life, upon a single thought of what would in the end be the best for all.

This decision has been made less difficult to me by the sure knowledge that my brother, with his long training in the public affairs of this country and with his fine qualities, will be able to take my place forthwith, without interruption or injury to the life and progress of the Empire. And he has one matchless blessing, enjoyed by so many of you and not bestowed on me – a happy home with his wife and children.

During these hard days I have been comforted by my Mother and by my Family. The Ministers of the Crown, and in particular Mr Baldwin, the Prime Minister, have always treated me with full consideration. There has never been any constitutional difference between me and them and between me and

Parliament. Bred in the constitutional tradition by my Father, I should never have allowed any such issue to arise.

Ever since I was Prince of Wales, and later on when I occupied the Throne, I have been treated with the greatest kindness by all classes, wherever I have lived or journeyed throughout the Empire. For that I am very grateful.

I now quit altogether public affairs, and I lay down my burden. It may be some time before I return to my native land, but I shall always follow the fortunes of the British race and Empire with profound interest, and if at any time in the future I can be found of service to His Majesty in a private situation I shall not fail. And now we all have a new King. I wish him, and you, his people, happiness and prosperity with all my heart. God bless you all. God Save the King.

Appendix C

The Duke of Windsor's Consultations of Jowitt
on the Question of the Duchess's Title

Opinion given by Sir William Jowitt and Mr Patrick Devlin, May 1937

The Duke of Windsor has been advised that the Letters Patent dated 27th May, 1937, have no effect upon the rank and precedence to be accorded to the Duchess of Windsor.

So far as the Duke's rank and precedence are concerned, these are governed by the Stat. 31, Hen. 8 Cap. 10 and by immemorial custom a wife is entitled to assume the same rank and precedence as her husband, unless such rank and precedence be merely official. In His Majesty's Declaration of Abdication Act, 1936, it was expressly provided that the Royal Marriages Act, 1772, should not apply to the Duke of Windsor. There is, accordingly, no reason why in the case of the Duke's marriage this immemorial custom should not be given its full force and effect.

Nor do the Letters Patent purport to deal with questions of rank and precedence.

With regard to the question of the 'title style or attribute' of Royal Highness with which the Letters Patent of the 27th May, 1937, do deal, it is to be observed that the Letters Patent of 27th May, 1937, are issued on the assumption that it is only by their operation that the Duke of Windsor is entitled to this form of address.

The Duke of Windsor is advised that since 1898 he has always been entitled to this form of address and has never ceased to be so entitled.

He first became entitled in this form of address by the Letters Patent of May, 1898, as a child of the eldest son of the then Prince of Wales.

On the accession of Edward VII in 1901 the Duke of Windsor came within the terms of the Letters Patent of January, 1864, as a child of a son of the Sovereign.

On the accession of George V the Duke of Windsor – apart from any patents – further became entitled to this form of address as a son of the Sovereign by established usage – a usage which is recognised in the Letters Patent of 1864.

The Letters Patent of 1917 did not affect the Duke's position.

There are no words in the operative part of any of the Letters Patent to restrict the title of Royal Highness to those only who are 'in succession to the throne'.

The Duke, during his reign as King Edward VIII naturally allowed the attribute 'Royal Highness' to be supplanted by the higher attribute of 'His Majesty' – but upon his abdication he automatically resumed his earlier attribute of 'Royal Highness' as a son of a former sovereign.

Accordingly, the Duke is advised that his right to the attribute of 'Royal Highness' is derived from sources which remain unaffected by the Letters Patent of 27th May, 1937; and this advice is fortified by the fact that in his speech of 12th December, 1936, upon his accession, His Majesty referred to the Duke as 'His Royal Highness'. In common with the wives of all other members of the Royal Family the Duchess of Windsor cannot lay claim to the attribute of 'Royal Highness' by reason of the provision of any Letters Patent, but only by reason of that immemorial usage which accords to every wife the style and title and attribute of her husband. Inasmuch as the Duke derives this attribute from sources wherein no limitation is imposed upon the use of it by his wife and inasmuch as the Letters Patent of 27th May, 1937, do not purport to deprive the Duke of rights acquired prior to their issue, the Duke is advised that the Duchess of Windsor is by virtue of her membership of the Royal Family entitled in the same way as other royal Duchesses to be known by the style and title of 'Her Royal Highness'.

Earls of Strathmore and Kinghorne

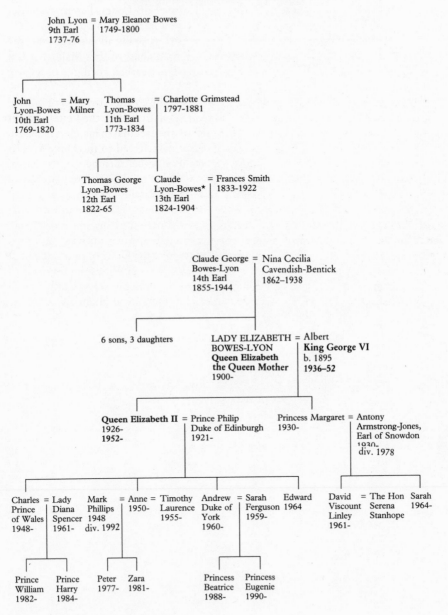

* Afterwards changed to Bowes-Lyon

The Royal House of Windsor

The Royal House of Hanover (1714)
The Royal House of Saxe-Coburg (1901)
The Royal House of Windsor (1917)
The Royal House and Family of Windsor (1952)
And the Family of Mountbatten-Windsor (1960)*

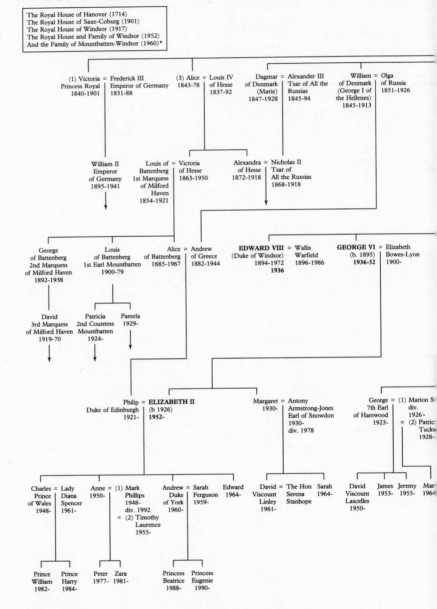

(1) Victoria = Frederick III
Princess Royal | Emperor of Germany
1840-1901 | 1831-88

(3) Alice = Louis IV
1843-78 | of Hesse
1837-92

Dagmar = Alexander III
of Denmark | Tsar of All the
(Marie) | Russias
1847-1928 | 1845-94

William = Olga
of Denmark | of Russia
(George I of | 1851-1926
the Hellenes)
1845-1913

William II
Emperor
of Germany
1895-1941

Louis of = Victoria
Battenberg | of Hesse
1st Marquess | 1863-1950
of Milford
Haven
1854-1921

Alexandra = Nicholas II
of Hesse | Tsar of
1872-1918 | All the Russias
1868-1918

George
of Battenberg
2nd Marquess
of Milford Haven
1892-1938

Louis
of Battenberg
1st Earl Mountbatten
1900-79

Alice = Andrew
of Battenberg | of Greece
1885-1967 | 1882-1944

EDWARD VIII = Wallis
(Duke of Windsor) | Warfield
1894-1972 | 1896-1986
1936

GEORGE VI = Elizabeth
(b. 1895) | Bowes-Lyon
1936-52 | 1900-

David
3rd Marquess
of Milford Haven
1919-70

Patricia
2nd Countess
Mountbatten
1924-

Pamela
1929-

Philip = **ELIZABETH II**
Duke of Edinburgh | (b 1926)
1921- | **1952-**

Margaret = Antony
1930- | Armstrong-Jones
Earl of Snowdon
1930-
div. 1978

George = (1) Marion S
7th Earl | div.
of Harewood | 1926-
1923- | = (2) Patric
Tuckw
1928-

Charles = Lady
Prince | Diana
of Wales | Spencer
1948- | 1961-

Anne = (1) Mark
1950- | Phillips
1948-
div. 1992
= (2) Timothy
Laurence
1955-

Andrew = Sarah
Duke | Ferguson
of York | 1959-
1960-

Edward
1964-

David = The Hon
Viscount | Serena
Linley | Stanhope
1961-

Sarah
1964-

David
Viscount
Lascelles
1950-

James
1953-

Jeremy
1955-

Mar
196

Prince
William
1982-

Prince
Harry
1984-

Peter
1977-

Zara
1981-

Princess
Beatrice
1988-

Princess
Eugenie
1990-

* On 8 February 1960 the Queen declared in Council that her descendants, other than descendants
enjoying the style, title or attribute of HRH and the titular dignity of Prince or Princess, and female
descendants who marry, and their descendants shall bear the name of Mountbatten-Windsor.

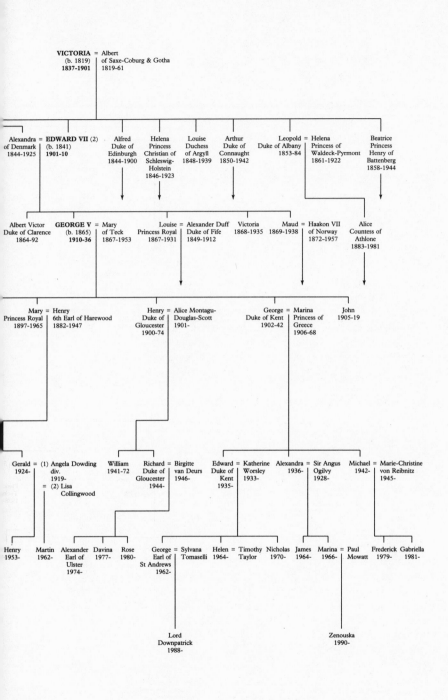

VICTORIA = Albert
(b. 1819) | of Saxe-Coburg & Gotha
1837-1901 | 1819-61

Alexandra = **EDWARD VII** (2)   Alfred   Helena   Louise   Arthur   Leopold = Helena   Beatrice
of Denmark | (b. 1841)   Duke of   Princess   Duchess   Duke of   Duke of Albany | Princess of   Princess
1844-1925 | **1901-10**   Edinburgh   Christian of   of Argyll   Connaught   1853-84 | Waldeck-Pyrmont   Henry of
1844-1900   Schleswig-   1848-1939   1850-1942   1861-1922   Battenberg
Holstein   1858-1944
1846-1923

Albert Victor   **GEORGE V** = Mary   Louise = Alexander Duff   Victoria   Maud = Haakon VII   Alice
Duke of Clarence | (b. 1865) | of Teck   Princess Royal | Duke of Fife   1868-1935   1869-1938 | of Norway   Countess of
1864-92 | **1910-36** | 1867-1953   1867-1931 | 1849-1912   1872-1957   Athlone
1883-1981

Mary = Henry   Henry = Alice Montagu-   George = Marina   John
Princess Royal | 6th Earl of Harewood   Duke of | Douglas-Scott   Duke of Kent | Princess of   1905-19
1897-1965 | 1882-1947   Gloucester | 1901-   1902-42 | Greece
1900-74   1906-68

Gerald = (1) Angela Dowding   William   Richard = Birgitte   Edward = Katherine   Alexandra = Sir Angus   Michael = Marie-Christine
1924- | div.   1941-72   Duke of | van Deurs   Duke of | Worsley   1936- | Ogilvy   1942- | von Reibnitz
1919-   Gloucester | 1946-   Kent | 1933-   1928-   1945-
= (2) Lisa   1944-   1935-
Collingwood

Henry   Martin   Alexander   Davina   Rose   George = Sylvana   Helen = Timothy   Nicholas   James   Marina = Paul   Frederick   Gabriella
1953-   1962-   Earl of   1977-   1980-   Earl of | Tomaselli   1964- | Taylor   1970-   1964-   1966- | Mowatt   1979-   1981-
Ulster   St Andrews   1964-
1974-   1962-

Lord   Zenouska
Downpatrick   1990-
1988-

Index

Index

Index

Harewood, 6th Earl of (formerly Viscount Lascelles), 54, 90
Harewood, 7th Earl of, 161
Harlech, 4th Lord, 126
Harris, Sir Arthur, Bt., 125
Hartnell, Sir Norman, 110, 111, 113, 157
Harvey, Oliver (Lord Harvey of Tasburgh), 88, 89, 94, 99, 121
Heald, Tim, 170
Helena, Princess (Princess Christian of Schleswig-Holstein), 65
Henry II, 4, 80
Henry VI, 92
Henry VIII, 4, 39, 59, 80
Henry of Wales, Prince (great-grandson of QM), 185, 189
Hepburn-Stuart-Forbes-Trefusis, Hon Fenella (Hon Mrs John Bowes-Lyon, sister-in-law of QM), 53
Herbert, Hon David, 178, 179
Hess, Rudolf, 97
Himmler, Heinrich, 97
Hitler, Adolf, 95-8, 110, 113–115, 118
Hoare, Rt Hon Sir Simon (Viscount Templewood), 20
Holden, Anthony, 187
Hore-Belisha, Rt Hon Leslie, 11
Horner, David, 63
Howard, Catherine (consort of Henry VIII), 59
Howarth, Patrick, 63
Hyde, Lady Anne (consort of Duke of York, later James II), 59

Ingrid of Sweden, Princess, 110

Jamagne, Marie-Luce (Mrs Peter Townsend), 153
James I, 51
James II, 59, 92, 101
John, Augustus, 148
John XXIII, Pope, 157
John, Prince, 6, 67
Jones, Mrs Arthur, 119

Jowitt, Rt Hon Sir William (Earl Jowitt), 93
Juan Carlos, King of Spain, 64
Juliana of the Netherlands, Princess, 85

Kent, Princess Victoria, Duchess of (mother of Queen Victoria), 95, 147
Kent, Prince Edward, Duke of, 38
Kent, Prince George, Duke of, 6, 10, 14, 33, 39, 43, 46, 67, 74, 81, 86, 90, 92, 98, 108, 120, 131, 132
Keppel, Alice, 185
Kerr-Smiley, Maud, 9
Knatchbull, Hon Amanda, 170
Knatchbull, Hon Nicholas, 170

Lang, Rt Rev & Rt Hon Lord, 1–5, 7, 12, 15, 22, 34, 40, 74, 88, 91, 107, 109, 114, 115, 125, 126, 128, 129, 134
Lascelles, Rt Hon Sir Alan, 6, 13, 27, 40, 79, 96, 116, 139, 151, 152, 156
Lascelles, Hon Gerald, 14, 161
Latimer, Catherine (consort of Henry VIII), 59
Lebrun, Albert, 110
Lees-Milne, James, 76, 131, 133, 155, 176
Leicester, 3rd Earl of, 8
Leopold III of the Belgians, 119
Leveson-Gower, Lady Rosemary, 8
Lillie, Beatrice, 133
Lincolnshire, 1st Marquess of, 56
Lindsay, Sir Ronald, 96
Llewellyn, Roddy, 170
Lloyd George, 1st Earl, 56, 62, 187
Logue, Lionel, 75–7
Louise, Princess, Duchess of Fife, 55, 56
Lowry, L. S., 148
Lygon, Lady Mary, 119

Macclesfield, Countess of, 104
MacDonald, Rt Hon Malcolm, 42
MacDonald, Margaret, 20
MacDonald, Rt Hon Ramsay, 36, 43, 108
Malcolm II of Scotland, 51

Index